AN ACCOUNT

OF

THE POLYNESIAN RACE

ITS ORIGIN AND MIGRATIONS

AND THE

ANCIENT HISTORY OF THE HAWAIIAN PEOPLE
TO THE TIMES OF KAMEHAMEHA I.

BY

ABRAHAM FORNANDER,

CIRCUIT JUDGE OF THE ISLAND OF MAUI, H.I.

VOL. I.

British Library Cataloguing-in-Publication Data
A catalogue record for this book is available from the
British Library

"As made up of legendary accounts of places and personages, it (mythology) is history; as relating to the genesis of the gods, the nature and adventures of divinities, it is religion."—*Native Races of the Pacific States*, H. H. Bancroft, vol. iii. p. 14.

"It is now a recognised principle of philosophy, that no religious belief, however crude, nor any historical tradition, however absurd, can be held by the majority of a people for any considerable time as true, without having in the beginning some foundation in fact." . . . "We may be sure that there never was a myth without a meaning; that mythology is not a bundle of ridiculous fancies invented for vulgar amusement; that there is not one of those stories, no matter how silly or absurd, which was not founded in fact, which did not once hold a significance."—*Ibid.*, vol. iii. pp. 16, 17.

"The fact of an immigration, and the quarter from which it came, are handed down from father to son, and can scarcely be corrupted or forgotten, unless in the case where the people sink into absolute barbarism."—Essay ii. book vii. of *Herodotus*, edited by G. Rawlinson.

TO MY DAUGHTER

CATHERINE KAONOHIULAOKALANI FORNANDER,

This Work

IS AFFECTIONATELY DEDICATED,

AS A REMINDER OF HER MOTHER'S ANCESTORS

AND AS

A TOKEN OF HER FATHER'S LOVE.

ABR. FORNANDER.

CONTENTS.

VOL. I.

CONTENTS.

PREFACE.

WHEN a gentleman, whose genius and talents have secured for himself one of the curule chairs in the republic of letters, introduces a blushing aspirant, his name becomes a voucher for the respectability of the latter, and his "*favete linguis*" ensures an attentive hearing until the close of the performance. But we are not all born with a silver spoon, and many an author, like myself, has had to bear the double burden of introducing himself as well as his subject. But when a writer presents himself with new discoveries, and new ideas based upon them, the reader has a right to inquire who the writer is, and if his dis..overies are genuine, before he exercises his judgment upon the ideas submitted for his acceptance. It is meet and proper, therefore, on entering upon ground so little travelled as that of Polynesian Archæology, on presenting myths and legends to the inspection of the literary world some of which have never darkened a sheet of paper before, that I should state my right to present them, how I came by them, and also the lights which guided and the aids which assisted me on the journey.

Thirty-four years' residence in the Hawaiian group; nineteen years' position in various offices under the Government; a thorough local and personal knowledge of every section of the group, acquired during numerous journeys; my knowledge of the language, and the fact—though with all due modesty I state it—that I am well known, personally or by reputation, to every man within the group, from the King on the throne to the poorest fisherman in the remotest hamlet;—all these considerations give me a right to speak on behalf of the Polynesian people, to unveil the past of their national life, to unravel the snarled threads of their existence, and to pick up the missing links that bind them to the foremost races of the world,—the Arian and the Cushite.

Thus much, though reluctantly, I have felt bound to say in vindication of my right to be the spokesman of a people whom no one knew till a hundred years ago, and whom no one even now recognises as a chip of the same block from which the Hindu, the Iranian, and the Indo-European families were fashioned.

When first I entertained the idea of preparing myself for a work on Polynesian Archæology, I employed two, sometimes three, intelligent and educated Hawaiians to travel over the entire group and collect and transcribe, from the lips of the old natives, all the legends, chants, prayers, &c., bearing upon the ancient history, culte, and customs of the people, that they possibly could get hold of. This continued for nearly three years. Sometimes

their journeys were fortunate, sometimes rather barren
of results; for the old natives who knew these things were
becoming fewer and fewer every year, and even they—
as is well known to every one that has had any experience
in the matter—maintain the greatest reserve on such subjects, even to their own countrymen; and to a foreigner,
unless most intimately and favourably known, any such
revelation is almost impossible. The labours of my em-
ployees, however, were crowned with results exceeding my
expectations, and I am now in possession of probably the
greatest collection of Hawaiian lore in or out of the Pacific.
It took me a long time, during leisure moments from offi-
cial duties, to peruse, collate, and arrange these materials,
and, though they are filled with much that was worthless
for my purpose, yet I found very many pearls of invalu-
able price to the antiquarian and historian.

To this *exposé* of my own pursuits, I would only add
that, during my many journeys from one end of the group
to the other, I never omitted an opportunity in my intercourse with the old and intelligent natives to remove a
doubt or verify a fact bearing upon the work I had in
hand.

Among Hawaiian authors and antiquarian literati, to
whom I gratefully acknowledge my obligations, are, in the
first place, his Majesty King KALAKAUA, to whose personal
courtesy and extensive erudition in Hawaiian antiquities
I am indebted for much valuable information; the late
Hon. LORRIN ANDREWS; and the late DAVID MALO, whose

manuscript collections were kindly placed at my disposal by the Honourable Board of Education; the late Dr. JOHN RAE of Hana, Maui, who, in a series of articles published in the "Polynesian" (Honolulu, 1862), first called attention to the extreme antiquity of the Polynesian language; the late Hon. S. M. KAMAKAU, with whom I have conferred both often and lengthily; the late Rev. Mr. DIBBLE, whose "History of the Sandwich Islands" (1843) contains many gems of antiquarian value; the late Hon. NAIHE of Kohala, Hawaii, and the late S. N. HAKUOLE. Mr. J. KEPELINO has furnished some valuable chants, and the groundwork of the "Kumuhonua" legends, most of which was confirmed by the late Mr. Kamakau above referred to. The current communications, from time to time, in the Hawaiian journals on antiquarian subjects, by different authors, have been carefully culled, and are thankfully remembered. Mr. JULES REMY is personally and kindly remembered since his *sejour* on the Hawaiian islands, and his Introduction to and edition of the "Moolelo Hawaii" (Paris and Leipzig, 1862), as well as his "Recits d'un vieux Sauvage, pour servir a l'Histoire ancienne de Hawaii" (1859), have been carefully considered and found of great value.

From the Marquesas group, the author is under obligation to Professor W. D. ALEXANDER for access to a collection of ancient legends and chants as told to and written down by the late Mr. T. C. LAWSON, for many years a resident of Hivaoa (St. Dominica).

From the Society group, and several others of the South-

Pacific Islands, Rev. Mr. ELLIS's "Polynesian Researches" is replete with much and valuable legendary lore. Mr. MOERENHOUT's "Voyage aux Isles du Grand Ocean" has been carefully referred to; and in Lieutenant DE BOVIS's "Etat de la Societé Taitienne a l'arrivée des Européens," was found a cautious, critical, and reliable author, though on some points we must necessarily differ.

From the Tonga group, "Mariner's Voyage" has furnished the greatest amount of information.

From New Zealand, DIEFFENBACH's "Travels," and SIR GEORGE GREY's "Polynesian Mythology," and "Proverbial and Popular Sayings of the Ancestors of the New Zealand Race," not only bring up the common property of the Polynesian race in its legendary lore, but throw an unexpected light on some very ancient passages of Hawaiian history.

From the Samoan (Navigators') group, I regret to say that I have but scant information, collected piecemeal from various sources. What I have, however, coincides strongly with the leading features of the legendary lore of the other groups.

From the Fiji group, the "Fiji and the Fijians," by THOMAS WILLIAMS and JAMES CALVERT, has been found to be good and reliable authority.

Various other utterances from Polynesian folklore have been collected and utilised from the best accounts obtainable of voyages undertaken at public expense or prompted by private enterprise; and among the former, I consider the highest praise is due to the Ethnological and Philological section of the United States' Exploring Expedition under Commodore Wilkes, prepared by Mr. HORATIO HALE; and among the latter, I have found Mr. M. G. L. DOMENY DE RIENZI'S work "Oceanie" (Paris, 1836), which is a *resumé* of his own and other voyages in Malaysia and Polynesia, still stand unrivalled for fulness and accuracy.

Touching the philological questions arising from a consideration of the Polynesian language and its relation to others, I have consulted the great work of WILLIAM V. HUMBOLDT, "Über die Kawi Sprache;" that of FRANCIS BOPP, "Über die Verwandtschaft der Malayisch-Polynesischen Sprachen mit den Indo-Europäeischen;" J. CRAWFURD'S "Grammar and Dictionary of the Malay Language;" ADOLPH PICTET'S "Origines Indo-Européennes;" Professor MAX MÜLLER'S "Lectures on the Science of Language," and his "Chips from a German Workshop," and such dictionaries as I could procure.

Mr. GEORGE SMITH'S "Assyrian Discoveries," and his "Chaldean Account of Genesis;" Colonel HENRY YULE'S edition of, and notes to, "The Travels of Marco Polo;" Mr. G. RAWLINSON'S edition of "Herodotus," and his "Five Great Monarchies;" and Sir STAMFORD RAFFLES'S various essays and writings, have furnished me many valuable points of contact and much light, where otherwise I must have groped my way in darkness.

But, while such are my right to speak, and the lights

which aided me in compiling this work, yet the work itself might possibly never have been published, had not the Hon. H. A. WIDEMANN, an acquaintance and friend of thirty years' residence in the Hawaiian group, kindly exerted himself in my behalf to procure the means to defray the cost of publication. And to him and to those who so promptly came forward to aid the enterprise my grateful acknowledgments are herewith tendered.

Painfully conscious that my long seclusion from literary labours has cramped my hand, even though the spirit be unflagging as ever, yet with the treasures of legendary lore around me, with my affection for the people with whom I have associated my lot in life for so many years, and with the certainty that each year is fearfully diminishing the chances of ever again procuring an equal collection of the Polynesian folklore, I submit this work without hesitation to the favourable regard of the Hawaiians and the Polynesians, whose past I have endeavoured to rescue from the isolation and oblivion which were fast closing over it, and whose echoes were growing fainter and fainter in the busy hum of a new era and a new civilisation, derided by some, disputed by others, unheeded by all.

To the literati of foreign lands I address myself with that respectful diffidence and cautious reserve which become a pioneer in an almost untrodden field. With the data before me, drawn from Polynesian sources, my conclusions could not well be other than what they are. If at times I have erred in comparative philology, mythology, or history, it will be kindly borne in mind that over forty years of an adventurous and busy life have crept between me and the Alma Mater on the Fyris, where the classics flourished, and where GEŸER taught history; that my own library is very small; and that there is no public institution worthy of the name within two thousand miles of the Hawaiian group. In attempting to solve the ethnic riddle of the Polynesian race, I may have stumbled in the path; but that path alone, I feel convinced, can lead to a solution.

ABR. FORNANDER.

LAHAINA, HAWAIIAN ISLANDS,
March 30, 1877.

ORIGIN AND MIGRATIONS

OF

THE POLYNESIAN RACE.

BEFORE I offer my contribution to Hawaiian history proper, I think it justice to the reader and to the cause of truth to state my view of the Origin and Migrations of the Polynesian Family, of which the Hawaiian is only one, though at present the foremost and best known branch.

The singular spectacle of a people so widely scattered, yet so homogeneous in its physical characteristics, in its language and customs, has not failed to exercise the minds of many learned and worthy men, both of past and present time, who have written much and differed widely about the origin of the Polynesian family. North and South Americans, Malays, Papuans, Chinese, and Japanese, and even the lost tribes of Israel, have all, at different times, and by different writers, been charged with the paternity of this family, and made responsible for its origin and appearance in the Pacific Ocean. These writers formed their opinions, undoubtedly, according to the data that were before them; but those data were too few, often too incorrect and too unconnected as a whole, to warrant the conclusions at which they arrived. A more intimate acquaintance with the Polynesian family itself, with its copious folk-lore, and its reminiscences of the past still

A

floating about with dimmer or brighter outlines through its songs and sagas; a better insight and a truer appreciation of the affinities of its language; and, lastly, a small amount of renunciation of national vanity on the part of those different writers, might have removed many of the errors and misconceptions in regard to this interesting family of mankind.

It would be presumption in me to pretend that I have fully solved so great a problem as the origin and descent of the Polynesian family. Yet I trust that the sequel will show that my conclusions are not only plausible, but extremely probable, and that, only by following the guide which the data now offered afford, can we account in a satisfactory manner for the ethnic, linguistic, and social phenomena connected with that family, for their appearance in the Pacific and their distribution within it—from New Zealand to Hawaii, from Easter Island to Rotuma.

That the reader may know at a glance the result to which my investigations in the Polynesian folk-lore, as well as its comparison with that of other peoples, have led me, it may be proper here at the outset to say that I believe that I can show that the Polynesian family can be traced directly as having occupied the Asiatic Archipelago, from Sumatra to Timor, Gilolo, and the Philippines, previous to the occupation of that archipel by the present Malay family; that traces, though faint and few, lead up through Deccan to the north-west part of India and the shores of the Persian Gulf; that, when other traces here fail, yet the language points farther north, to the Aryan stock in its earlier days, long before the Vedic irruption in India; and that for long ages the Polynesian family was the recipient of a Cushite civilisation, and to such an extent as almost entirely to obscure its own consciousness of parentage and kindred to the Aryan stock.

Were every other trace of a people's descent obliterated by time, by neglect, by absorption in some other tribe, race, or tongue, the identity of the nomenclature of its places of abode with that of some other people would still remain an *à priori* evidence of the former habitats of the absorbed or forgotten people. Were every other record and tradition of the descent of the present ruling races in America, North and South, obliterated, the names which they have given to the headlands, rivers, cities, villages, and divisions of land in the country they inhabit, would primarily, and almost always infallibly, indicate their European descent —English, Spanish, Portuguese, French, &c., &c. The practice of naming new abodes in memory of old homes is a deep-rooted trait of human nature, and displays itself alike in the barbarous as in the civilised condition of a people. We find it in the wake of all great migrations, from the most ancient to the most recent. History is full of illustrations to this effect, to prove the presence of the mother race, through its migrations, in foreign lands where every other vestige, except this one, has been trodden out by time or by succeeding migrations of other peoples and races.

Following the clue which this evidence affords, I hope to be able to show that the Polynesian family formerly occupied, as their places of residence, the Asiatic Archipelago, and were at one time in the world's history closely connected by kindred, commerce, or by *conquest* with lands beyond, in Hindustan, the shores of the Persian Gulf, and even in Southern Arabia.

From what I have been able to glean of the old Javanese annals, and of their ancient language, the Kawi, I am led to believe that of the two words, which in the present Malay tongue signify an island—"Nusa" and "Pulo"— the former is by far the older, and obtained exclusively before the latter was introduced by the comparatively modern Malays. In those old annals may be found such names for Jawa, or different portions of it, as "Nusa-Kindang," "Nusa-Hara-Hara,"[1] and "Nusa-Jawa;" "Nusa-Kautchana" for Borneo; "Nusa-Antara" for Madura; "Nusa-Kambargan" for Bali, &c., and in several of the eastern parts of the archipelago, such as Ceram, Bulu, Amboyna, the ancient word "Nusa" still prevails over the modern "Pulo."

This word "Nusa," the old ante-Malay designation of an island, reappears under a Polynesian form in various quarters of the Pacific. We have "Nuka-tea," one of Wallis' group; also "Nuka-tapu," "Nuka-lofa," the principal town on Tonga-tabu; "Nuka-Hiwa" (in some dialects contracted to "Nuuhiwa"), one of the Marquesas group; "Nuku-nono"[2] of the Union group; "Nuku-fetau" of the De-Peyster's group; "Nuku-ta-wake" and "Nuku-te-pipi" of the Paumotu Archipel; and some others in the Eastern portion of the Viti group, which has received so large a portion of its vocables from Polynesian sources. But in none of the Polynesian dialects does the Malay word for island, "Pulo," obtain, nor has it left any marks of ever having been adopted.

In regard to this word "Nusa," as signifying an island, among the old ante-Malay inhabitants of the Indian Archipelago, and having been brought by them into various parts of the Pacific, it may be interesting to remark that we meet with the same word, signifying the same thing, in the Mediterranean, at a time anterior to the Hellenic predominancy, as far back as the Phœnician supremacy over that sea, and probably older. We thus find that "Ich-nusa" was one of the oldest names of Sardinia; "Oe-nusæ," some islands in the Ægean Sea, off Messene; "Sire-nusæ," islands off Cape Surrentum, Campania, Italy; "Argi-nusa," below Lesbos, off the Æolian coast, and others. Of this word I have found no etymon in the Greek lan-

[1] "Hara," or "Hara-Hara," was one of the many names of Siwa.
[2] This may derive from *Nuku* or *Nuu*, elevated, raised; but in the present case it may be as much a corruption of "Nuka-nono" as "Nuu-hiwa" is a corruption of "Nuka-hiwa."

guage, and it is no kin to Nasos or Næsos, the Doric and Ionian names for island. It is justifiable, therefore, to trace it back to the Cushite Arabs, who traded, colonised, and conquered up to and beyónd the pillars of Hercules in the West, as well as to the confines of the Pacific in the East.[1]

I will now give the names of a number of places within the Polynesian area, which I think may be identified with others situated in the Indian Archipelago and beyond. Were my acquaintance with the older pre-Malay names of the latter greater than it is, I have no doubt the number could have been greatly increased.[2]

1. The first island whose name I will thus trace back will be the island of *Hawaii*, the principal one of the Hawaiian or Sandwich Islands.

That name in the principal Polynesian dialects is thus pronounced :—

[1] In The Five Great Monarchies of the Ancient Eastern World, by G. Rawlinson, vol. i. p. 112, the author says : " We can scarcely doubt but that, in some way or other, there was a communication of beliefs, a passage in very early times, from the shores of the Persian Gulf to the lands washed by the Mediterranean, of mythological notions and ideas." If so, why not of names of places, capes, islands, &c., also?

In Col. Yule's edition of "Marco Polo," London, 1875, vol. ii. p. 406, it is said that the people of St. Mary's Isle, off the east coast of Madagascar, in lat. 17°, as a sign of their Arab descent, "call themselves the children of Ibrahim, and the island *Nusi Ibrahim.*"

[2] Mr. Crawfurd's Grammar and Dictionary of the Malay Language, vol. i. p. 282, says : " With the exception of a few places in the Philippines and Madagascar, no Malay or Javanese names of places are to be found beyond the limits of the Archipelago. We look for them in vain in the islands of the Pacific." As Mr. Crawfurd properly distinguishes the Malay and Javanese languages from the pre-Malay and pre-Javanese languages of the Archipelago, he is probably correct; but the names which I am going to refer to, came without doubt with the earliest Polynesian settlers from the Indian Archipel, and their not being Malay or Javanese is another proof that the Polynesians had departed from the Archipel before the Malays and Javanese had been so long domiciled there as to introduce their own nomenclature of islands and places. The number of old names of places retained and adopted by these invaders must have been very great, though perhaps now impossible to define.

In Hawaiian,	.	.	.	.	.	*Hawa-ii.*
„ Society group,		.	.	.	.	*Ditto.*[1]
„ Somoan (Navigator's),		.		.	.	*Sawa-ii.*
„ South Marquesan and New Zealand,						*Hawa-iki.*
„ Rarotonga,	.	.	.	.	.	*Awa-iki.*
„ Tonga (Friendly Island),				.	.	*Habai.*

This word is manifestly a compound word : *Hawa* and *ii* or *iki*. Whether the *ii* or *iki* is accepted as meaning " small, little," the apparent sense of the New Zealand, Rarotongan, and South Marquesan form of the word, or " raging, furious with heat," the sense of the word in the North Marquesan, and which has its analogy in the Tahitian and Hawaiian, it is evidently an epithet, a distinguishing mark of that particular " Hawa " from any other. I am led to prefer the North Marquesan sense of the word, in as much as in a chant of that people, referring to the wanderings of their forefathers, and giving a description of that special Hawaii on which they once dwelt, it is mentioned as :

Tai mamao, uta oa tu te Ii; " a distant sea (or far off region), away inland stands the volcano " (the furious, the raging).

This " Hawa," referred to by the Polynesians of all the principal groups as an ancient place of residence, corresponds to *Jawa*, the second of the Sunda islands, which name, however, seems to have been applied principally to the eastern part of that island, the western portion being known from ancient times as " Sonda."

In the second century A.D., Ptolomy called the Sunda Isles by the general name of *Jaba-dios insulæ,* or *Jaba-din.*

In the ninth century A.D., two Muslim travellers, reported by Renandot, spoke of the island and its grandeur as the empire of *Zaba-ya* or *Zapa-ge,* evidently an Arabic pronunciation of *Jaba* or *Jawa.*

---

[1] An ancient name of the sacred place " Opoa," in the island of Raiatea, Society group, was " Hawa-ii."

In the fourteenth century A.D., Marco Polo mentions the island under the name of *Ciawa*, and refers to both Sumatra and Java under that name.[1] Javanese historians indicate that the name of "Java" was given to the island by emigrants from Kling, Kalinga, or Telinga, on the north-east coast of Deccan, who in the first century A.D. invaded and settled on the island, under one Aji Saka, or Tritestra; but it is understood that *Java*,

[1] On this subject, Colonel Yule in his edition of "Marco Polo," 1875, vol. ii. p. 266, remarks : "Polo by no means stands alone in giving the name of Java to the island now called Sumatra. The terms *Jawa, Jawi,* were applied by the Arabs to the islands and productions of the Archipelago generally, but also specifically to Sumatra. Thus Sumatra is the *Jawah* both of Abulfeda and of Ibn-Baluta, the latter of whom spent some time on the island. *Javaku* again is the name applied in the Singhalese chronicles to the Malays in general. *Jau* and *Dawa* are the names still applied by the Battaks and the people of Nias respectively to the Malays, showing probably that these were looked on as Javanese by those tribes who did not partake of the civilisation diffused from Java. De Barras says that all the people of Sumatra called themselves by the common name of *Jauijs.* There is some reason to believe that the application of the name Java to Sumatra is of very old date. It is by no means impossible that the *Jabadin* or Yavadvipa of Ptolomy may be Sumatra rather than Java." In a note to page 359, same work, Colonel Yule says, "Sònagar or Jònagar is a Tamil corruption of *Yavanar*, the Yavanas, the name by which the Arabs were known, and is the name most commonly used in the Tamil country to designate the mixed race descended from Arab colonists."

As names of places and peoples are older than the chronicles which record them, it is well to bear in mind that the Singhalese and the Tamil speaking peoples of Southern India recognised a Jawa to the east of them, the land of the "Javaku," and a Jawa to the west of them, the land of the Yavanar or Jònagar. But the Singhalese chronicles were written after the Malays had occupied the Sunda Isles, became the leading people there, and appropriated the name of the country to themselves ; while the Tamil appellation of the Arabs must have been infinitely older than the commercial revival during the early Mohammedan times, seeing that Arab intercourse with India was frequent and continuous as far back as the times when the Cushite race ruled supreme in Arabia, and their Zaba was yet an emporium of commerce and a cradle of colonisation. The inference, therefore, seems to me almost irresistible that the people, known to the Tamils as "Yavanar," extended their operations to the Sunda Isles, and called that country after their own home, a name which in after ages was borne back to Ceylon by Malay cruisers and invaders. The Tamil expression "Java-ku," is thoroughly Polynesian. In Hawaiian legends (for the words are obsolete in modern parlance), the suffixes *ku* and *moe* to names of places indicate east and west. Thus *Kahiki-ku* and *Kahiki-moe, Holani-ku, Holani-moe,* signifying "Eastern Kahiki, Western Kahiki," &c., &c.

which in Sanskrit means *barley*, does not grow on the island. Evidently those emigrants found the name already existing, and with national vanity found a meaning for it in their own language, and in process of time believed the fiction. The name occurs, however, in other parts of the Archipelago, as

Djawa, a river on the east coast of Borneo, near Coti; as

Sawa-it, a place in south-west Borneo; as

Sawa-i, a place on the north coast of Ceram; and as

Awaiya, a village on the south coast of Ceram.

For the origin of the name, and its expansion in the Asiatic Archipelago, and thence into Polynesia, we must look beyond the Kalinga invasion, beyond India, to that nation and race whose colonies and commerce pervaded the ancient world in pre-historic times—the Cushite Arabians; and among them we find as a proto-nom the celebrated *Saba*, or *Zaba*, in Southern Arabia, a seat of Cushite empire and commercial emporium "from the earliest times," according to Diodorus Siculus and Agatharcides. We shall see in the sequel how Polynesian legends confirm the opinion of an early intercourse between the Polynesians and the Cushites, and the close adoption by the former of the culture, and many of the beliefs and legends, of the latter. That the influence of this Cushite "Saba," as a name-giver, extended to the nations of the West as well as in the East, may be inferred from the epithet of Dionysius "Sabazius," and probably also from the names of the town "Saba-te," in Etruria, and of the "Sabini," one of the most ancient indigenous peoples of Italy, and of their god "Sabus," from whom Cato derived their name.

2. The next case of identity will be found in the name of the island of *Oahu*, one of the Hawaiian group, which evidently refers to

Ouahou, a tract of country in Central and South-east Borneo, occupied by Dyak tribes; and to

Ouadju,[1] a State or territory in Central Celebes, occupied by a Buguis population. We shall see further on that both the Dyaks and the Buguis, as well as other tribes in that Archipelago, are pre-Malay inhabitants, and kindred to the Pacific Polynesians.

3. We now come to *Molokai,* another island of the Hawaiian group; in the ancient songs and sagas called *Molokai-a-Hina.* This island finds a striking confirmation of the derivation of both the names in

' *Morotay, Moroty, Morty* (according to different orthographies), one of the Moluccas, north-east of Gilolo. The Moluccas were called by ancient geographers the *Sindas,*[2] and this name is, referred to by Spanish navigators in the sixteenth century, as having obtained before the islands were called collectively the Moluccas. The "Molokai-a-Hina," therefore, or "Molokai-a-Sina," as it would be called in the Samoan dialect of the Polynesian, points with remarkable directness to the derivation of the name, and to the people who named it; and, allowing for phonetic variation, we find the same name in

Borotai, a place or village among the Sadong hill-Dyaks inland from Sarawak, Borneo.

4. *Lehua, Lefuka,* and *Levuka,* of the Hawaiian, Tonga, and Fiji groups respectively, and *Lefu,* one of the Loyalty Islands, refer themselves to

Labouk, a province on the north side of Borneo.

5. *Niihau,* one of the Hawaiian group, corresponds to *Lifao,* a place on the island of Timor.

---

[1] By other writers called and written *Wajo.* See Asiatic Journal, August 1825. Mr. Crawfurd, in his Grammar and Dictionary of the Malay Language, vol. i. p. 85, says: that the Bugis call themselves *Wugiss.* As we shall observe more than one reference to Celebes in this work, it is not improbable that the Hawaiian appellation of *Wohi,* as a title for a certain rank of chiefs, principally on the island of Oahu, may refer to some half-forgotten remembrance of a former national appellation of *Wugi.*

[2] In the Histoire de la Conquête des Isles Moluques, par d'Argensola, Amsterdam, 1706, vol. iii., it is said that the Moluccas were formerly called "Sindas" by Ptolomy, especially Amboyna, Celebes, and Gilolo.

6. *Morea*, or Eimeo, one of the Society group, west of Tahiti, corresponds to

Morea, name of a mountain range in the east of Jawa, and east of Mount Ardjouna.

7. *Bora-Bora*, one of the Society group, and *Pola-pola*, name of lands in Ewa, Oahu, in Koolau, Molokai, and in Lahaina, Maui, of the Hawaiian group, refer to

Pulo-Pora, an island off the coast of Menangkabau, in Sumatra.

8. *Huahine*, one of the Society group, refers to

Oujein or *Ujein*, a town in Malva, on the Nerbudda river, India; in Sanskrit called *Ujjayini*, also called "Visala." Oujein was also called "Avanti." This town boasted of a most remote antiquity. It is mentioned in the Puranas, also in the Periplus of the Erythrean Sea, and Ptolomy mentions it under the name of "Ozene."[1]

9. *Vavao* or *Wawao*, one of the Habai group in the Friendly Islands, in other dialects pronounced "Wewau" or "Vevau;" and *Mature-Wawao*, or Acteon Island of the Paumotu group, correspond to

Babao, an ancient name of the Bay of Coupang, Isle of Timor; also of a village and district there, and probably the name of the whole island before the Malays *conquered* it, settled, and named it Timor.

10. *Namuka*, one of the Tonga islands (Friendly Island), also one of the Fiji group, refers to

Namusa, one of the Menguis group in the Moluccas.

11. *Kauai*, one of the Hawaiian group, refers to

[1] In the Asiatic Journal, February 1821, p. 118, B. Tytler, speaking of Vikramaditya, says: "Although he is called king of Oujein, this does not by any means prove him to have been monarch of any portion of Hindostan; because Oujein·is uniformly made use of by the natives of the upper provinces in the sense of 'the west.' Consequently 'King of Oujein' means in part nothing more than sovereign of some undefined country situated in the west, or to the westward of India." Its other name "*Avanti*," being an equivalent of Oujein as meaning west, confirms the above reasoning. "*Avanti*," from Sanskrit *Ava*, away, off, down; *Avanati*, setting of the sun.

Tawai, one of the Batchian islands, west of Gilolo, in the Moluccas; *Kawai,* in south-west of Sumatra.

12. *Pangai-motu,* one of the Tonga islands; *Pango-pango,* or *Pago-pago,* harbour and·village on the island of Tutuila, Samoan group, and *Pao-pao,* a land in Kohala, Hawaii, Hawaiian group. *Paopao,* or Cook's Harbour, on the island of Eimeo, Society Islands, correspond to

Pampanga or *Papango,* a district in Luzon, Philippine Islands, and to *Pagai* or *Poggi,* two islands off the west coast of Sumatra.

13. *Puna,* name of districts on the islands of Hawaii and Kauai, Hawaiian group; and *Puna-auia,* a district in Tahiti, Society group, and *Puna-he,* district on Hiwaoa, Marquesas group, refer themselves to

Puna, the name of a mountain tribe ·in the interior of Borneo, and to

Puna, a district in Deccan, India, south of Bombay, as well as to a river of that name in Northern India, supposed by Remusat to be the Jamuna or Jumna. It recalls, moreover, the old Egyptian name of *Pun* for Yemen, in South Arabia; a name older than the twelfth dynasty.

14. *Kohala,* a district on the island of Hawaii, Hawaiian group; also name of a land in Kumuele, Molokai, Hawaiian group; also *Ta-hara,* the south-west point of Matawai Bay in Tahiti; also *Haraike,* one of the Paumotu Islands, correspond to

Koshala or *Kosala,* the ancient name of the kingdom of Oude, in India. I mentioned above that Ujjayini or Oujein, in Malva, India, was also formerly called "Vi-sala;" and Arrian mentions an island off the coast of Mekran, the present Beluchistan, called "No-sala," whence the Ichthyophagi were said to derive

Sohár, or Soer as Marco Polo calls it, the former capital of Oman, Arabia, shows another singular family likeness to the constituent part of the above names, Hara, Hala, with different prefixes.

15. *Ka-papala,* name of a land in Kau, Hawaii, Hawaiian

group; also a district called *Papara* in Tahiti, Society group, find their reference to

Papal, name of a district in Borneo, inhabited by Dyaks.

16. *Anahola,* a land in the district of Koolau, Kauai, Hawaiian group, refers to

Ankola, one of the six districts of the Batta country, Sumatra.

17. *Laie,* a land in Koolauloa, Oahu, Hawaiian group, and a land in Kula, Maui, Hawaiian group, recalls

Laye, a place in the country of the Reyangs, in Sumatra.

18. *Mana,* a district of Kauai, Hawaiian group, points to *Mana,* a district near Bencoolen, Sumatra.[1]

19. *Ninole,* name of lands in Kau and in Hilo, Hawaii, also on Molokai, Hawaiian group, refers to

Ninore, a place in the Rajpootana, north-west India, in the Bheel country.

20. *Kipu,* name of lands on Molokai and at Keei, Kona, Hawaii, Hawaiian group, correspond to

Tibuu, the south-west point of the Island of Buru, in the Moluccas.

21. *Hana;* name of numerous districts and lands in the Hawaiian, Marquesas, and Tahitian groups, either singly or in compounds, as "Hana," "Hana-vi," "Hana-manu," "Hana-pepe," "Mala-e-ka Hana," "Olo-hana," and others, refer themselves ultimately, doubtless, to

Sana, one of the ancient Cushite emporiums in Southern Arabia. I am not aware of any place in the intermediate Indian Archipelago that has preserved the single form of this name, but there are several places with the compound name, such as *Rata-han* on the north-east prong of Celebes, *Asa-han* in the north of Sumatra.

22. *Taioa;* name of place and bay in Nukahiwa, Marquesas group; and *Kaioa,* a land in Koolau, Oahu, Hawaiian group; refer plainly to

Kaioa, one of the Molucca Islands, west of Gilolo.

---

[1] Also to *Mana-toa,* a place in northern part of Timor.

23. *Lawai*, a land on Kauai, Hawaiian group, corresponds to

Lawai, a river in Borneo, province of Succadow, near the centre, inhabited by Dyaks.

Besides these references — and their number could be greatly increased were my means of knowing names of localities in the Asiatic Archipel, their present and more ancient names, greater—there are numerous places on all the principal Polynesian groups which preserve the name of water, *wai*, under various combinations, in their names, such as "Wai-kapu," "Wai-luku," "Wai-aka," "Wai-ehu," "Wai-pa," "Wai-pipiha," "Wai-tiarea," Wai-rao," &c., while the same combination still obtains in many of the islands 'of the Asiatic Archipelago, as "Wai-gama" in Mysol, "Wai-puti" and "Wai-apo" in Buru, "Wai-kiu" in Timor, &c. The formation of names of places in Polynesia with the final compound of *hai*, as "Ka-wai-hai" on Hawaii, "Tai-o-hai" on Nukahiwa, &c., has its counterpart in such names as "Wa-hai" in Ceram, and "Ama-hai" in Celebes, all showing the ethnic current of the people who named them.

I now have to refer to some names which occur several times in the ancient Hawaiian chants, legends, and prayers, as the names of places or islands inhabited and visited by the remote ancestors of those who composed said chants or legends, but whose location is very vaguely defined, and of which, with one exception, I have not been able to find a name-sake among the present Polynesians, though, possibly, many such existed in former times. I note, first—

24. *O-lolo-i-mehani*, in some legends said to have been the residence of Wakea. The word is composed of the vocative *O*, the name proper *Lolo*, and the epithet *Mehani*. The latter, so far as I know, has no kindred now existing in the Polynesian dialects; but it remains entire in the Amblaw dialect, where "Mehani" means "Red;" and in the Ceram, Ahtiago dialect, "La-hanin" means also "Red." This name refers itself to the island of

Gi-lolo or *Ji-lolo,* the principal of the Moluccas.

In other Hawaiian legends (that of "Keanini"), reference is made to a group or country called the *O-pae-Lolo,* literally, "the Lolo group," thus indicating that *Lolo* is the proper, original name, and "Mehani" but a subsequent and descriptive appellation. This reference of "O-lolo-i-mehani" to "Ji-lolo," receives a farther confirmation from another legendary name of Wakea's residence, which in other legends is said to have been in

25. *O-lalo-waia,* and which finds its counterpart and original in

Lalo-da, a village or district on that same island of "Ir-lolo," on the west coast, opposite Galela. I know not the meaning of the Jilolo suffix-*da;* the Hawaiian *waia* means "strong smelling, filthy, dirty."

26. *Fatu-hiwa,* one of the Marquesas group, refers itself to

Batou, a place on the south side of Timor; and to *Batou-bhara* in the north of Sumatra.

27. *Halawa;* name of several lands in the Hawaiian group, refers to

Salaway, the north-east cape of the island of Jilolo, of the Moluccas; also to two districts in Beluchistan, mentioned in Lieutenant Pottinger's travels under the names of *Jhalawan* and *Sarawan.* One of the ancient names of the island of Sawaii, Samoan group, was *Salafa-ii,* which, as well as the Hawaiian "Halawa," indicates its connection with the Jilolo nomenclature of places.

28. In the western part of the Fiji group occur the names of such places as *Oto-wawa* and *Ka-wawa,* and in Hawaiian legends reference is made to places named *Wiwa* and *Wawa.* The comparison "Wawa" probably refers to

Baba, an island south of the Banda group, Indian Archipelago.

29. *Kepa,* a land on Kauai, Hawaiian group, refers itself to

Tepa, a village on the above mentioned island of Baba.

30. *Manoa,* a valley on Oahu, Hawaiian group, points to *Manoa,* islands off the south-east prong of Celebes.

31. *Holani-ku* and *Holani-moe,* corresponding to East and West Holani, also occurring in the chants as *Helani;* refers to the island of Ceram, which, according to Crawfurd and others, was formerly called *Sirang,* and is still so called by the natives. Another ancient Indonesian name might also stand sponsor to the Polynesian appellation, viz., *Siren-dwip,* the ancient name for Ceylon. For the etymology of Ceylon, see "Travels of Marco Polo," edited by Colonel Henry Yule, C.B., vol. ii. p. 296.

Under this head of evidence—properly, perhaps, called the geographical evidence—of the previous residence of the Polynesian family in the Asiatic Archipelago, and, probably, lands beyond, the following observations may be worthy of consideration.

While the present names for the north and south points of the compass may, or may not, have been adopted by the Polynesians since their irruption and dispersion in the Pacific; yet, in the ancient Hawaiian chants and legends, with which I am best acquainted, there occur names for north and south which indicate a residence on islands or lands whose configuration and physical surroundings were different from those which they now inhabit. Thus for the north we find such names as *Ulu-nui, Uli-uli, Haka-lauai, Mele-mele;* but these are known and handed down by tradition as having been names of lands as well, situated to the north of some former habitat of the people, of which all knowledge and remembrance were lost, save this that they were so situated to the north of them, and were visited at one time by that famous voyager, "Kaulu-a-Kalana," whose exploits survive in song and saga. Of *Ulu-nui* and *Mele-mele,* I shall have occasion to speak hereafter. Of *Hakalauai* I find no further mention in Polynesian legends and manuscripts; but the Dyaks in

the province of Succadow, Borneo, on the river Lawai,
have a tradition that, having been driven out by war from
a country which they called *Lawai*, they embarked in
canoes or praus, and arriving at Borneo, settled there and
named the river after their former home.[1] The geographical relation of Borneo to Jawa, or the Sunda Isles
generally, gives point and application to the Hawaiian
legends, that *Lauai* or some particular portion of it, distinguished as *Hakalauai*, was situated to the north of
some of their former habitats, and in course of time
became synonymous with north.

The other Hawaiian legendary name for the north, just
referred to, was *Uli-uli*. This word throughout the Polynesian dialects means " a dark colour, black, blue, dark-
green, dusky, sombre," and its application to the northern
point of the heavens recalls the observation of M. de
Rienzi, when, speaking of the most ancient Javanese
division of time into weeks of five days, he says:[2] "Les
denominations de noir et de Nord demontrent d'une
manière incontestable que cette subdivision a pris naissance dans l'Hindustan, où le soleil n'est jamais boreal
comme à Java et dans les contrées equinoxiales."[3] May
not the Hawaiian denomination of the north suggest the
same inference ?

[1] Asiatic Journal, August 1821,
p. 118.

[2] Oceanic, vol. i. p. 167.

[3] The five days of the Ancient Javanese week were called respectively—
(1.) *Laggi*, (2.) *Pahing*, (3.) *Pon*, (4.)
Wagi, and (5.) *Kliwon;* and representing, 1st, the blue and the east;
2d, the red and the south; 3d, the
yellow and the west; 4th, the black
and the north; and 5th, a mixed
colour and the hearth or centre.
This division of the week is said to
have obtained before the Hindus introduced the Brahminical week of
seven days. This division and those
names, then, belong to the people
that inhabited Jawa before the Hindus invaded and obtained supremacy
in the island; and the etymology of
those names plainly indicate their
Polynesian affinity. Thus the *Laggi*,
blue, is the Polynesian *Langi*, *Lani*
(Fiji), *Lagi*, the sky, the blue expanse; *Pahing*, red, doubtless refers
to the same root as the Polynesian
Hina or *Sina*, white, bright, in Fiji,
Siga, the sun, *Siga-Sigau*, white,
while in Ceram (Wahai), *Mo-sina* is
red; *Pon*, yellow, finds its relation in
the Polynesian; Hawaiian, *Poni*, a
mixture of colours, purple, the early
dawn of the morning; *Waggi*, black,
refers to the Polynesian *Wake* and
Wake-wake, the black liquid of the
squid.

Among the Hawaiian names for the south occur those ancient ones of *Lisso*,[1] and *Lepo*. The former signifies "blue, black, or dark," and hence "the deep water in the ocean; the latter is synonymous with ' *Moana*,' the deep, open ocean." But there is no land to the north of the present Hawaiian islands, within reach or ken, that could have suggested those other names as epithets or synonyms for the north only: the "Moana-lipo," the dark fathomless ocean, approaches them, not on the south only, but on every side. Nor were these names acquired or adopted while the Hawaiians yet lived in some of the southern groups of the Pacific, for the situation and surroundings of none of these would justify such designations for either north or south. Those names, therefore, refer to a period when the Polynesians occupied the Asiatic Archipelago, and probably lands further west, with the Indian Ocean as their "Moana-lipo," their "dark, unbounded sea," their southern quarter of the heavens, *Kuana-lipo*, their south; and with lands of various names all along their northern horizon.

The expressions *Tonga, Kona, Toa* (Sam., Haw., Tah.), to indicate the quarter of an island or of the wind, between the south and west, and *Tokelau, Toerau, Koolau* (Sam., Tah., Haw.), to indicate the opposite directions from north to east—expressions universal throughout Polynesia, and but little modified by subsequent local circumstances—point strongly to a former habitat in lands where the regular monsoons prevailed. Etymologically "Tonga," "Kona," contracted from "To-anga" or "Ko-ana," signifies "the setting," seil. of the sun. "Toke-lau," of which the other forms are merely dialectical variations, signifies "the cold, chilly sea." Mr. Hale, in the Ethnological portion of the United States Exploring Expedition under Commodore Wilkes, considers the application of *Tonga* to the south-western quarter as subsequent to the dispersion

---

[1] One of the Greek names for the south-west wind was Lips, *g*. Libos (Λιψ, λιβος).

of the Polynesians in the Pacific (*vid.* p. 180). But Mr.
Hale, in the very same article, has very lucidly shown that
" Tonga " was a term applied to the very first settlement
of the Polynesians in the Pacific, on Viti-lewu, signifying
" the Western," seil. people, in contradistinction from the
Viti proper, or " Eastern " people. Hence it is reasonable
to infer that the Polynesians brought the term with them
as an already existing appellation of the western quarter,
as much so as they did the other term of " Toke-lau," to
designate the eastern quarter.

In the Tonga Islands, *Hahagi* means the northern and
eastern side of an island, and *Hihifo* means the southern
and western side. The first is derived from the preposition *Hagi*, " up, upward; " the latter from the preposition
Hifo, " down, downward." In many of the other Polynesian groups the expressions " up " and " down " (Haw.,
iluna or *manae* and *ilalo*) are used with reference to the
prevailing trade-winds. One is said to " go up " when travelling against the wind, and to " go down " when sailing
before it. But the relative situation of the Tonga Islands
reverses this order of things, and thus precludes the idea of
its application being original there. These terms, then, are
older than the residence of the Polynesians in the Tonga
Islands, and indicate, in connection with other considerations, that they originated in some continental abode, or on
the southern side of one of the larger Asiatic islands,
where, from time immemorial and from constant use, they
had hardened into synonyms with the cardinal points,
and where to go to the northward was equivalent to " going
up," to ascending an upland or mountain, and where the
south became identified with the idea of descent, of " going
down," towards the sea, from the interior highlands.[1]

[1] In Malay *Utara* means north,
evidently derived from the ancient
and universal Polynesian word *Uta*,
Uka, meaning "inland" from the sea-
shore, up the mountain side.

In New Zealand the north was conventionally called *Raro*, " down,"and
the south *Runga*, or "up." Leaving
the Samoan islands, when bound to
New Zealand, they were going to the
south, or " up "against the south-east
trades; when going back to the north-

Among the many traditions and legends which obtained currency among the Polynesian groups, it is not always easy to distinguish which are of an earlier and which of a later date. Almost every group of any note—that does not confessedly derive its inhabitants from some other group, like New Zealand, the Hervey Islands, Rotuma, and some others—has more than one tradition upon the creation of the world and of man, &c. Many of these traditions are not exempt from the vanity of sister nations in the Old World, and make the first inhabitants autochthones of their respective groups. But even those who thus begin their national history almost invariably derive their gods and demi-gods from some far off western country. The Tonga islanders say that they were created, or rather descended on their group, from their gods, but that the gods themselves dwelt on an island far to the north-west, called *Pulutu*. This name strikingly points to the island of "Buru," near Ceram, of the Banda group in the Asiatic Archipelago.

In the Fiji group, where so much of early Polynesian tradition as well as language was engrafted on the Papuan stock, the abode of departed spirits is called *Mbulu*, and the Fijian Elysium is called *Mbulotu*, thus bringing the Tonga tradition back to the time of the Polynesian sejour on the Fiji group. And the tenacity of the tradition, as well as the universality of a western original home of gods or ancestors, is evidenced by the fact that in all the prin-

---

ward, they were going before the wind, or "down."

According to Dieffenbach, Travels in New Zealand, the natives also call the south by the name of *Tonga*. But as none but the Samoans and Tahitians call the south by that name, it indicates the source whence the New Zealanders came, and thus confirms their own traditions.

In the Hawaiian group, the western portion or side of an island was called "the front," *ke alo*, of the land, and the eastern side was called "the back," *ke kua*. The reason of such designations must be sought in the fact of the arrival of the inhabitants from the west. Compare with this the practice of the Aru Islanders in the south-east of Malaysia, who also call the eastern parts of their group "the back of the islands." See *Voyages of the Dutch brig of war "Dourga," by D. H. Kolff, jun.*, p. 175. London: 1840.

cipal groups, on the western or north-western side, there are certain places, set off from time immemorial, as the points of departure from which the spirits of the dead plunged in the unknown hereafter to join the society of the gods or to be food for them.

The Marquesans are the only people who own to a distinctive national name, and retain a tradition of the road they travelled from their original habitat, until they arrived at the Marquesas Islands. They call themselves *te Take,* "the Take nation." They say that they were created in a country far far to the west, *iao-oa,* called *Take-hee-hee;* and of two different traditions reporting the same fact, one mentions thirteen places of stoppage and sejour during their migration eastward, *iuna,* ere they arrived at the Marquesas, and the other mentions seventeen places.

In one of their legends [1] or religious chants, that of the creation of the world, *te Pena-pena,* by the god Atea, the then known world extended from Vavau to Hawa-ii, "*me Vevau i Hawaii,*" and after the earth was made, or rather, brought to light, the order was given—

> "*Pu te metani me Vevau*
> *A anu te tai o Hawa-ii ;*
> *Pu atu te metani me Hawa-ii*
> *A anu te ao o Vevau.*"

(Blow winds from Vavao and cool the sea of Hawaii ; blow back winds from Hawaii, and cool the air or region of Vavao.) And the burden of each stanza or act of creation is—

> "*O Vevau me Hawa-ii.*"

Again, in the Marquesan chant of the Deluge, *Tai-Toko,* it is said that after the flood the ribs of the earth and the mountain ridges of "Hawa-ii" and of "Matahou" [2] rose up, and extended far and near over the sea of Hawaii—

---

[1] Collected by T. O. Lawson, Esq. of Hivaoa, Marquesas Islands, in MS. kindly furnished the author by Professor W. D. Alexander, formerly of Punahou College, Oahu, Hawaiian Islands.

[2] New Zealand legends and proverbs also refer to a country called

" Una te tai o Hawa-ii."

I know not the age of these chants; but from the absence of any mention or allusion in them to the present Marquesas Islands, or the *" Ao-Maama "* as they are called in other chants, specially that of the Migrations, where they are brought in as the closing scene, so to say, of the epic period of this remarkable branch of the Polynesian family—I infer that they were composed in some other habitat, under physical and geographical conditions entirely different from any that the Polynesian groups afford for the solution of the question which were the Vevau and Hawa-ii to which the chants refer. To seek for them in the Vavau of the Tonga group, and the Sawa-ii or Hawa-ii of the Samoan and Hawaiian groups, would be an arbitrary distortion of the obvious sense of the legend, and incorrect as to the relative position of those islands among themselves and in regard to the prevailing winds. We must therefore seek the scene of these chants beyond the Pacific, where the winds alternate regularly—in fact, where the monsoons blow; and by so doing we not only conform to the sense of the chants, but we also find that the relative position of these two points was east and west, and not north and south.

I have already stated that the large bay of Coupang, on the island of Timor, was formerly called Babao. This bay and surrounding country were, at the time of the first European settlements there, an independent kingdom or state, and it is highly probable that in ancient times, before the Malay element preponderated in the Asiatic archipelago, it had given its name to the whole island. But *Babao* is and would be *Vavao* or *Vevau* in any of the Polynesian dialects, and as such is preserved in the names of several places within the Polynesian area of the Pacific. It thus becomes intelligible why Vavao or Timor should have been

---

"Mataaho," destroyed by a flood, "*te hurianga i Mataaho.*" *Vide* Proverbs and Popular Sayings of the Ancestors of the New Zealand Race, by Sir George Gray, p. 85.

quoted in the chant as the one terminus of the known world to the people then occupying the Asiatic Archipelago from there to Jāwa or Sumatra. To those people, at that time, it was the eastermost land then known, and when subsequently the Malays became dominant, they called it *Timor* or "the East," plainly indicating thereby that it was also by them at that time considered, as the extreme east. They merely translated the old name, or the idea associated with it, into their own language.

I have before stated that I consider the Polynesian word *Hawa-ii* or *Sawa-ii* as corresponding to *Jawa*, whether applied to Jawa proper or to Sumatra, or both, and the frequent allusion made in the chant referred to the "sea of Hawa-ii," *te tai o Hawa-ii*—the Jawa sea points with sufficient accuracy to those islands as the western terminus of the world as known to those who composed that chant, unless future investigations may enable us to extend that boundary so as to include the Arabian *Saba*.

In this way the expression used, regarding the winds, receives a force and application which, under no other construction, it could have received; and it then applies to the regular monsoons which blow over that part of the world : " Blow winds from Vevao (from the east) and cool the sea of Hawa; blow back winds from Hawa (from the west), and cool the region or air of Vevao."

The Hawaiian traditions which bear upon the origin of the islands and the derivation of the inhabitants are many and diversified, both in substance and colouring. National or dynastic vanity and priestly speculations have apparently at different periods re-cast and re-arranged some old primordial tradition, whose features either retreated to the back-ground of by-gone ages, or were overlaid or altered to suit local necessities, or the pressure of newer ideas. Enough, however, remains of that old primal tradition, the groundwork of nearly all the others, to show that the earliest reminiscences of the Hawaiian branch of the Polynesian family refer to a far western habitat on some very large island or islands, or perhaps continent, as the birth-place of their ancestors. This land was known under many names, but the most frequently occurring is "*Kapa-kapa-ua-a-Kane.*" It is also called "*Hawaii-kua-uli-kai-oo*" (Hawaii with the green back, banks or upland, and the dotted sea). It is said to have been situated in *Kahiki-ku*, or the large continent to the east of *Kalana-i-Hau-ola*, or the place where the first of mankind were created, while *Kahiki-moe* was the name of the large land or continent to the west of this same "Kalana-i-Hau-ola." According to the tradition, there lived many generations after the flood (*ke kai-a-Kahinalii*), on the east coast of a country situated in or belonging to "Kapakapa-ua-a-Kane," and called *Ka Aina Kai Melemele-a-Kane,*[1] "the land or coast of the yellow or handsome sea," a chief of high renown and purest descent called *Hawa-ii-loa*, or, also, *Ke Kowa-i-Hawaii.* This chief was a noted fisher-man and great navigator, and on one of his maritime cruises, by sailing in the direction of the star *Iao* (Jupiter when morning star) and of the Pleiades, he discovered land, arrived at the eastermost of these islands which he called after his own name, and the other islands he called after his children. Delighted with the country, he returned to his native land after his wife and family, and having performed the same eastern voyage, in the direction of the

[1] "Among the various traditions regarding the manner in which Jawa and the eastern islands were originally peopled, and the source whence the population proceeded, it has been re-lated that the first inhabitants came in vessels from the Red Sea (*Laut Mira*), and that in their passage they coasted along the shores of Hindostan, that peninsula then forming an unbroken continent with the land in the Indian Archipelago, from which it is now so widely separated, and which, accord-ing to the tradition, has since been divided into so many distinct islands by some convulsions of nature or re-volution of the elements." History of Jawa, by Thomas S. Raffles, chap. x., *vide* Asiatic Journal, December 1817, p. 586. The mention of the "Laut Mira" or Merah by the Ja-vanese tradition as the direction whence their ancestors came, gives a singular confirmation and importance to the "Kai Melemele" of the Hawa-iian legend; but whether it should refer to the Red Sea or the Erythrean may be a question which, under the bearing of the Hawaiian legend, I should be inclined to answer in favour of the latter.

morning star and the Pleiades, crossing the ocean which is called by the diverse names of *Kai-holo-o-ka-ia*, " the sea where fish do run," *Ka Moana-kai-Maokioki-a-Kane*, " the spotted, many-coloured ocean," and also *Moana-kai-Popolo*, " the blue or dark-green ocean,"—he arrived the second time to the Hawaiian Islands, and he and his family and followers were their first human inhabitants. So runs the legend.

That this legend embodies the oldest remembered knowledge of the Hawaiian people regarding the origin of the world, the creation of mankind, the deluge and some principal events in the national life of that branch of the human family which we now call " the Polynesian," there will, in my opinion, be little room for doubting. The principal facts, and some of the episodes connected with them, are repeated or alluded to, *mutatis mutandis*, yet in a recognisable shape—and thus corroborated as an heirloom of the entire Polynesian family, previous to its dispersion in the Pacific—in the traditions and legends of the principal groups. The universality of the tradition proves its antiquity.

This is not, perhaps, the proper place to critically consider the historical merits of the Hawaiian legend of *Kumuhonua*, of which the story of *Hawaii-loa* is but an episode; but, admitting the antiquity of the legend, it shows that, according to the earliest recollections of the Hawaiian people, as handed down by tradition, they sprang from a country lying far to the westward of their present abode, and that, whether the Hawaii to which the legend refers be the Hawaii of the North Pacific, the Sawaii of the Samoan group, or the Jawa of the Asiatic Archipel, they did not come there from the east, north, or south, but from lands and seas in the far distant west. The Hawaiians considered themselves as emigrants, not as autochthones, of the Hawaii of which the legend speaks.

But there are three of the Polynesian groups, the

Hawaiian, the Samoan, and the Tongan, having each an island whose name, with a slight dialectical difference, is precisely the same—Hawa-ii—and each one claiming for itself the honour of having been the first peopled and first named in the Pacific. Yet all concur, however, in pointing to the far west as the birthplace of their ancestors, or the abode of their gods.[1] In the far west, therefore, beyond the Pacific, we must look for the original "Hawa" or "Hawa-ii," after which they named their new abodes in the various quarters of the Pacific. And here the legend, to which I have already referred, gives another landmark which, in a peculiar manner, points out the direction in which to look for the special and primary "Hawa" which the Polynesians so fondly remembered. The name of that wandering chief, who is said to have discovered the Hawaiian islands and first settled upon them, is not only *Hawaii-loa,* "the great burning Hawa," but his name is also repeatedly given as *ke Kowa o Hawa-ii,* "the straits of the great burning Hawa." If, as I think, there is sufficient ground for identifying the Polynesian Hawa-ii with Jawa in the Asiatic Archipel, then this "Kowa-o-Hawa-ii" can be no other than the Straits of Sunda, or a personified remembrance of them.

The Polynesian mind had also another mode of expressing this vague remembrance of a far off home. In many, if not most of the groups, the *Moku-Huna* or *Aina-Huna-a-Kane,* "the hidden, concealed land of Kane," was as much a reality as the existence of Kane himself. This land of plenty and bliss would occasionally loom up in the far off western horizon to the sight of the gifted and faithful. In the Hawaiian traditions its situation was vaguely indicated to be in a north-westerly direction from the group or the particular island of the beholder, and though firmly believed in, yet the belief seldom stimulated

---

[1] According to M. de Bovig, "Etat de la Société Taitienne à l'arrivée des Européens," the Tahitian traditions expressly state that the cradle of the human race was where the sun sets.

to action. But in the Marquesas group numerous expeditions have from time to time, up till quite lately,
been started in search of this traditional land of mys-
tery and bliss, and their course was invariably to the
westward.[1]

This looking to the west, this longing after the home of
their forefathers, was doubtless brought by the Polynesians from their earlier Asiatic homes. From India to the
Arran Isles, off the coast of Ireland, the belief in some
" happy island of the west" was a conspicuous trait of
the Indo-European family; and whether the Polynesians
derived it from Aryan or Cushite sources, or whether it
developed itself on each particular group as a common
expression of regret and desire after that happier land
where they had formerly dwelt, its existence as a fact is
none the less pertinent to the argument for their western
origin.

The physical resemblance, and the uniformity of usages,
customs, modes of thought, not to mention language, of
which I shall speak more fully hereafter, between the
Polynesians and the Dayahs, Battas, Buguis, and other
tribes still living in the Malay Archipelago, and whom I
look upon as pre-Malay remnants of the Polynesian
family, are too many and too striking not to indicate a
close relationship, a common origin, and a lengthened
period of residence in the same place, to give time for
their development and spread. In the " L'Univers " sec-

---

[1] As late as the commencement of
this century the Nukahivans were
every now and then fitting out exploring expeditions in their great
canoes in search of a traditional land
called *Utupu*, supposed to be situated
to the westward of their archipelago,
from which the god Tao first introduced the cocoa-nut tree, *vide* L'-
Univers Pittor., Oceanie, by D. de
Rienzi, vol. ii. p. 230.

tion " Oceanie," by Mr. G. L. Dominis de Rienzi, this subject is fully and well-treated. The Javanese and Malays
themselves, who arrived in the archipelago at a later date
than the above tribes—conquering, extirpating, driving
them out, or driving them into the mountain fastnesses of
the different islands—also acknowledge their priority by
calling them the *Orang-Benoa,* "the aborigines of the
country."

Speaking of the different races which now inhabit
Malaysia, M. de Rienzi says, "Oceanie," vol. i. p. 18:

"La seconde race est celle des Polynésiens. Nous cro-
yons avoir trouvé dans la race des Dayas et autres peuples
de Borneo, le berceau des peuple Malaisiens, Mélanésiens
et Polynésiens. Leur teint blanc-jaunâtre plus ou moins
foncé, l'angle facial aussi ouvert que celui des Européens,
la haute stature, la physionomie régulière, le nez et le
front élevés, les cheveux longs et noirs, la beauté, la grace,
les manières souples et lascives de leurs femmes, et surtout des danseuses, les rapports quoique altérés de leurs
langues, l'habitude de l'agriculture, de la chasse et de la
pêche, l'habilité à construire leurs pirogues et à fabriquer
leurs ustensiles, leurs immenses cases, leurs croyances
religieuses, les sacrifices humains, leurs coutumes et une
sorte particulière de consécration ou *tapou,* tout indique la
plus grande ressemblance entre les Dayas et les Polynésiens. La comparaison serait même plus exacte entre
ceux-ci et les Touradjas et les Bouguis de Célèbes ; mais
les Touradjas et les Bouguis, chez lesquels les propriétés
des grands et des prêtres sont reputées sacrées, ainsi que
dans la Polynésie et parmi les Dayas, nous paraissent,
ainsi que nous l'avons déja dit, appartenir a la race Daya,
de même que les Balinais, les peuples des îles Nias, Nassau
ou Poggy, les Ternatis, les Guiloliens et ceux d'une partie
des Moluques, de l'archipel de Holo, des îles Philippines et
des îles Palaos. Ces trois derniers surtout paraissent etre
originaires de Célèbes et de Borneo ; mais la ressemblance
des Taïtiens, des Nouveaux-Zeelandais et surtout des

Battas avec les Dayas est frappante, selon le récit des voyageurs les plus dignes de foi."

This striking resemblance, physical and social, between the pre-Malay inhabitants of Malaysia—those remnants of an anterior population, found more or less pure—and the Polynesian family, I have found corroborated by nearly every competent traveller. It is a *prima facie* evidence of consanguinity which every inquiry only tends to strengthen, and greatly leads to the conclusion that during some previous epoch these *disjecta membra* constituted one great family, occupying the Asiatic Archipel from Sumatra to Ceram, from Luzon to Timor. From Javanese and Malay chronicles or records it may be gathered that there was a time when the Malay and the Hindu had no permanent foothold in the present Malaysia; that about the commencement of the present era, and possibly earlier, they arrived from the country of Kling or Talinga, on the east coast of Hindustan, and established themselves by force on Java and Sumatra; that they found there a people whom they called Rakshasas or demons—a Hindu complimentary term for those of non-Brahminical belief—and whom they exterminated, subdued, or expelled. That this people, thus stigmatised by the conquering Hindus and Brahminical historians, were the ancestors of the Polynesian family there seems to me now to be little room for doubting, and I hope subsequent pages will make it still clearer.

Great as the similarity is in other respects between the Polynesian in the East Pacific—from Hawaii to New Zealand—and his unmistakable blood-relations in Malaysia, the Battas, Reyangs, Nias, Dayahs, Buguis, Tagals, Moluccans (in places), Saouans and others, the linguistic conformity is equally remarkable, and it gives us, moreover, a clue to the high antiquity of that branch of the family now found in the Pacific, and enables us to decide its priority in time, irrespective of other proofs, over the Malay and Hindu intruders in the Asiatic Archipelago.

I must not, however, ignore the fact that not a few writers, and some of great reputation even, have classed the Polynesians as an offshoot, as descendants, of the Malay stock; and that at least one naturalist of high and well-deserved renown, in writing on the " Malay Archipelago," has come to the conclusion that the Polynesian race is " a modification of the Papuan, superinduced by an admixture of Malay or some light-coloured Mongol element." Reserving my remarks on both these classes of writers to another division of this work, and merely referring to the physical resemblance of some of the pre-Malay, or rather non-Malay, tribes in the Asiatic Archipelago, to the Polynesians of the north and south Pacific, I find that in the work above quoted, Mr. R. A. Wallace, speaking of the Galela men of Gilolo,[1] one of the Moluccas, says that they are of light complexion, with Papuan features, resembling the drawings of Tahitians and Hawaiians more than any that he has seen. Again, on page 323, the same author finds that the people of northern Gilolo, or Alfuras, as he calls them, are "radically distinct from all the Malay races," and thinks that they "unmistakably proclaim a Papuan type," and considers them as a comparatively recent immigration, and that they had come from the north or east, perhaps from some of the islands of the Pacific. Again, on page 269, speaking of the people of the plateau of Tondano, Celebes, Mr. Wallace says, "the plateau of Tondano is chiefly inhabited by people nearly as white as the Chinese, and with very pleasing semi-European features. The people of Siam and Sanguir much resemble these, and I believe them to be perhaps immigrants from some of the islands of north Polynesia." Again, on page 249, Mr. Wallace describes the people of Minchasa and Menado, of north-east Celebes, as differing "from any other people in the archipelago. They are of a light brown or yellow tint, often approaching the fairness of the European; rather short stature, stout and well made, open

---

[1] Page 331.

and pleasing countenance, more or less disfigured as age increases by projecting cheek-bones, with the usual long straight jet-back hair of the Malay races." On page 203, speaking of the inhabitants of Timor, Mr. Wallace calls the mountaineers "a people of Papuan type, slender forms, bushy frizzled hair, and skin of a dusky brown colour. Long nose with overhanging apex, so characteristic of the Papuan, and so absolutely unknown among races of Malayan origin." Finally, on page 195, Mr. Wallace considers the people of Savu, south-west from Timor, as probably of Hindu descent; at least they were different from either Malay or Papuan; had well-formed features, straight, thin noses, and clear brown complexion.[1]

Though Mr. Wallace, in two or three places of the work referred to, intimates a belief that the Polynesians emigrated from the Pacific, and settled in the Malay Archipelago, at least in the eastern portions of it, instead of deriving their origin from that direction, yet it is sufficient for my present purpose that he admits the resemblance and consanguinity of the Polynesians to tribes still existing in the said archipelago:

[1] Lieutenant Kolff, in Voyages of the Dutch brig of war "Dourga," 1825-26, speaking of the heathen inhabitants of Lette, an island near Kissa, in the southern Moluccas, says, "They are tall and well formed, with light brown complexions; their noses are pointed, and their foreheads high, while their hair, naturally black, is rendered yellow by rubbing in a composition of lime. It is confined by means of a bamboo comb. The men wear no other dress than a piece of cloth, made from the bark of a tree, wrapped round the waist. The women, in addition to this article of clothing, sometimes wear a sort of Kabya, or short gown, open in front," p. 60.

Speaking of the inhabitants of the Tenimber group in the same sea, Mr. Kolff says, "They are usually well formed, and possess a fairer complexion than most of their neighbours, while their features display few of the characteristics of the inhabitants of the Indian Archipelago, generally being more in accordance with those of Europeans, to whom they would bear much resemblance were it not for the dark colour of their complexion," p. 239.

In Voyage au Pale Sud, vol. ii. p. 280, &c., Captain d'Urville describes the Harfouras of Celebes (Menado) as identical, physically, with the Polynesians.

I believe that it is now established by the best philologists, that all languages, in their development, proceed from the simple to the complex, from monosyllables to polysyllables, from agglutinative to inflectional. Thus considered, the Polynesian language, through its various dialects, as found in the Pacific, is one of the oldest living on the face of the earth.[1] Its identity with the pre-Malay dialects still existing in Malaysia is now fully established; and not only so, but it is especially and manifestly the older surviving form of a once common tongue. Thanks to its isolation for long un-numbered ages, it has preserved the ancient simplicity of its structure, and suffered less phonetic corruption than its congeners and pre-Malay cousins, the Dayahs, Battas, Buguis, &c., subject as these latter have been, for 1800 years at least, to a constant and harassing intrusion from, and intercourse with, Arab, Kawi, Malay, and Chinese. The absence in the Pacifico-Polynesian branch of those abbreviations of syllables, elisions of vowel-sounds, and the abundance of terminal consonants which characterise the Asiatic branch, besides the rudimentary simplicity of its alphabet, attest the early age at which it separated from its kindred in the Asiatic Archipelago.

Having shown by various facts that the Polynesian family in the Pacific—from Easter Island to Rotuma, from the Hawaiian group to New Zealand—can be traced directly to the Asiatic Archipelago, and that in a majority of cases they themselves refer not only the residence of their gods, but also the homes of their immediate ancestors, to those islands and lands in the far off west which they so

---

[1] " The Polynesian language is, in its whole formation and construction, by far more primitive than the Malayan and the rest of the Javano-Tagalo languages. It belongs to a primitive state of society." Dieffenbach, Travels in New Zealand, p. 299.

fondly remembered in naming their new habitats in the
Pacific, and the glamour of which still haunts the popular
mind in song and saga, there is still an objection which at
first sight appeared to me, and may appear to others, as an
incomprehensible fact, if not a fatal demurrer to the conclusion above set forth.   It is this—and the question may
pertinently be asked—how came the Polynesians in their
migrations, whether forcible or voluntary, from any part of
the present Malay Archipelago, to push past the entire
space of Papuasia—from New Guinea to the Viti group—
some thousands of miles into the Pacific, before they established themselves in their new homes ?   That question
involves a consideration of the origin and habitats of the
Papuan race which I do not feel thoroughly competent to
engage in.   This much, however, I think may be safely
asserted, and will in part be borne out by facts, that at some
remote period the Papuans inhabited the islands of the
Asiatic Archipelago as far west at least as Borneo, and probably extending up on the mainland on the side of Siam,
the Malacca peninsula, and perhaps as far as Burmah ; that
they held those islands at a time previous to the arrival
and occupation of them by the ante-Malay family, whom I
designate as the Polynesian race : that as this race advanced to the eastward through the archipelago, the Papuans
were driven before them, either out of the islands altogether, or into the interior of the larger ones, where remnants of them still are found ; and that, thus expelled or
conquered, they found an asylum and a home in the Papuan
Archipelago; unless we assume that they had already spread
so far east before they came in hostile contact with the
Polynesians in the west.   And when, in the course of time,
these latter were in their turn crowded out by the en-
croachments of Malay and Hindu immigrations, and left
from various points, entering the Pacific in quest of new
abodes, they found their ancient foes in superior force along
their route, and, unable to effect permanent settlements on
the Papuan islands, they were obliged to push on eastward

until the Eastern Pacific islands, at that time probably uninhabited,[1] afforded them that shelter and rest which in vain they had sought on Papuan coasts.

When the Polynesians entered the Pacific there were two routes open to them, and they probably followed both —according to the different points of departure within the Asiatic Archipelago—Torres Straits and the Gilolo Passage. On either route they have left mementoes of their passage in the Polynesian names of various places, and in outlying remnants of their own race on scattered points of the Papuan Archipel. The islands of Lefu and Uea of the Loyalty group, Nuumea on New Caledonia, and other names, recall their Polynesian origin; while the inhabitants of St. David's or Freewill Island, of Stewart Islands or Sikyana and How's group, along the northern extent of Papuasia, are unquestionably of Polynesian descent, both in appearance and language.[2]

If not the first, at least the last and best confirmed attempt of the Polynesian wanderers at permanent settlements on Papuan soil, was at the Viti or Fiji Islands. The number of Polynesian names by which these islands and places in them are called, even now, by their Papuan inhabitants, argues a permanence of residence that cannot well be disputed. The large infusion of Polynesian vocables in the Fijian language, and the mixture of the two races, especially in the south-eastern part of the group, indicate a

---

[1] The indications that the various Pacific groups were inhabited at the time that the Polynesians occupied them, are very faint indeed ; and yet the import of some of their traditions cannot be otherwise construed. That the majority of the groups were uninhabited at the time referred to seems to me quite clear; but I think it equally clear also that the people which left their architectural remains on the Ladrone islands, and their colossal statues on Easter Island, had swept the Pacific Ocean before that time, and possibly may have left some remnants of themselves to which the traditions refer, but which were absorbed or expelled by the new-comers.

[2] Late discoveries on the south-east coast of New Guinea have brought to light several tribes of undoubted Polynesian affinity, both in physique and language.—*Vide* Journal of Rev. Mr. Lawes in the Missionary Steamer "Ellengowan," from Port Moresby to China Straits, published in "Town and Country Journal," Sydney, June 3, 1876.

protracted sejour, and an intercourse of peace as well as of war.[1] But after some time—how long cannot now be expressed in generations or in centuries—the Papuans succeeded in driving the Polynesians out of their group, and then, if they had not before, they occupied the island groups still farther eastward, simultaneously or successively.

Of that intercourse, contest and hostility between the Papuan and Polynesian races, on the south-west fringe of the Pacific, there are several traditionary reminiscences among the Polynesian tribes, embodied in their mythology, or retained as historical facts, pointing to past collision and stimulating to future reprisals. The Tongá Islands have a tradition, recorded by Mariner,[2] that *Tanga-loa,* one of their principal gods, had two sons, of which the elder was called *Tu-po,* the younger was called *Vaka-ako-uli.* The first was indolent and shiftless, the other industrious and prosperous. Jealousy induced the former to kill the latter. Then "Tanga-loa" called the older brother and the family of the younger before him, and thus addressed the latter : "Your bodies shall be fair as the spirit of your father was good and pure ; take your canoes and travel to the eastward, and all good things attend you." And to the older brother the offended god thus spoke : "Thy body

---

[1] We now know from New Caledonian traditions, as reported by Dr. V. de Roehas ("La Nouvelle Calédonie," &c., Paris, 1862), that in olden times joint and singular expeditions of Fijians and Tongans frequently invaded New Caledonia and conquered tracts of land for themselves, and that the higher aristocracy and subordinate nobles of to-day claim descent from the chiefs of those predatory parties ; that, owing to this influx, the language presents a great variety of idioms ; that the main stock, however, of the population is of the original Papuan ; and, as circumcision is also practised among them, it may, for want of more precise knowledge of its origin and introduction there, with great plausibility be ascribed to that same Tonga-Vitian element.

In further confirmation of the settlement and protracted stay of Polynesian tribes on the Fiji group, the reader is referred to United States Exploring Expedition, Ethnography and Philology, by Horatio Hale, p. 174, &c.; a writer whom I have found as valuable, trustworthy, and cautious as any who has attempted to write upon the Polynesian family in the Pacific.

[2] Account of the Natives of the Tonga Islands, vol. ii. pp. 123 and 402. London, 1817.

shall be black as thy soul is wicked and unclean: I will raise the east wind between you and your brother's family, so that you cannot go to them, yet from time to time I will permit them to come to you for the purposes of trade."

Whether this legend was of purely Tongan and limited origin,[1] or merely a chip from the old Cushite storehouse of primitive legends, yet, when we consider that from the earliest times the Tonga islanders have kept up a more or less continuous intercourse with the Viti group, either warlike or commercial, it is not difficult to apply the tradition, or to point the moral.

That the hostilities in the early days of Polynesian settlements in the Pacific was remembered by other tribes as well as the Tonga, and looked upon as a national vendetta, may be inferred from a remark made by Quiros in his account of the expedition of Mendana (1595), while at the island of Santa Christina (*Tahuata*), one of the Marguesas group. He says:—I quote from "Voyage de Marchand," vol. i. p. 227—that the natives, having observed a negro on board of the Admiral's ship among the Spaniards, said that to the south of their island there was land inhabited by black men; that these were their enemies; that they used the bow and arrow; and that the big war-canoes then lying in the bay of Madre de Dios were destined and being fitted to make war upon them. Quiros, not then knowing the existence of the Viti group, dis-

---

[1] I am inclined to believe this legend to be older than the expulsion of the Tongans from Viti, because I have found references, though more or less distorted, to similar early fratricide in both New Zealand and Hawaiian traditions, and I therefore look upon it as a common heirloom of the Polynesian family before its dispersion in the Pacific. The Hawaiian legend states that the oldest son of *Kumuhonua*, the first man, was called *Laka*, and that the next son was called *Ahu;* that *Laka* was a bad man, and killed his brother *Ahu.*

The New Zealand legend states that the New Zealanders descended from two brothers, *Maui-mua* and *Maui-potiki;* that the former, being the elder, killed the younger brother and ate him, whence the custom of cannibalism among them.—Oceanie, par G. L. D. de Rienzi, vol. iii. p. 161.

The old legends of the Island of Madura, north of Jawa, mention a King called *Rawson Dawa*, who had two children, one white and called *Kakra Sana*, the other black, and called *Krisna.*—"Monde Maritime," par G. A. Walkenaer.

credited their story of the black men. The specialty, however, of these using the bow and arrow, points them out as of the Papuan race, to whom that weapon was and is familiar, while by the Polynesians generally it is never, or very seldom, used for purposes of war.

Whether the Marquesans of Quiros' time actually carried on so distant a warfare, as between their group and the Viti or any other Papuan island, may fairly be called in doubt, and is, in my opinion, quite improbable. But the fact that they were acquainted with the existence of the Papuan race in the Pacific as distinct from their own, and with the peculiar weapon of war of the former, and that that acquaintance was one of ancient and intense hostility, cannot be doubted. That acquaintance probably dated back to the time when they were dwelling in the Samoan group to the north-east of the Viti; or perhaps older still, when coasting along the shores of the Papuan Archipel, before their arrival at Viti.

How long the Polynesian family had dwelt in the Asiatic Archipelago ere it debouched in the Pacific there are now small means of knowing, hardly of forming even a conjecture. Its reminiscences of that period are not many, and are confused with memories of older date and of other habitats. There are many allusions in their sagas and songs to events and persons previous to their arrival in the Pacific, and which they evidently brought with them from that far western home. But whether these allusions were born there, so to say, or acquired there by intercourse with other peoples still farther west, or brought with them as reminiscences of a previous national life in some other land, before they explored and spread over the Asiatic Archipelago, are points extremely difficult to decide, and enveloped in great obscurity. Glimpses of Cushite Zabaism; religious symbols of the Siwa worship; Hindu myths, but of Vedic simplicity and Iranian colouring, or rather fraternity; legends derived from both Cushite and Iranian sources; customs largely bespeaking the same mixed origin; but, above all, a language fundamentally Arian,[1] but Arian of a pre-Vedic and pre-Iranian era—all these cumulative yet many-sided evidences of a foreign extraction, beyond the Asiatic Archipelago, meet us at every step in Polynesian folk-lore and Polynesian archæology. Let us collect these scattered lights; let us endeavour to read the riddle they present, and lift a corner of the curtain that shrouds the cradle of the Polynesian race. These lights are dim, and they are few; but though they may not illumine the landscape, yet I think they are sufficient to show the path.

Of the peculiar extension, development, and influence of the ancient Arabic civilisation in pre-historic times, it is not my object, nor wholly within my ability, to treat. That it was a power in the world, and felt as such, from beyond the pillars of Hercules to the furthest East, modern researches are making more and more evident. This remarkable race of people—whom the earlier Greek writers mentioned as Ethiopians, whom Iranian traditions designated as inhabiting "Cusha-Dwipa," and who claimed for themselves a descent from the twelve sons of Chan—had overrun the then known world with their conquests, their colonies and commerce, long before the Arian and Semitic stocks had issued from the barbarism of ethnic infancy.[2]

[1] According to Professor Max Müller (Lectures on the Science of Language, 2d Series, p. 192. London, 1864), "the original elements of the Arian language consisted of open syllables of one consonant followed by one vowel, or of a single vowel." As the Arian was then, so is the Polynesian to this day.

[2] "Recent linguistic discovery tends to show that a Cushite or Ethiopian race did in the earliest times extend itself along the shores of the Southern Ocean, from Abyssinia to India. The whole peninsula of India was peopled by a race of this character before the influx of the Arians. It extended from the Indus along the sea-coast through the modern Beloochistan and Kerman, which was the proper country of the Asiatic Ethiopians; the cities on the northern shore of the Persian Gulf are shown by the brick inscriptions found among their ruins to have belonged to this race; it was dominant in Susiana and Baby-

They were the first to navigate and explore the coasts and islands of the Mediterranean as well as of the Indian seas. They called many of those places by names drawn from their own tongue, and which have come down to our own time as vestiges of their presence, as fossilised specimens cropping out through successive strata of overlying nationalities and languages, awaiting some philological Cuvier to collect and classify them. Wheresoever they went they inoculated the barbarous tribes with whom they came in contact with their religious notions, their social customs, their arts, their knowledge. Time, the natural disintegration of overgrown empires, and the irruption over the same area of other systems—religious and political—of other progressive and self-sustained races, have effaced much and absorbed more of this early civilisation, whose shreds and patches may still be found hanging on many an ethnic bush, and thus attesting the influence and intellectual activity of this wonderful race.[1]

My object in thus specially referring to this Cushite-Hamitic-Arabian race and its wide-spread influence in prehistoric times, is to call an increased attention of eminent Orientalists to the elucidation of the past of this singular race, because I have found in the traditions, religious notions, and modes of expression, social customs of the Polynesian family, not a few indications and startling co-

lonia until overpowered in the one country by Arian, in the other by Semitic intrusion; it can be traced, both by dialect and tradition, throughout the whole south coast of the Arabian peninsula, and it still exists in Abyssinia, where the language of the principal tribe (the *Galla*) furnishes, it is thought, a clue to the cuneiform inscriptions of Susiana and Elymais, which date from a period probably a thousand years before our era."—Herodotus, by George Rawlinson, vol. i. p. 529, n. 8.

[1] In speaking of ancient Arabian commerce with India, Mr. Lenor-

mant, in the Manual of Ancient History, vol. ii. p. 301, says: "It dates from so remote an antiquity that it is impossible to determine its origin. Both countries, the shores of the Indian Ocean as well as those of the Persian Gulf, were even anterior to the Arian migrations and the establishment of the Ioktanite Arabs in Yemen, inhabited by populations of the same race, Cushites and Canaanites, those people to whom all historical traditions agree in attributing the first development of commerce and navigation."

incidences tending to show that at some time in its early trans-Pacific life, in Deccan or beyond the Vindhya mountains, this family had been subject to Cushite influence, and received more or less of Cushite blood into its veins.

With the dim and intermittent light which present knowledge throws upon that Cushite empire, it is difficult, nay impossible, to arrange these indications and coincidences properly as to locality of origin or sequence of time. And the same remark will apply to whatever in Polynesian folk-lore may be found corresponding or akin to modes of thought or social usages, whether of early Arian growth or of later Hindu development. I simply present them, therefore, in bulk, so to say, as the stock in hand yet remaining among the Polynesian tribes from its former connection with the Cushite and Arian races.

According to the old Arab, pre-Semitic tradition, the Cushite race consisted originally of twelve tribes.[1] Their names were Ad, Thamud, Tasm, Djadis, Amlik, Oumayim, Abil, Djourhoum, Wabar, Jasm, Autem, Hashen. Another tradition mentions Ad as the son of Chan; and as a general expression, "old as Ad," conveyed a sense of the highest antiquity to the Arab mind. When the Semitic or Semitised Arabs, at a later epoch, had obtained the predominancy in Arabia and Syria, they moulded their genealogical descent on the Cushite pattern. We find that the Semitic Arabs claimed descent from Jaktan, through his twelve sons; that the Ishmaelites claimed through the twelve sons of Ishmael; that the Edomites claimed through the twelve dukes of Edom, sons and grandsons of Esau; that the Hebrews claimed through the twelve sons of Jacob; the Babylonians of historic time had twelve gods besides Ra or Il, their tutelar deity or supreme god; the Etruscans

[1] "Pre-historic Nations," by John D. Baldwin, A.M., sect. iii., passim.

had twelve great gods; and we find this mystic number twelve obtaining in the myths and theogonies of several branches of the Arian race; the Du "Majores" or Consentes of the Romans and Greeks,[1] and the Asa family of gods among the Scandinavians. Now, whether that idea of twelveship in human descent or divine economy was merely a development and after application of the primary Zabaism, of which those old-world Cushite Arabians were among the earliest, if not the original professors, I leave others to determine. It is sufficient for my present purpose that that idea, of evidently Cushite origin, and so widely diffused and so variously applied by both the Semitic and Arian races, is also found among the Polynesian tribes, and found too in the peculiar form used by the Arabian Cushites and neighbouring Semites, to indicate their human descent from some noted progenitor.

In the Hawaiian legend of *Kumuhonua* and his descendants, we find that the Hawaiian people claim descent from the youngest of the twelve sons of *Kini-lau-a-Mano*.

In the Marquesan legends the people claim their descent from *Atea* and *Tani*, the two eldest of *Toho's* twelve sons, whose descendants, after long periods of alternate migrations and rest in far western lands, finally arrived at the Marquesas Islands.

In the famous legend of *Aukele-nui-a-Iku*, known in some form or other on several of the Polynesian groups, the hero's father *Iku* or *Aiku*, and his mother *Ka Papai-akea*, king and queen of a country called *Kua-i-helani*, had twelve children, of which "Aukele" was the youngest son.

But the legend of "Aukele-nui-a-Iku," so ancient and so popular among the Polynesians, presents more indications and coincidences of Cushite extraction than the application of the number twelve as a family or genealogical

---

[1] Sir Henry Rawlinson, in Essay x. App. Book i. of G. Rawlinson's "Herodotus," considers that much of the Greek and Roman mythology, beside what is of purely Arian element, may be traceable to the banks of the Tigris and Euphrates, and was brought to Europe from there by what he calls "Scythic or Scytho-Arian" emigrants.

division. We know from Indian lore that far off in pre-historic times a famous king ruled over Arabia and Upper Egypt, whose name was *It* or *Ait*, and whose fame and exploits were introduced and retained upon the early Greek traditions, where he is called *Aetus*.[1]

The recollection of that Cushite King "Ait" or "Aitu," of whom the Greeks in the west, and the Iranians in the east, had heard so much as to retain his name upon their ancient traditions—survives, also, not only in this Poly-nesian legend, but even in the nomenclature of several places north and south in Polynesia, which bear his name, simply or composite. We thus find *Aitu-take*, one of the Hervey group; *A-fare-a-Aitu*, a bay and village on Hua-hine, of the Society group; *Aiku*, name of a tract of land between Hamakua and S. Kohala, on Hawaii, Hawaiian group; *Fare-a-Aitu* was the name of the house of worship in heathen times on Rakahanga, one of the Manahiki group; in the Samoan and Rotuma dialects *Aitu* signifies a spirit, and so does *Maitu* in the Paumotu group.[2]

The idea of royalty or sovereignty attached to this word "Iku" or "Aiku," as of Cushite origin, is, moreover, ob-served in the old Hawaiian tradition, according to which the chiefs were divided into two classes or pedigrees: the class *Iku-pau* and the class *Iku-nuu*. The former appear to have been considered as descendants in direct line from

---

[1] Baldwin's Pre-historic Nations, p. 280.

As the etymology of the word Aethiopians or Αιθιοπες is not yet satisfactorily determined by philolo-gists, I may be permitted to suggest its derivation from this same King Ait, It, or Aitu, and the early Hel-lenic, or, perhaps, pre-Hellenic term Opes, signifying peoples, tribes, as-semblages; the word Aethiopes thus being of analogous formation to Pel-opes, Dol-opes, Cere-opes, &c., and equivalent to "the people of Ait or Aitu."

In Rawlinson's Herodotus, vol.

ii. p. 35, n. 8, I read: "Αιδιοψ was evidently a corruption of the Egyptian name for Southern Ethiopia or Nubia, 'Ethaush' or 'Ethosh,' the ps being substituted for sh, a sound the Greeks could neither write nor pro-nounce. The Greeks (like the Arabs) often adopted a word having some signification in their own language, if it resembled a foreign one, and the Greek derivation of Αιδιοψ is on a par with that of Isis, from εισις, 'know-ledge,' and many others."

[2] In Tahitian *Taefei-a-itu* is the name of a bird sacred to the god *Tane*.

"Kane," the god, or "Kumuhonua," the first man, and possessed both spiritual and temporal power; the latter appear to have corresponded to collateral or cadet branches of the royal families, and possessed only temporal power.

As regards the country in which this renowned King "Ait" or "Aitu" is said to have lived, the cumulative evidence of a Cushite connection induces me to collate the first component part of *Kua-i-helani* with "Cusha" in the Vedic and later Sanskrit *Cusha-Dwipa*, the division of the earth between the Mediterranean and the Indian Ocean and Persian Gulf. If this be correct, there can be little difficulty in collating the second component of the name with *Hiran* or *Iran*, the ancient name of parts of Persia, and the whole name would then correctly express the extent of country over which King "Ait" ruled according to the Puranas.[1]

I will refer again to this legend of "Aukele-nui-a-Iku" when treating of the so-called Hebrew affinities of the Polynesian race.

Of ancient Zabaism, or rather solar worship, traces may be found in the legends and in expressions of the language. In the Hawaiian legend of "Kumuhonua," it is said "that when, after the flood ('Kai a Kahinalii'), *Nuu* left his vessel in the evening of the day, he took with him a pig, cocoa-nuts, and awa (piper methyst) as an offering to his god *Kane*. As he looked up he saw the moon in the sky, and he thought that that was the god, saying to himself: 'You are *Kane*, no doubt, though you have transformed yourself to my sight.' So he worshipped the moon, and offered his offerings. Then *Kane* descended on the rainbow and spoke reprovingly to *Nuu*, but on account of the mistake *Nuu* escaped punishment, having asked pardon of *Kane*. Then *Kane* ascended to heaven and left the rainbow as a token of his forgiveness."

In ancient Hawaiian poems (meles) and prayers the East is called *he ala nui hele a Kane*, "the great highway

---

[1] Baldwin's "Pre-historic Nations," *loc. cit.*

of Kane," and the West or the setting sun is designated as *he ala nui o ka make*, "the great road of death or the dying." In other chants the East is called *Ke ala-ula a Kane*, "the bright road of Kane, the dawning, the morning light;" and the West is called *Ke ala nui maaweula a Kanaloa*, "the much travelled highway of Kanaloa," he being, according to the elder Hawaiian mythology, considered as the god of death and the ruler of the deep.

Other names of the West, only occurring in the older chants and prayers, and referring to the same symbolism and identification of Kane with the sun, are found in *Kaulana a Kane*, "the resting-place of Kane," and in *Kane nee-nee*, "the moving, the departing sun."

I have found no trace in Polynesian folk-lore that the moon was ever regarded as an object of adoration, nor, though the planetary stars were well known and named, that these latter ever received religious consideration. In the mythology of the Marquesas Islands, the god which corresponds to "Kane" in the Hawaiian group is called *Atea*, a personification of light, as the word itself indicates.

How old creeds will linger in popular customs, long after they have been superseded in the popular mind, will find another illustration in the fact that in olden times, on the Hawaiian group, the front door of the dwelling-houses was facing the east and the rising sun, as a special sign of the "Kane" worship; and another door or opening was facing the west, in remembrance of their arrival from that direction.

Traces of serpent-worship, another peculiarly Cushite outgrowth of religious ideas, occur in Polynesian legends, when reference is frequently made to *Moko* or *Moo*, enormous, powerful reptiles or serpents, evil beings generally, to be propitiated by sacrifices and offerings. In the Fiji group, where much of ancient Polynesian lore, now forgotten elsewhere, is still retained, the god "Ndengei," according to some traditions, is represented with the head and part of the body of a serpent, the rest of his form being stone.[1]

But to whatever extent either solar or serpent worship may have formerly obtained among the Polynesians in pre-Pacific habitats, it is tolerably certain that at the time, and after their entrance in the Pacific, it had faded from the national mind, and only remained in the form of some cherished customs, or some hateful, dreaded recollections.

If the ideas of solar worship, embodied in the Polynesian "Kane"—as the sun, the sun-god, the shining one, and thus synonymous with the Marquesan "Atea," the bright one, the light—were of Cushite origin, yet the name itself is of Arian kindred, and refers itself to some primary root expressed in the Sanskrit *Kan*, to shine, *Chand*, to light up, shine, to the Latin *Canus*, bright, clear, white, to the Greek, Eανθος, golden yellow, to the Welsh *Can* or *Cain*, bright, fair, white; and, I doubt not, recurs again with the same Cushite association of ideas in the Greek Eαv, Eαvω, and the Latin, primarily Etrurian, *Janus* and *Jana*, are terms for the solar and lunar deities. Though *La* and *Ra* are Polynesian terms, designating the sun and the day, as well as in Egyptian and old Babylonian, yet there are few traces in Polynesian lore that he ever was associated with religious ideas, or deified, so to say, as he was both in Egypt and ancient Chaldea.[2] The inference, therefore, is that the Polynesians at some early period of their life accepted the solar culte from the Cushites, but clothed it in terms of their own language; and that, having once raised the term of "Kane" to the power of a deity, it

---

[1] Fiji and the Fijians, by Thomas Williams, p. 170.

[2] The only place in Polynesia where I found that the sun was worshipped under the name of *La* or *Raa*, is on the small island of Tupai, the westernmost of the Society group, where a Marae was dedicated to him. A Tahitian legend, according to M. de Bovis, says that *Hiro*, the first king of Raiatea, was the son of *Haehi*, who was son of *Uruumatamata*, who was the son of *Raa*, the sun. And the same author remarks that on the island of Borabora (Society group) the god *Raa* was a secondary deity, and adds: "Mais il parait avoir été déchu d'une splendeur antérieure." The Society islanders seem at all times to have been prone to depose their gods, or to subordinate them to other deities.

never again reverted to the primary, secular sense which it retained among kindred Arian tribes; and when the culte died out the original sense was forgotten, and in subsequent cultes the term was retained as an expression of deity, of godship.

In the Polynesian Pantheon there are not many gods whose names can be directly traced to a Cushite origin. I find, however, *Oro, Olo,* or *Koro,* as differently pronounced. He was a grand and important deity among the Southern Polynesians. He was the war-god of the Society group, the terrible, exacting human sacrifices. He is said by some to have been the brother of "Tane" or "Kane," whose worship in that group he seems to have in a great measure superseded;[1] by others he is said to be not one of the gods who sprang from night (*mai ka Po mai*), or existed during the primal chaos or darkness, but was the son of the mighty and wondrous *Taaroa* or *Tangaloa,* the Demiurgas of some of the southern groups.[2] His name is probably of Cushite origin. We have the Egyptian *Hor,* the son of Osiris and Isis, the conqueror of Typhon and the "God of Victory." By a strange coincidence of name and attributes, the war-god of the Rajpoots in north-west India is also called *Hor.*

On all the Polynesian groups, from New Zealand to Hawaii, their legends refer to a god or demi-god called *Maui,* whose exploits and adventures were numerous and wonderful. Though the narrative differs in detail on almost every group, yet all agree in ascribing to him the arresting the progress of the sun and regulating its course, and the introduction of fire among mankind.[3] The universality of

[1] Does *Oro-tal,* whom Herodotus, iii. 8, calls one of the two gods of Arabia in his time, and whom he likens to Bacchus, bear any relation to the Egyptian *Hor?* Was it an old Cushite appellation handed down from time immemorial to their Semitic successors who held Arabia when Herodotus wrote?

[2] Other legends say he was the son of the god *Taiau.*

[3] M. Moerenhout, in his Voyage aux Iles du Gr. Ocean, vol. i. p. 446, gives the Tahitian version of the Maui or Mahui legend; how "he brought the earth up from the depths of the ocean; and, when mankind suffered from the prolonged absence

the legend, and the fact that each group has endeavoured
to localise the god and his exploits on its own domain,
proves to me that the legend was one of many which the
Polynesians brought with them to the Pacific before their
dispersion there, and that its origin and the name of the
hero must be looked for in their former habitats in the
West. What Cushite or Hindu legend may have formed
the basis of the Polynesian I am unable to say; but I find
that one of the twelve gods of the second order in Egypt
was called *Moui*, " apparently the same as *Gom* or Hercules,
the splendour and light of the sun, and therefore called a
' son of Re.' "[1]

In a recent work, called " Pre-historic Nations," by Mr.
J. D. Baldwin, the author establishes with much learning
and research that the Hindu deity Siwa, and his worship
and symbols, were not of Vedic origin, but peculiar to the
ante-Arian population, whose civilisation he assigns to
Cushite sources. He shows, moreover, that in early Vedic
times, before the Arians had crossed the Ganges, they
looked with horror and disgust on the Siwa worshippers
and the impure rites of the Lingam or Phallus; but
that after they had crossed the Ganges, extended to the
Vindhya mountains and entered Deccan, an amalgamation
with the conquered peoples had began to take effect, and
then Siwa was adopted in the Brahminical theogony as a
compromise and conciliation with his ancient worshippers;
yet that for long ages afterwards the original repugnance
was still so great that no true officiating Brahmin would
serve at the altars or before the idols of Siwa.

How far any distinct remembrance of the Siwa worship
may be traced in Polynesian traditions and customs is not
easy to determine precisely. The blood-thirsty wife of

of the sun and lived mournfully in
deep obscurity, and when fruits would
not ripen, how he stopped the sun and
regulated its course, so as to make
day and night equal." Does not that
legend indicate that the Polynesians

formerly lived in a zone where the
inequality of day and night was
greater than in the tropics?

[1] Rawlinson's Herodotus, vol. ii.
p. 243.

Siwa still survives in name and attributes in the Tongan God of War, "*Kali-ai-tu-po.*" The name itself of Siwa recurs in the Polynesian word *Hiwa*, primarily "dark-coloured, black or blue;" secondarily, "sacred," as a sacrificial offering. In different dialects the word occurs as *Siwa, Hiwa*, or *Heiwa*, and is applied as an adjective with derivative meanings, but in all the idea of sacredness underlies and characterises its application. Thus *Nuka-Hiwa*, one of the Marquesas, undoubtedly meant originally the "dark or sacred island;" *Fatu-Hiwa* or *Patu-Hiwa*, another of the same group, meant the "sacred rock or stone;" *Hiwaoa*, still another of the same group, meant the "very sacred or holy." In Hawaiian *Puaa-Hiwa* means the "black or sacred hog," offered in sacrifices. *Hiwa-hiwa* was an epithet applied to gods and high chiefs. The name of the Siwaite *Lingam* has unquestionably its root and derivation from the same source as the Tongan *Linga*, the Hawaiian *Lina*, occurring in such words as *Ta-ringa*, "the ear," *Papa-lina* "the cheek," et al.

What the Hawaiians called *Pohaku-a-Kane*, upright stones of from one to six and eight feet in height, the smaller size portable and the larger fixed in the ground, and which formerly served as altars or places of offering at what may be called family worship, probably referred to the Lingam symbolism of the Siwa culte in India,[1] where similar stone pillars, considered as sacred, still abound.[2] But Siwa, as before observed, was not a Vedic

[1] Dieffenbach, in his Travels in New Zealand, p. 64, says that Phallic sculptures are common there on tombs, symbolic of the vis generatrix of male and female originals.

In the Fiji group, also, rude stones resembling milestones are consecrated to this or that god, at which the natives deposit offerings, and before which they worship.—Fiji and the Fijians, by Thomas Williams, p. 173.

[2] In the "Asiatic Journal," February 1828, I find that in Deccan and in the collectorship of Punah, the Koonbees, living to the eastward of the western Ghauts, worship their principal gods in the form of "particular unshapen stones." A black stone is the emblem of Vishnu; a grey one of Siwa or Maha-deo. So, also, stones are consecrated to or emblematical of Mussooba, the god of revenge; of Vital, the god of demons; of Bal-Bheirow or Bharoo, the beneficent god; Khun-dooba, the principal household god of the whole Deccan, is represented at Jejourg by a Lingam.

god, and his rites were held in abomination by the earlier
Vedic Arians. These stone symbols refer, therefore, to a
period of pre-Arian occupation of India, and to the Cushite
civilisation or race. In the Hawaiian group these stone
pillars were sprinkled with water or anointed with cocoa-nut
oil, and the upper part frequently covered with a black
native tapa or cloth, the colour of garment which priests
wore on special occasions, and which was also the cloth in
which the dead were wrapped. Singularly enough, the
Greeks called Priapus the "black-cloaked," and the
Phallus was covered with a black cloth, signifying the
nutritive power of night. The veil of Latona, the mother
of Apollo and Diana (Sun and Moon), was black. The
Hindus of north-west India still worship "Suria," the sun,
under the emblem of a black stone.

The colour of the Egyptian bulls Apis and Mnevis was
black, and in the hieroglyphic representations of acts of
consecration or anointing, the officiating priest is painted
black, and the recipient of the ceremony is painted red;
this more especially in upper Egypt. Hence the black
colour would seem to indicate superior sacredness. It is
possible that from these or similar considerations of supe-
riority or sacredness arose the Polynesian proverb (in
Hawaiian), "*he weo ke kanaka, he pano ke alii*," red is the
common man, dark is the chief.[1]

---

[1] In "Polynesian Researches" the
Rev. Mr. Ellis explains a similar expression in Tahiti, from the fact that
a dark and bronzed complexion was
looked upon, among the chiefs, as a
sign of manliness, hardihood, and ex-
posure to fatigue and danger, and a
pale complexion was considered a
sign of effeminacy. The probable
reason and explanation of the proverb may be found in the greater
amount of tattooing with which the
bodies of the chiefs were adorned.
As late as the time of Kamehameha
I. of Hawaii, his rival Kahekili,
King of Maui, had one half of his
body entirely blackened by tattooing.

The connection of the black colour
with Siwa's symbols may be found
in the Hindu legend, according to
which, at the churning of the sea of
milk for the production of Amutham
(the Ambrosia of immortality) Siwa,
the supreme, was appealed to by the
other gods to remove the poison
vomited in the Ambrosia by the serpent Vasuke. He complied with
their request by drinking up the
poison, but from that time he was
known by the name of "the azure-
necked one," because the colour of
the poison remained on his neck as a
sign of what he had done.—See Oriental Illustrations, by J. Roberts, p. 6.

That these sacrificial stones were closely connected with the Phœnician *Bœtylia*, dedicated to the same purposes, and indicative of a similarity in creeds and symbols, may be shown from the name itself. "Bœtylia," or *Βαιτυλια*, is evidently a composite word, but may not, as some lexicographers indicate, be of Semitic-Hebrew extraction. The thing and its name must be older than the adoption of a Semitic dialect by the Phœnicians. But, as often happens in transition periods, the term "Bœtylia" may be a compromise between the older Cushite and later Semitic languages spoken by the Phœnicians. I consider, therefore, the word as composed of *Batu* and *Il, Illu* or *El*. The latter term is evidently Semitic, and, through all its dialects, signifies God, the God. The former, however, I take to be a Cushite word. It certainly has no Arian connections. But in nearly all the Polynesian congeners we find this word retaining both its primary and derivative sense, both "Stone" and "God" or Lord. In the ancient Madura dialect "Batu" means a stone. At Pulo Nias "Batu" is used as a name for the deity who has charge of the earth, and is called *Batu-da-Danau*. The expression *Battala*, used by the pre-Malay Battas in Sumatra, and *Bitara* of the Bali Islanders, for their deities, may reasonably be referred to the same origin. In the Polynesian dialects proper, we find *Patu* and *Pata-patu*, "stone," in New Zealand; *Fatu* in Tahiti and Marquesas signifying "Lord," "Master," also "Stone;" *Haku* in the Hawaiian means "Lord," "Master," while with the intensitive prefix *Po* it becomes *Pohaku*, "a stone."

But these stones of religious import, and symbolic of an indwelling God, were common in Arabia, Syria, and Greece. In the "Manual of Ancient History of the East," by Lenormant, vol. ii. p. 325, speaking of the religion of Yemen, the author says, that the ancient Arabs in some of their temples or high places, or on top of pyramids like those in Chaldea, worshipped the stars of heaven in preference to idols, though these were also used; and then adds: "They also in some temples adored, as natural images of the gods, or more accurately as objects in which resided the divine essence—in the same way as in Syro-Phœnician religions — certain stones believed to have fallen from heaven, and similar to the Bœtylia of Phœnicia."

Common to the Syrian as well as the Phœnician Baal worship, was the setting up of the *Astera* "on every high hill and under every green tree," as we are told in 1 Kings xiv. 23, was the reprobated practice in Judah.

In Harwood's "Grecian Antiquities," p. 139, I find that in ancient Greece the idol of the temples was but a rude stock or stone cut square, of a black colour, and called *Zanis* as well as Bactylia; and that Dœdalus is said to have been the first who made two feet to these stone idols.

The emblem of Siwa, in Hindu mythology, is the double trident. On a hill called *Kaulana-hoa*, back of Kalae, island of Molokai, of the Hawaiian group, are a number of large, irregularly-shaped volcanic stones, standing on the brow of the hill. One is shaped like a high-backed chair, and, judging from analogy to others like it in other parts of the group, may have served as a seat for the chief, or his priest, from which to look out over the ocean, or to watch the stars. On the east side of this, and near to, stands another large stone, marked with a double trident (⊞) in two places. Who marked this stone, and what the import of the mark? Tradition is silent; and in the absence of other marks of similar character, or of corroborative nature, I forbear to offer a conjecture.

But if the name, attributes, and symbols of Siwa at one time were known to and obtained currency among the Polynesians, through their connection with the Cushite race during their residence in India or before, that fact is further strengthened by the Polynesian legend from Raiatea, Society group, which states that the Deluge was óccasioned by the wrath of *Rua-Haku* (Rua, the Lord), the great Ocean God of that group. To those acquainted with the phonetic peculiarity—a peculiarity especially archaic —of the Polynesian dialects in the Pacific, and their aversion to double and terminal consonants, it is not difficult, nor will it be considered as an etymological crotchet, to connect *Rua*, in his character of an ocean god, with *Rudra*, one of the many names of the Hindu pre-Arian Siwa, whose permanent emblem, the trident, indicates his maritime character, and that at some time, perhaps the earliest period of his culte, he was looked upon as lord of the sea. Whether this name, *Rudra, Rua*, is of Arian or Cushite origin, I know not. If of Arian, it must be of highest antiquity, for in the Celtic-Irish mythology I find that *Ruad* was the name of the deity presiding over the waters. If of Cushite, it proves the immense extent of the influence of that race, from the borders of the Atlantic to the heart of the Pacific.

There is another Hindu god of pre-Vedic origin, and presumably of Cushite extraction, called *Yama*, or *Dhermarajah*, the Hindu Pluto, lord of the infernal regions ("Patala"), who finds his counterpart in attributes and emblems, if not in name, in Polynesia. In India he is represented with a snare in one hand, and a club in the other, looking out for the souls of the dying; and one of his epithets is "the catcher of the souls of men." In the Hervey group, South Polynesia, *Tangaroa*, one of the principal gods in that place, is represented with a net in one hand, wherewith to catch the souls of the dying, and a spear in the other, wherewith to kill them.

The Hawaiian tradition of *Pele*, the dreaded goddess of volcanic fires, analogous to the Samoan *Fée*, is probably a local adaptation in aftertimes of an older myth, half forgotten and much distorted. The contest, related in the legend, between "Pele" and *Kama-puaa*, the eight-eyed monster demi-god, indicates, however, a confused knowledge of some ancient strife between religious sects, of

which the former represented the worshippers of fire, and
the latter those with whom water was the principal element worthy of adoration. Though the contest, according to the legend, ended in a compromise, and both sides
claimed the victory, yet the worship of "Pele" held its
ground to the latest times, while that of "Kama-puaa"
disappeared, and the monster-god himself is said to have
left for foreign lands. In the invocations by the respective parties, addressed to their gods, superior and associate,
the symbolism of the legend is clearly brought out. These
two prayers, replete with archaic expressions, appeal directly to the gods of fire and of water for assistance in the
contest. In that of "Kama-puaa" reference is made to
"the storm-clouds of Iku," *ka punohu nui a Iku;* in that
of "Pele" reference is made to "the bright gods of night
in Wawao, the gods clustering thick round Pele,"

> "*Liolio i Wawao na 'Kua o ka po,*
> *Ae-ae na 'Kua no Pele.*"

The name itself, *Pele*, deserves some attention when
considering the probable connection of the myth to the
modes of thought, of speech, and of creed of those peoples
in India or in Chaldea, from whom this myth was derived,
along with so much other heterogeneous and unacknow-
ledged lore among the Polynesians.

In the Hawaiian, *Pele* is a personification of the forces
of volcanic fires; the fire goddess who dwells in the volcanoes. In Samoan, *Fée* is a personage with nearly similar
functions. In Tahitian, *Pere* is simply a volcano, the
myth seemingly being unknown or forgotten there. But
the Hawaiian, Samoan, Tahitian, "Pele," "Fée," "Pere," I
consider, etymologically, as nearly allied to the general
Polynesian word *Wera*, *Wela*, which in different dialects
signifies "fire, conflagration; to be hot, as from fire or the
sun; to be on fire, to burn," &c.; and this relation is made
more evident from the pre-Malay dialects of the Indian
Archipelago, where the Mysol *Pelah* signifies "hot," the

Sunda *Belem* "to burn," the Ceram (Gah) *Woleh* "the sun."

But this word has evidently travelled further than from Java to Tahiti. It meets us again in the far West, in the Celtic *Bel* or *Belen,* "the sun-god;" in the old Spartan *Bela* (Βελα), "the sun;" in the old Cretan *A-belios* (Αβελιος), "the sun;" and in the Phœnician and Syrian *Bel,* itself an offshoot and adaptation of the Babylonian *Bel,* the planet Jupiter, and the principal deity worshipped by the later Babylonians.

I am not aware that the Polynesian word, or its cog‑nates, with radical or derivative sense, occur in the San‑skrit or Indo-European languages. It is true that the Hindus call the morning star Velle, and a legend in the Scanda Punâna describes him as the leader of the Asuras in their war upon the Devas or gods.[1] But that very cir‑cumstance induces me to consider his name as a foreign one, and the legend as having reference to the contention and separation of the Vedic and Zend speaking branches of the Arian race, incident to the reformation of Zoroaster. The Hindu and the Polynesian legends, however, if re‑ferring to the same event, seem to be as much distorted the one as the other, with this difference, that the former relates the defeat of "Velle," the latter relates the victory of "Pele," thus showing the different streams on which the legend descended from the battle-field.

National appellations are not common among the Poly‑nesian tribes. They generally distinguish each other by the name of the island or group to which they belong. *Kai Viti, Kai Tonga,* "Fiji people," "Tonga people," &c., or they designate themselves as *Maori,* "indigenous, native," in contradistinction from foreigners, *Papalangi,* or *Haole,* or *Papaa.* The Marquesans and the Hawaiians,

[1] Oriental Illustrations, by James Roberts, p. 411. London, 1835.

however, form two exceptions. The former have preserved in their legends, and still retain for themselves, a
national appellation which is *te Take*, " the Take." According to the legend they claim " Tane," one of the twelve
sons of " Toho," or the original " Take," as their immediate progenitor, and the country of *Take-hee-hee* or *Ahée-
take* as their ancient home, the birth-place of their race.
It is possible that at one time this national name was
common to other tribes as well as the Marquesan, for in
the Hervey group, which was confessedly settled by emigrants from the Samoan and Society groups, we find an
island bearing the name of *Aitu-Take*, and a place on the
same island called *Oni-Take*.[1]

Marquesan legends offer no explanation of whence this
name was derived, or how it came to be adopted as a
national designation, beyond the fact that " Take " apparently was a soubriquet of " Toho," the father of the famous
twelve. With other Polynesian tribes the word has
become obsolete and meaningless.

This name, as well as the legend of " Toho," the first
" Take," like so many other Polynesian legends, was probably of Cushite extraction, infiltered by prolonged contact into the Polynesian mind, adopted and believed in,
and retained as a national distinction long after its origin
had been forgotten. I am not aware that this word
" Take," under any dialectical variation, is or has been
current among the Polynesian congeners in the Asiatic
Archipelago, unless the Tagal *Taga*, " native, indigenous,"
be a relation or an adaptation of it. But among the

---

[1] Dieffenbach, in his " Travels in
New Zealand," mentions that a title
or appellation of the chiefs there was
" *Taki o te wenua*," and explains it
to mean " the root of the land." As
the New Zealanders also came from
the Samoan group, it seems as if
what once was a national appellation,
in course of time became the title of
a chief. If Dieffenbach's interpreta-
tion of the title is correct, it corresponds to the Hawaiian *Kumu-honua*,
the name of the first man. The same
author also mentions, p. 67, a place
where chiefs go after death, and says
it is called *Taki-wana*. If the name
does not refer to the old national
appellation of the Polynesians, or a
portion of them, I do not see that it
has any meaning at all.

Cushite peoples or tribes, of pure or mixed descent, who inhabited the Mesopotamian basin, and constituted the confederation of the *Rot-u-nu* in the time of Thotmes III. of Egypt, circa 1430 B.C., mention is made of the *Takœ*, a people living in the neighbourhood of " Is," on the Euphrates.[1] Such a people or tribe has disappeared from history, and would probably never have been heard of but for the inscriptions on the great tablet of Karnak. Was it a namesake or an ancestor of the "Take," after whom the Polynesians called themselves? At what period of their existence did they receive it; and where were they dwelling at the time? History and tradition are silent. But the fact is almost certain that the Polynesians brought the name with them into the Pacific from their former habitats in the Asiatic Archipel, or beyond.

In the Hawaiian legend of "Kumuhonua" and his descendants, the Polynesians are distinguished by the appellation of *ka poe Menehune*, "the Menehune people," said to be descended from "Menehune," son of "Lua Nuu," and grandfather of the twelve sons of "Kinilau-a-mano," and thus in a measure, though with altered names, it conforms to the Marquesan legend. But this name, as a national appellation, was apparently dropped at a very early period. In Tahiti it became a distinctive name for the third class into which the people were divided, the labouring class, the commoners, the *Manahune*, and as such remains to this day. In Hawaii it disappeared as a national name so long ago, that subsequent legends have converted it into a term of reproach, representing the Menehune people sometimes as a separate race, sometimes as a race of dwarfs, skilful labourers, but artful and cunning.

I am inclined to consider the "Menehune" of the legend as a personification of "the people of Mene," for such is the literal signification of the word; and then *Mene* alone becomes in reality the national appellation which still

[1] Rawlinson's Herodotus, vol. ii. p. 302.

lingers in Hawaiian legends and Tahitian usage. Our knowledge of the legendary lore of the pre-Malay Polynesian relations in the Asiatic Archipel, is too limited to enable us to say if any trace or remembrance there exists of either " Take " or " Mene " as national appellations; but as the latter, like the former, was evidently an older appellation than Polynesian residence in the Pacific, we must look to the west for some former habitat or connection, which may account for the adoption of the name.

Though the Hawaiian legend makes the name-giver of the race the grandfather of the famous twelve, and the Marquesan legend makes him the father; yet the similarity of origin of both legends cannot well be doubted; and that origin, as we shall see plainer as we proceed, was Cushite—Chaldean or Arabian. There, then, we must look for the name as well as the legend.

Diodorus Sic. and Agatharcides relate[1] that in southern Arabia there lived a people called *Minœi*, whose capital or chief place was named *Karana.* When it is borne in mind that in the time of these writers the Himgarites, descendants of the Cushite Arabs, still ruled in that part of Arabia, the similarity, not only of the name of the people, but also of their chief place—which gives a clue to the name of the Hawaiian paradise, *Kalana-i-Hauola*—becomes of no small importance in ethnic inquiries.

In the "Transactions of the Ethnological Society," London, vol. ii. p. 262, article "Ethnology of Egypt," by R. S. Poole, it is stated that the paintings of the tombs of the kings give four races, of which the first or Egyptian proper is called *Men;* the second *Aamu*, representing Asiatics generally but specially Arabs; the third is called *Nahsee*, representing negroes; and the fourth *Temhu*, or the Libyans of north and north-west Africa.

It appears, then, that this word *Mene, Minœi,* and *Men,* is an old-world national appellation, claimed by Polynesians, Arabians, and Egyptians. It may not prove the

---

[1] *Vide* Anthon's " Classical Dictionary," *sub voce.*

ethnic descent of the former from either of the latter; but it forcibly indicates a once common possession of legends, traditions, and national existence, that could only have been obtained through an intimate and protracted intercourse, or from the political ascendancy of one over the other.

As another coincidence of national appellations, it may be noted that the ancient Chaldean and Assyrian inscriptions call Arabia and upper Egypt by the name, as variously read, of *Mirukh, Miruki,* and *Milu-ka,* as well as "Kusu" or Cush. In Hawaiian mythology, according to some traditions, *Milu* was a god who dwelt beneath the sea and ruled over the regions where departed spirits were said to dwell; and the direction in which this realm of "Milu" was situated was in the west. The spirits of those who died on the eastern shore of an island never started for "Milu's" abode in that direction, but invariably crossed over to some one of the points of departure on the western shore.[1] In the far west, then, we must look for the origin or analogy of the myth. But it is a long way from Hawaii to the land of Cush. Let us see if any traces of the myth can be found on the road.

The people of Pulo Nias, an island off Sumatra, like the Battas and Dyaks, a pre-Malay remnant of the Polynesian race, called the sky or heaven by the name of *Holi-Yawa,* and peopled it with an order of beings whom they

[1] A similar legend seems to have existed in Tahiti. According to Rev. Mr. Ellis, Tour around Hawaii, p. 205, I find that "the spirits of the Areois and priests of certain idols were not eaten by the gods after the death of their bodies, but went to *Miru,* where they lived much in the same way as the departed kings and heroes of Hawaii were supposed to do, or, joining hands, they formed a circle with those that had gone before, and danced in one eternal round."

In Dieffenbach's Travels in New Zealand, it is related, p. 67, that when a chief dies he goes first to *Taki-wana,* where his left eye remains and becomes a star. Then he goes to *Reinga* and further. Spirits sometimes leave the nether world and come back on earth and communicate with the living. For Hawaiian legends to same effect, see p. 83, note 1 of present work. *Reinga* was a place near the North Cape, New Zealand, where the spirits of the dead collected previous to their final departure.

called *Baruki,* superior to mortals, gifted with wings, and invisible at their pleasure. And they relate that in olden time a king of these "Baruki," called *Luo-mehu-hana,* arrived from that "Holi-Yawa, and was the first who taught them arts and civilisation, and also how to speak.[1]

This legend, doubtless, refers to their former intercourse with the early Cushite Arabians, who are said to have dwelt in, and to have come from, the sky, *i.e.,* from beyond the visible horizon, and the name of whose abode they called "Holi-Yawa." Here again the word "Yawa" points to its Cushite source, "Zaba" or "Saba;" and the name of the king, whose benefits the legend records, forcibly recalls the name of *Nuu-(Lolo-i)-Mehani* who, according to the Hawaiian legend, was the person that escaped from the Flood and repeopled the earth.

What kindred or connection, if any, except in name, there may be between the "Baruki" of the Pulo Nias legend and the *Beloochees* on the Persian Gulf, I am not able to determine. Lieutenant Pottinger, in his "Travels," states that the Beloochees claim descent from Arabia, although they were not like the Arabs, and their language bore affinity to the Persian. Canon Rawlinson, in his Appendix, Book VII. of "Herodotus," vol. iv. p. 181, considers the Beloochees as consisting of two ethnic divisions: The "Beloochees" proper, inhabiting the interior and of Arian descent, and the "Brahuis" of the Cushite race, inhabiting the coast-land; that the latter formerly penetrated much further inland, but were driven out and confined to the sea-board by the former. The same author, in his "Five Great Monarchies," vol. i. p. 50, connects the name of the Beloochees with that of "Belus" or Bel, the great Cushite-Chaldean Divinity. However that may be, there is no misconstruing the import of the Pulo Nias "Yawa." That points unmistakably to the west and the Cushite race as the source of their knowledge and culture.

[1] Memoirs of Sir Stamford Raffles, vol. ii. chap. 17.

The various readings of the cuneiform inscriptions, *Milu-ka, Miru-ki, Mirukh,* would seem to indicate that the word originally was a composite, and, judging from analogy, akin to the Egyptian *kah,* signifying "land," as in *Cham-kah,* "the land of Cham" (Egypt), *San-cha* in "San-cha-dwipa," "the land of San," and others. In Cushite parlance "Miruki" or "Miluka" would thus signify "the land of Milu," by which the Chaldeans understood Arabia and Upper Egypt.[1] Of this "Milu" with his realm of deep shadows[2] beneath the sea, in the west, the Polynesians retained the recollection in their folk-lore, and the Hawaiians converted him into a god of departed spirits; while more rationalistic legends assert that he was a very wicked king who was thrust down into *Po,* the original chaos, for his many misdeeds on earth.

Among the Dyaks on the north-west coast of Borneo, the future world, to which the dead are journeying, and where they hope to arrive, is called *Sabayan;* and with remarkable fidelity to Chaldean imagery, this heaven of theirs is said to be "seven-storied." Here also the recollection of the ancient "Saba," "Sabai," "Sabagi," has survived amid the wreck and debasement of subsequent ages.

CREATION.

The symbolism of "Kane" and his compeers in the Hawaiian group, of "Atea" in the Marquesas group, and of "Tane" and "Hina" in the Society group, plainly indicate a former religious development among the Polynesian family, when Zabaism, planet-worship and the adoration of the forces of nature, was yet in its simplest form.

[1] In Rawlinson's Herodotus, Essay i., Appendix, Book I., p. 518, note 3, I find that in analysing one of the ancient names of Babylon, "the old Hamitic name, or, at any rate, one of the old Hamitic names of the city of Babylon, must have been read *Din Tir ki, din,* 'a city,' and the final *ki* being the mere affix of locality." It thus appears that *ki* is but a variant of *ka,* and that I am correct in construing *Miruki* as "the land or place of Miru."

[2] In Hawaiian *Milu,* "shaded, grand, solemn."

Numerous prayers, invocations, and "meles" (religious poems), interspersed in the legends and handed down by tradition among the Hawaiians, with whom I am best acquainted, abundantly prove this. Throughout the grosser idolatry and the cruel practices springing from it in subsequent ages, these shreds of a purer culte were still preserved, soiled in appearance and obscured in sense by the contact, it may be, yet standing on the traditional records as heirlooms of the past, as witnesses of a better creed,[1] and as specimens of the archaic simplicity of the language, hardly intelligible to the present Hawaiians.

This "Kane" creed, such as it has been preserved in Hawaiian traditions, obscured by time and defaced by interpolations, is still a most valuable relic of the mental status, religious notions, and historical recollections of the earlier Polynesians. No other group in Polynesia has preserved it so fully, so far as my inquiries have been able to ascertain; yet I have met with parts of it on nearly all the groups, though more or less distorted, and in that case I hold that the universality of a legend among so widely scattered tribes proves its antiquity. This "Kane" legend, or rather series of legends, treating of *Kane* and the creation of *Kumuhonua* or the first man, of *Nuu* or *Kahinalii* in the time of the deluge, of *Lua Nuu* or *Kanehoalani* and his descendants, from whom the Hawaiians and Tahitians are said to have sprung; this legend, with accompanying prayers, invocations, genealogies, and half-forgotten "meles," has been partially and at different times reduced to writing in the Hawaiian language by David Malo, S. M. Kamakau, Kepelino, and other Hawaiian scholars, who obtained their information from the ancient chiefs and priests who flourished before the introduction of

---

[1] "It could be shown that even among the South-Sea Islanders, and other tribes who have been driven farthest from the original settlements of man, there were many religious customs of which those who practised them did not know the origin or the meaning, and which clearly indicated their derivation from an older, a more intelligible, but a forgotten faith."—Primeval Man, by the Duke of Argyle, p. 196.

Christianity, some fifty years ago. Among the Hawaiian missionaries who endeavoured to preserve the ancient traditions from oblivion, the greatest credit is due to Rev. Messrs. S. Dibble and Lorin Andrews; and my own collection of Hawaiian folk-lore, gathered from the lips of the old people, is both large and varied.

Collating the different narratives thus preserved, I learn that the ancient Hawaiians at one time believed in and worshipped one god, comprising three beings, and respectively called *Kane, Ku*,[1] and *Lono*,[2] equal in nature, but distinct in attributes; the first, however, being considered as the superior of the other two, *a primus inter pares;* that they formed a triad commonly referred to as *Ku-kau-akahi*, lit. " Ku stands alone," or " the one established," and were worshipped jointly under the grand and mysterious name

---

[1] Surnamed *Ka-Pao*, " the builder," " the architect."

[2] Surnamed *Noho i ka wai*, " dwelling on the water." Traces of the worship of these three deities are found throughout the Southern groups, though in later times it had fallen in abeyance in many places, or been entirely superseded by the worship of other gods.

The following remnant of what may be called the ancient Hawaiian Liturgy, recited by the priest and the congregation at the time of the great festivals, has been preserved. It runs:—

" *The Priest.*—O Kane me Ku-Ka-Pao, e oia nei?

The Congregation.—Hooia, e oia.

The Priest.—O Lono-nui-noho-i-ka-wai, e oia nei?

The Congregation.—Hooia, e oia.

The Priest.—Ho-eu, kukupu, inana, ku iluna o ka moku, e oia nei?

The Congregation.—Hooia, e oia, Hooia, e oia, Hooia, e oia, ke Akua oia.

All together.—Kane-Po-Lani, O Lani-makua, me Ku-Ka-Pao i Kiki-lani, me Lono-nui-maka-oaka, he

Akua, ke Akua i huila, malamalama paa ka Lani, Ku i ka honua, i ka honua a Kane-kumu-honua, he Akua. Hooia, e oia, Hooia, e oia; Oia ke Akua oia."

It may be translated thus :—

" *The Priest.*—O Kane and Ku, the builder, is it true?

The Congregation.—It is true, it is so.

The Priest.—O great Lono, dwelling on the water, is it true?

The Congregation.—It is true, it is so.

The Priest.—Quickened, increasing, moving. Raised up is the continent (island, division). Is it true?

The Congregation.—It is true, it is so; it is true, it is so; it is true, it is so; the true god.

All together. —Kane-Po-Lani, O heavenly father, with Ku the builder in the blazing heaven, with great Lono of the flashing eyes, a god, the god of lightning, the fixed light of heaven, standing on the earth, on the earth of Kane-kumu-honua, he is god. It is true, it is so; it is true, it is so; he is the true god."

of *Hika po loa,* while another ancient name was *Oi-e,* signifying "most excellent, supreme," sometimes used adjectively as *Kane-oi-e.* These gods existed from eternity, from and before chaos, or, as the Hawaiian term expresses it, "*mai ka Po mai*"—from the time of night, darkness, chaos. By an act of their will these gods dissipated or broke into pieces the existing, surrounding, all-containing *Po,* night or chaos, by which act light entered into space. They then created the heavens—three in number—as a place for themselves to dwell in, and the earth to be their footstool, *he keehina honua-a-Kane.* Next they created the sun, moon, stars, and a host of angels or spirits—*i kini akua*—to minister to them. Last of all they created man on the model or in the likeness of "Kane." The body of the first man was made of red earth—*lepo ula* or *ala-ea*—and the spittle of the gods—*wai-nao*—and his head was made of a whitish clay—*palolo*—which was brought from the four ends of the world by "Lono." When the earth-image of "Kane" was ready, the three gods breathed into its nose and called on it to rise, and it became a living being. Afterwards the first woman was created from one of the ribs—*lalo puhaka*—of the man while asleep, and these two were the progenitors of all mankind. They are called in the chants and in various legends by a large number of different names, but the most common for the man was *Kumu-honua,* and for the woman *Ke Ola ku honua.* Such is the general import of the Kumuhonua legend.

Another legend of the series, that of *Wela-ahi-lani,* states that after "Kane" had destroyed the world by fire,[1]

---

[1] "Of the Egyptian theory of creation some notion may perhaps be obtained from the account given in Ovid (Met. i. and xxv.), borrowed from the Pythagoreans; as of their belief in the destruction of the earth by fire, adopted by the Stoics. (Ovid. Met. i. 256; Seneca, Nat. Quœst. iii. 13 and 28; Plut. de Placit. Phil. iv. 7). They even thought it had been subject to several catastrophes, 'not to one deluge only, but to many;' and believed in a variety of destructions 'that have been, and again will be, the greatest of these arising from fire and water.'" (Plut. Tim. pp. 466, 467). "The idea that the world had successive creations and destructions is also expressly stated in the Indian Manu."—Hero-

on account of the wickedness of the people then living, he organised it as it now is, and created the first man and the first woman, with the assistance of "Ku" and "Lono," nearly in the same manner as above narrated. In that legend the man is called *Wela-ahi-lani*, and the woman is called *Owe*.[1]

The Marquesas islanders have a legend called *Te Vanana na Tanaoa* (the prophecy or record of Tanaoa), which relates that in the beginning there was no life, light, or sound in the world, that a boundless night, *Po*, enveloped everything, over which *Tanaoa*, which means "darkness," and *Mutu-hei*, which means "silence," ruled supreme. In course of time the god *Atea*, which means "light," evolved himself, sprang from or separated himself from "Tanaoa," made war on him, drove him away and confined him within limits. Light—*Atea*—having thus been evolved from darkness—*Tanaoa*—the god *Ono* or "sound" was evolved from "Atea," and he destroyed or broke up "Mutuhei." But from the foregoing struggle between "Tanaoa" and "Atea," "Ono" and "Mutuhei," arose *Atanua* or the dawn. "Atea" then took "Atanua" for wife, and from them sprang their first-born *Tu-mea*. After that "Atea" created the host of inferior deities, fixed or created the heavens and earth, animals, man, &c. Another legend mentions "Atea" and his wife *Owa* as the progenitors of the Marquesans.[2]

Although the Society islanders, like most of the South Polynesian tribes, held that the earth was fished up out of the ocean by *Taaroa*—Tangaloa—who with them was the source of all things, the father of gods and men,[3] yet the remnant of a legend, collected by M. de Bovis,[4] for many years a resident on that group, bespeaks an older creed

---

dotus, by G. Rawlinson, vol. ii. p. 250, New York, 1875. Of the future destruction of the world by fire, the Scandinavian descendants of the Arian stock preserved a vivid impression in their mythical poem, the "Volu-spa."

[1] *Vide* Appendix, No. I.
[2] See Appendix, No. III.
[3] See Appendix, No. II.
[4] "Etat de la Société Taitienne à l'arrivée des Européens," par M. de Bovis, Lieutenant de vaisseau, "Revue Coloniale," annee 1855.

and a clearer conception, and harmonises more with the Hawaiian, Marquesan, and Samoan cosmogonies of more ancient date. The extract of the legend, preserved by M. de Bovis, reads thus: " In the beginning there was nothing but the god *Ihoiho;* afterwards there was an expanse of waters which covered the abyss, and the god *Tino Taata* floated on the surface." It is to be regretted that no more of that interesting legend has been preserved. It has the ring of the true antique, ere the primal myth was shattered into fragments. M. de Bovis translates *Ihoiho* with " le vide," the empty space, as a better rendering of sense than "image de soi meme." I know not if the Tahitian word *Ihoiho* has also the sense of "le vide"— a void, empty space—but it certainly has the meaning of the "manes, ghosts or remains of the dead," and in the legend was probably a trope expressive of a dead and perished world, the wreck of which was covered by water; and the god *Tino Taata,* which I think M. de Bovis correctly renders by " the divine type or source of mankind," floated on the waters.

It is with some hesitation that I thus correct a writer whose article shows him to have been well-informed, exact, and cautious. But the expression, "le vide," seems to me misleading. Through all the Polynesian cosmogonies, even the wildest and most fanciful, there is a constant underlying sense of a chaos, wreck, *Po,* containing all things, and existing previous to the first creative organisation; the chaos and wreck of a previous world, destroyed by fire according to the Hawaiian legend, destroyed by water according to the Samoan legend; a chaos, ruin or night, *Po,* in which the gods themselves had been involved, and, only in virtue of their divine nature, after continued struggle, extricated themselves and re-organised the world on its present pattern.

The generally current tradition on the Society group is, that man was a descendant of *Taaroa,* through sundry demi-gods; but others, more in accordance with the

Hawaiian legends, make him a direct creation of *Taaroa*, who made him out of red clay—*araea*—and made the first woman from one of his bones, and hence she was called *Iwi*, lit. "the bone."

In the Paumotu group, or, as the natives themselves call their group, the Tuamotu, the ancient tradition relates that "the earth was composed of three separate parts or strata, super-imposed one above the other. Each stratum had its particular heaven. The upper stratum was destined for fortunate souls or spirits; the middle was inhabited by the living; and the third was the place where spirits wandered in pain. Many restless spirits, however, sometimes escaped by hiding in the bodies of birds."[1] As the Paumotu or Tuamotu group was doubtless originally peopled from the Society group, and also by occasional arrivals from the Marquesas, it is fair to infer that the same or a similar legend obtained in either of those groups in olden time, though forgotten in later ages. The allusion to the three heavens connects it with the Hawaiian legend, *vide supra*, p. 61.

Of Samoan legends bearing on the creation but little has been published. One legend,[2] however, states that in the beginning the earth was covered with water, and the heaven alone was inhabited. *Tangaloa*, the great God, sent his daughter in the form of a bird called the *Kuri*, "the snipe," to look for dry land. She found a spot, and, as it was extending, she visited it frequently. At one time she brought down some earth and a creeping plant. The plant grew, decomposed and turned into worms, and the worms turned into men and women. Another legend states that man was formed from the vine of "Kuri" by a god called *Ngai*.[3] In the Samoas and in Rotumah, the name of the first woman is given as *Iwa*, thus connecting

---

[1] Annuaire des Etablissements Français de l'Oceanie, Papeete, 1863, p. 95.

[2] "Nineteen Years in Polynesia," by Rev. Mr. Turner.

[3] "United States Exploring Expedition, Ethnology," by Hor. Hall.

itself with the Tahitian "Iwi," the Marquesan "Owa," the Hawaiian "Owe."

Some of the New Zealand legends [1] ascribe the origin of all things to *Rangi* and *Papa*, "heaven and earth," but admit that *Po*, "night chaos," enveloped everything, heaven and earth included. Still, under such unfavourable conditions, with "Rangi" and "Papa" packed close together, these latter generated six children. The first was *Tu-mata-uenga*,[2] or the progenitor of man; next, *Tane-mahuta*, the father of forests, &c.; next, *Ta-whiri-ma-tea*, the father of winds; next, *Rongo-ma-tane*, the father of cultivated food; next, *Tanga-roa*, the father of fishes and reptiles; and last, *Haumia-tikitiki*, the father of wild-grown food. The close position of heaven and earth to each other, without interval or separation, greatly annoyed and inconvenienced their offspring, and after several ineffectual attempts, "Tane-mahuta," exerting his strength, succeeded in rending "Rangi" and "Papa" asunder, and, pushing the former up into space, let in light on the earth. "Ta-whiri-ma-tea disapproved of the separation of his parents, and followed his father "Rangi" up in the sky, but the other brethren remained with their mother, "Papa," and multiplied and developed indefinitely. War, however, soon arose between

---

[1] "Polynesian Mythology," by Sir George Gray.

[2] That the name of this god, and his character as the forefather of the human family, are older than the arrival of the Polynesians in the Pacific, is plainly shown in the fact that among some of the pre-Malay dialects of the Indian Archipelago, as in Saparua, Ceram, Salibabo, and Celebes, we find the words *Tu-mata*, *To-mata*, *Tau-mata*, and *Tau*, as expressing the sense of "man" especially, and in a general way "mankind."

Professor Fr. Bopp, in his "Ueber die Verwandtschaft der Mal.-Polynes. Sprachen mit den Ind.-Europ.," refers this *Tau* or, contracted, *Tu* to the Sanskrit *Dhava*, man, a word which, in its compound form of *Vidawa*—without man, a widow—has survived in the principal Indo-European families of speech. Adolphe Pichet, in Origines Ind-Europ., vol. ii. p. 342, refers this *dhava* to the root *Dhû*, agitare, "aux rapports sexuels des époux," and calls in confirmation the other derivative *Dhûtâ*, "la femme comme agitata, nempe, in concubitu." I believe, however, that the Polynesian *Tu*, as the name of one of their most powerful gods, and the progenitor of mankind, if it has any affinity to the Sanskrit, refers itself rather to the Vedic *Tu*, "to be powerful," than to *Dhava* or any corrupted form of the same.

the brothers, and finally "Tu-mata-uenga"[1] subdued them all to his will and use, except "Ta-whiri-ma-tea."

Another New Zealand legend, according to Nicholas,[2] records three primitive gods, *Maui-Rana-Rangi*, the foremost god, the New Zealand Jupiter; *Tipoko*, god of anger and of death; and *Towaki* or *Tauraki*, lord of the elements and god of tempests. The same work intimates that these three created the first man, and afterwards the first woman from one of the man's ribs.

According to the foregoing versions of the creation of the world and of man, it is evident that the original Polynesian myth contemplated a pre-existing chaos, night, *Po*, containing within itself, according to the Hawaiian and Tahitian legends, the wreck and débris of a previously perished universe; and that out of this chaos the first great gods evolved themselves, and then set about organising and creating the world and man as now existing. The Samoan legend relates that in the beginning the world was covered with water; and the Tahitian legend, preserved by M. de Bovis, states in addition that "the god 'Tino Taata' floated on the surface."

This chaos idea among the Polynesian tribes bears a striking relationship to the old Babylonian and Hebrew accounts of the Genesis of the world. Every reader knows

---

[1] This *Tu-mata-uenga*, "Tu with the red face." This god, or demi-god, according to the legend, after having subdued his brothers, became known to his posterity by several other names, amongst which was *Tu-mata-wha-iti*, "Tu with the four small faces." In Hawaiian mythology, *Kama-puaa*, the demi-god opponent of the goddess Pele, is described as having eight eyes and eight feet; and in the chants and legends *Maka-walu*, "eight-eyed," is a frequent epithet of gods and chiefs. This specialty of four faces or heads, and of corresponding limbs, is peculiar to some of the principal Indian deities. Brahma is represented with four faces, Dourga with eight arms, &c. I have no means of knowing whether this fourfold representation of divine faces or limbs was of Arian or Cushite conception. It does not appear, I believe, in Egyptian mythology, nor generally among the Indo-European descendants of the Arian stock. The only analogy I can now remember, is that of Odin's horse "Sleipner," said to have had eight feet. I note the coincidence, however, as bearing upon the derivation of Polynesian myths and legends.

[2] L'Univers-Oceanie, par G. L. D. de Rienzi, vol. x. p. 161.

the second verse of "Genesis:" "And the earth was without form and void; and darkness was upon the face of the deep. And the Spirit of God moved upon the face of the waters." The Tahitian "*Tino Taata* who floated on the surface" may be the original or the copy of the Hebrew legend. The Babylonian legend, according to Berosus, states that "there was a time in which there existed nothing but darkness and an abyss of waters;" and according to the cuneiform inscriptions collected and translated by Mr. George Smith,[1] "Tiamat," the spirit of the sea and of chaos, "was self-existent and eternal, older even than the gods, for the birth or separation of the deities out of this chaos was the first step in the creation of the world." The Chaldean legend refers to a time

> " When above were not raisèd the heavens,
>   And below on the earth a plant had not grown up ;
>   The abyss also had not broken open their boundaries;
>   The chaos (or water) Tiamat (the sea) was the producing mother
>   of the whole of them.
>
>   .   .   .   .
>
>   When the gods had not sprung up, any one of them ;
>   A plant had not grown, and order did not exist."

The Hebrew legend infers that the gods, *Elohim*, existed contemporaneously with and apart from the chaos. The Marquesan legend makes the great god of all, *Atea*, the light, evolve himself from out of darkness, *Tanaoa*, the ruler of chaos, and from "Atea" sprung the next great god, *Ono*, or sound. The Hawaiian legend makes the three great gods, *Kane*, *Ku*, and *Lono*, light, stability, and sound, evolve themselves out of chaos, *Po*. The Babylonian legend makes the two gods *Lahmu* and *Lahamu*, the "male and female personifications of motion and production, issue from chaos, followed by the gods *Sar* and *Kisar*, "representing the upper and lower expanse;" which four deities, however, appear to be mere abstractions, and were followed by the first actual, personal gods, *Anu*, *Elu*

----
[1] The Chaldean Account of Genesis, by George Smith, chap. v.

or *Bel*, and *Hea*, representing heaven, earth, and the sea, the Babylonian triad, corresponding to the Hawaiian triad, as the first real creators and organisers of the universe.

The New Zealand legend, above referred to, of heaven and earth ("Rangi" and "Papa") being shut up together, as it were, and enveloped in darkness, "Po;" of their final separation, and the admission of light upon earth by one of their sons, who pushed the heavens (his father) far upward and away from the earth. This legend, though apparently forgotten or neglected in most of the groups, was still at one time common to the Polynesian family, and, as such, an heirloom brought with them from the West. Traces of it remain in the Samoan, where the legend tells us[1] that "of old the heavens fell down, and people had to crawl about. The plants grew, and pushed the heavens up a little from the earth. One day a man came along and offered to push the heavens up still higher for a drink of water from a woman's gourd. He did so, and they are now as he left them. The man's name was *Tiitii*."[2] In the Hawaiian group little remains of this legend but the old saying that at the hill of Kauwiki, not far from the eastern point of the island of Maui, the heaven was nearer to the earth than elsewhere; in fact, so close that it could be reached by a good strong cast of a spear; and the *lani haahaa*, "the low-lying heavens," is a soubriquet of the place to the present time. The Dyaks of Borneo—of whom the Bishop of Labuan says,[3] that "like many other uncivilised nations, they have legends of a better and loftier origin, something like the story of Cœlus and Terra"—still retain a legend that, up to the time of the birth of Tana-compta's daughter, the sky had been so

---

[1] "Nineteen Years in Polynesia," by Rev. Mr. Turner.

[2] *Tiitii* or *Tiki-Tiki* or *Kii* is a common expression throughout Polynesia, signifying spiritual beings, departed and deified ancestors, protectors of boundaries, and in compara- tively modern times, the idols or images of the gods.

[3] Transactions of Ethnological Society, vol. ii., London. "Wild Tribes of Borneo," by the Bishop of Labuan.

near the earth that one could touch it with the hand; but
she now raised it up and put it permanently on props.
The legend further states that "in the beginning there
was Solitude and *Soutan*, who could hear, see, speak, but
had no limbs or body. This deity is supposed to have
lived on a ball, and after some ages to have made the two
great birds called *Bullar* and *Erar*, who flew round and
round, and made the earth, sky, and rivers. Finding the
earth greater than the sky, they collected the soil with their
feet, and piled it up into mountains. Having tried to make
man out of trees and out of rocks, and not succeeding,
they took earth and mixed it with water, and so modelled
a man of red clay. When they called to him, he an-
swered; when they cut him, red blood came from his
veins. This first man was *Tana-compta*, who afterwards
brought to life a female child, who gave birth to offspring. Then the succession of day and night began,
and her progeny became numerous, sailing up and down
the river."

The juxtaposition of heaven and earth is not expressly
stated in the Chaldean and Hebrew legends, though it
doubtless is inferred, as both emerged from the primal
chaos; but in some of the hymns of the Rig-Veda the
idea is plainly held forth that at one time heaven and
earth were close together, and the separating them is
variously attributed to Varuna, to Vishnu, to Indra, and
Soma, who "propped up the sky with supports, and spread
out the earth, the mother."

The Polynesian legend of the creation of man shows too
remarkable an accord with the Hebrew account to be
lightly passed over. The former says that "Kane," "Ku,"
and "Lono," formed man out of the red earth, and breathed
into his nose, and he became a living being; *vide supra*.
The latter says, "the Lord God formed man of the dust of
the ground, and breathed into his nostrils the breath of
life, and man became a living soul" (Gen. ii. 7). The
Polynesian account offers details — the mixing of the

earth with the spittle of the gods, and the forming the head of man out of white clay, which do not appear in the Hebrew.

According to Mr. G. Smith, the Babylonian inscriptions, so far as yet discovered, are defective in that portion which treats of the creation of man; but it appears that the race of human beings spoken of in line "18," p. 82, chap. v. of "Chaldean Account of Genesis," is "the *zalmatqaquadi*, or dark race, and in various other fragments of these legends they here are called Admi or Adami, which is exactly the name given to the first man in Genesis." And the author further says, that "it has already been pointed out by Sir Henry Rawlinson that the Babylonians recognised two principal races: the Adamu, or dark race, and the Sarku, or light race, probably in the same manner that two races are mentioned in Genesis, the sons of Adam and the sons of God.[1] It appears incidentally from the fragments of inscriptions that it was the race of Adam, or the dark race, which was believed to have fallen; but there is at present no clue to the position of the other race in their system." The Hebrew word *Adam* signifies "Red," and may thus help us to connect the Polynesian first man, made of "red earth," with the Babylonian "dark race;" but the Polynesian reference to the head of man being made of "white clay," although a myth, may yet have a historical substratum, and indicate a lingering reminiscence of a mixed origin, in which the white element occupied a superior position. In regard to the creation of the first woman, the Polynesian and the Hebrew narratives coincide perfectly, even to the very name.

Of the ancient Hawaiian chants, referring to the Creation, and which were at once the rythmical, sacerdotal expression of the ancient creed and the crystallised form of the primal tradition—two only, so far as I know, have been preserved and reduced to writing. With the prac-

---

[1] How other writers have handled this curious passage in Genesis vi. 2, see Primeval Man, by the Duke of Argyle (New York, 1874), p. 104, &c.

tice and observance of the ancient culte, vanished also
in great measure the ancient metrical formulas, though
the prosaic tradition lingers still in the minds of some of
the old people where the hymns have been forgotten. Of
these two, which from intrinsic evidence I should judge to
be older than the influx into the Hawaïian group of South
Pacific emigrants about 800 years ago, I offer the following translations. They are but portions of longer chants,
and would probably in a few years more have been
entirely forgotten; but, *ex pede Herculem*, and they are
extremely interesting.

The first reads :—

> " O Kane, O Ku-ka-Pao [1]
> And the great Lono, dwelling on the water,
> Brought forth are Heaven and Earth,
> Quickened, increasing, moving,
> Raised up into Continents. [2]
>> The great Ocean of Kane,
>> .The Ocean with dotted seas, [3]
>> The Ocean with the large fishes,
>> And the small fishes,
>> Sharks and Niuhi, [4]
>> Whales,
>> And the large Hihimanu [5] of Kane.

---

[1] *Ka-Pao* is an epithet of "Ku," the second deity, and is probably best rendered as "the architect, the constructor, the builder." *Pao*, v. signifies "to peck, as birds with the bill; to dig out, as from a rock or other substance; to dig down in the ground, as in making a pit." *Pao*, s. signifies "the arch of a bridge; the bridge itself; a prop; also a shallow pit, a place dug out." The original conception of the epithet *ka Pao* corresponds to the leading idea of the Marquesan legend of Creation, *te Pepena*, formerly referred to, where the great God "Atea" sets the inferior deities to work to pick out or dig out the earth from the surrounding chaos.

[2] *Moku*, primarily "a division, something cut off; a land separated from other land by water; an island; a district."

[3] *Kai oo*, "dotted, variegated sea," scèl. with islands or with coral patches. *Kai* is used in speaking of local seas, in contradistinction from *Moana*, the great circumambient ocean.

[4] *Niuhi*, a species of shark of the largest kind.

[5] *Hihimanu*, a large, broad, soft creature of the sea, one and a half or two feet in diameter. Both this and the foregoing "Niuhi" were forbidden, under the Kapu system, to be eaten by women, under penalty of death.

The rows of stars of Kane,
The stars in the firmament,
The stars that have been fastened up,
Fast, fast, on the surface of the heaven of Kane,
And the wandering stars,[1]
The tabued stars of Kane,
The moving stars of Kane ;
Innumerable[2] are the stars ;
The large stars,
The little stars,
The red stars of Kane.   O infinite space !
  The great Moon of Kane,
  The great Sun of Kane,
  Moving, floating,
  Set moving about in the great space of Kane.
The great Earth of Kane,
The Earth Kapakapaua[3] of Kane,
The Earth that Kane set in motion,
Moving are the stars, moving is the moon,
Moving is the great Earth of Kane."

Subjoined is the Hawaiian text :—

" *O Kane, O Ku-ka-Pao*
 Me Lono-nui noho i ka wai,
 Loaa ka Lani, Honua,
 Ho-eu, kukupu, inana,
 Ku iluna o ka moku.
  O ka Moana nui a Kane,
  O ka Moana i kai oo,

---

[1] *Kahakahakea*, lit., "that have been hewn off, chipped off ;" hence "set adrift, wandering." In Marquesan *Taha* is "to go, march." In Tahitian *Tahataha* is "to be declining as the sun in the afternoon, to be wondering as the eye on account of some evil intended."

[2] I have rendered by "innumerable," what in the text is expressed by *kini, ka lau, ka mano,* which literally means "40,000, 400, 4000."

[3] *Kapakapaua*, in Hawaiian legends designates in a general way the first land or country inhabited by man. If the word, however, is taken in its literal sense, one of the meanings of *kapa* in Hawaiian is "to gather up in the hands and squeeze, as awa dregs," the line may be read "the earth squeezed or strained dry by Kane," and in so far convey an ancient conception of the mode of creation analogous to the notion of the early Babylonians, who "evidently considered that the world was drawn together out of the waters, and rested or reposed upon a vast abyss of chaotic ocean which filled the space below the world."— Chaldean account of Genesis, G. Smith, p. 74.

O ka Moana i ka ia nui
I ka ia iki,
I ka mano, i ka niuhi,
I ke Kohola,
I ka ia nui hihimanu a Kane.
O na lalani hoku a Kane,
O na hoku i ka nuu paa,
O na hoku i kakia ia,
I paa, i paa i ka ili lani a Kane,
O na hoku i kahakahakea,
O na hoku kapu a Kane
O na hoku lewa a Kane,
O kini, o ka lau, o ka mano o ka hoku.
O ka hoku nui,
O ka hoku iki,
O na hoku ula a Kane. He lewa !
O ka Mahina nui a Kane,
O ka La nui a Kane,
A hoolewa, a lewa,
I hoolewa ia i ka lewa nui a Kane.
O ka Honua nui a Kane
O ka Honua i Kapakapaua [1] *a Kane,*
O ka Honua a Kane i hoolewa.
O lewa ka hoku, o lewa ka malama,
O lewa ka Honua nui a Kane."

The second chant reads as follows :—

" Kane of the great Night,
Ku and Lono of the great Night,
Hika-po-loa the King.
The tabued Night that is set apart,
The poisonous Night,
The barren, desolate Night,
The continual darkness of Midnight,
The Night, the reviler.[2]
O Kane, O Ku-ka-Pao,
And great Lono dwelling on the water,[3]

---

[1] See note 3, p. 73.

[2] *Hai-amu,* synon. with *Ku-amu-amu,* " to revile sacred things, curse the gods, blaspheme."

[3] "Dwelling on the waters," *noho i ka wai,* as a characteristic or epithet of the third great god of the Hawaiians, forcibly recalls to mind the Tahitian legend referred to on p. 64, according to which " the god *Tino-Taata* floated on the surface of the waters."

Brought forth are Heaven (and) Earth,
Quickened, increased, moving,
Raised up into Continents.
  Kane, Lord of Night, Lord the father,
  Ku-ka-Pao, in the hot heavens,
  Great Lono with the flashing eyes,
  Lightning-like lights has the Lord
  Established in truth, O Kane, master-worker ;
The Lord Creator of mankind :
Start, work, bring forth the Chief Ku-Honua.[1]
And Ola-Ku-Honua [2] the woman ;
Dwelling together are they two,
Dwelling in marriage (is she) with the husband, the brother."

The Hawaiian text reads :—

  " *Kane i ka Po-loa,*
   Ku a me Lono i ka Po-loa,
   O Hika-Po-loa ke Lii.
    Ka Po-kapu i hoano e,
    O ai-au ka Po,
    O kekaha ka Po anoano,
    O mau kulu ka Po-eleele,
    Ka Po ke haiamu.
  O Kane, O Ku-ka-Pao,
  Me Lono-nui noho i ka wai,
  Loaa ka Lani, Honua,
  Ho-eu, Kukupu, inana,
  Ku iluna o ka Moku.
   Kane-Po-Lani, O Lani Makisia,
   O Ku, O ka Pao i kikilani,
   O Lono-nui maka-oaka,
   Huila, malamalama, loaa ka Lani,
   Hooia i oia, O Kane kumu-hana.
  O ka Lani hookanaka,
  Hoi, hana, loaa ke Lii Ku-Honua,
  O ke Ola-ku-Honua ka wahine,
  Nonoho iho no laua,
  I hoi noho i ke Kane kaikunane.'

It will thus be seen that the order of creation, according to Hawaiian folk-lore, was that after heaven and earth had been separated, and the ocean had been stocked with its

[1] One of the many names of the first man. [2] The corresponding name of the first woman.

animals, the stars were created, then the moon, then the sun. In this order the Marquesan legend agrees with the Hawaiian, and both agree exactly with the Babylonian legend of the cuneiform inscriptions. Mr. G. Smith, l. c. p. 75, says: "The Babylonian account of the creation gives the creation of the moon before that of the sun, in reverse order to that in Genesis; and evidently the Babylonians considered the moon the principal body, while the book of Genesis makes the sun the greater light. Here it is evident that Genesis is truer to nature than the Chaldean text." Granted that it be truer; but may not that very fact indicate also' that the Hebrew text is a later emendation of an older but once common tradition ?

On the creation of animals these chants are silent; but from the prose tradition it may be inferred that the earth, at the time of its creation or emergence from the watery chaos, was stocked with vegetable and animal life. The animals specially mentioned in the tradition as having been created by Kane were hogs, *Puaa*; dogs, *Ilio*; lizards or reptiles, *Moo*. *Puaá* (in South Polynesian dialects *Puaka*) seems at one time to have been a general name for beasts and animals, but after the isolation of the Polynesians in the Pacific to have been limited to the hog species. *Ilio* was a general name for dog and his kindred, obsolete in the southern groups.[1] Besides the common domesticated dog, *Ilio holo*, the tradition speaks of *Ilio nui niho oi*, "the large dog with sharp teeth," and *Ilio 'lii a Kane*, "the royal dog of Kane." The *Moo* or *Moko* mentioned in tradition, reptiles and lizards, were of several kinds: the Moo with large, sharp, glistening teeth; the talking Moo, *moo-olelo*; the creeping Moo, *moo kolo*; the roving, wandering Moo, *moo-pelo*;[2] the watchful Moo, *moo-*

---

[1] The Hawaiian is the only group that has preserved the name *Ilio* for dog. In the southern groups the word *Kuri* is generally used, in the Marquesan *Nuhe*.

[2] The word *Pelo* is obsolete in the Hawaiian. It occurs, however, in the Tahitian *Pero-pero*, "to roam about, to wander."

kaala; [1] the prophesying Moo, *moo-kaula;* the deadly moo, *moo make a kane.* The Hawaiian legends frequently speak of moo of extraordinary size living in caverns, amphibious in their nature, and being the terror of the inhabitants. Now, when it is taken into consideration that throughout the Polynesian groups no reptiles are found much bigger than the common house lizard, it is evident that these tales of monster reptiles must have been an heirloom from the time when the people lived in other habitats where such large reptiles abounded.

The Hawaiian traditions are eloquent upon the beauty and excellence of the particular land or place of residence of the two first created human beings. It had a number of names of various imports, though the most generally occurring, and said to be the oldest, was *Kalana i Hauola*, "Kalana with the living or life-giving dew." It was situated in a large country or continent, variously called in the legends by the names of *Kahiki-honua-kele, Kahiki ku, Kapakapaua-a-Kane,* and *Mololani.* Among the many other names for this primary homestead or paradise, retained in the chants and traditions, are *Pali-uli,* "the blue mountain;" *Aina i ka Kaupo o Kane,* "the land in or of the heart of Kane;" *Aina wai Akua a Kane,* "the land of the divine water of Kane." The tradition says of "Paliuli" that it was "a sacred, tabued land; that a man must be righteous to attain it; that he must prepare himself exceedingly holy who wishes to attain it; if faulty or sinful, he will not get there: if he looks behind, he will not get there, if he prefers his family, he will not enter in Paliuli." Part of an ancient chant thus describes it:—

[1] This word in the present combination is not found in the Hawaiian. Its root is evidently *Ala,* "to wake, be watchful."

" O Pali-uli, hidden land of Kane,
  Land in Kalana i Hau-ola,
  In Kahiki-ku, in Kapakapa-ua a Kane,
  Land with springs of water, fat and moist,
  Land greatly enjoyed by the god."

" *O Pali-uli, aina huna a Kane,*
  O ka aina i Kalana i Hau-ola,
  I Kahikiku, I Kapakapa-ua a Kane,
  O ka aina i kumu, i lali,
  O ka aina ai nui a ke Akua."

The prohibition referred to above, not to look back when
starting on a sacred journey, under penalty of failure,
curiously enough recalls to mind the Hebrew legend of
Lot, *vide* Gen. xix. 17, &c., and the Greek legend of Orpheus
and Eurydice. None of the three legends was in all probability derived from or moulded by either of the others,
yet the family likeness between them seems to bespeak
a common origin in times anterior to the departure of
Abraham from "Ur of the Chaldees," and among a people
where superstition had already hardened into maxims and
precepts.

The *Aina wai Akua a Kane,* or, as it is more generally
called in the legends, *Aina wai-ola a Kane,* "the living
water of Kane," is frequently referred to in the Hawaiian
folk-lore. According to traditions this spring of life, or
living water, was a running stream or overflowing spring,
attached to or enclosed in a pond. " It was beautifully
transparent and clear. Its banks were splendid. It had
three outlets; one for Ku, one for Kane, and one for Lono
and through these outlets the fish entered in the pond. If
the fish of the pond were thrown on the ground or on the
fire, they did not die; and if a man had been killed and
was afterwards sprinkled over with this water, he did soon
come to life again." In the famous legend of " Aukele-
nui-a-Iku" the hero visits " Kalana i Hau-ola" and, by the
aid of his patron god, obtains water from this fountain of
life, wherewith he resuscitated his brothers who had been
killed a long time before.

The notion of a fountain of life is very old, and its origin and its *raison d'etre* are lost in the gloom of pre-historic times. The earliest allusion to it now known is found in the Izdubar legends of Chaldea,[1] where Ninkigal, the goddess of the regions of the dead, tells her attendant Simtar to pour "the water of life" over Ishtar and restore her to life and health and the company of the gods.

I have not the means of ascertaining if the conception of a fountain of life or life-giving waters was common to the Arian family. The Indus and, specially, the Ganges, were sacred rivers with the Hindus, but in how far the sacredness attributed to the latter was local, and posterior to the Arian invasion of India, or older than Vedic times, and transferred from some equally sacred river, lake, or spring in more ancient habitats, I am unable to say, nor am I positive that "Mimer's well" in Scandinavian mythology, where Odin sought wisdom, and pawned his eye to get it, or the "well of Vurdh," where the Nornas sat and watered the tree Ygdrasyl,—though somewhat analogous, are of kindred origin with the Chaldeo-Polynesian fountain of life or water of life.

The Chaldeans placed their waters of life in the realm of the dead; the Polynesians placed theirs in paradise. Which is the older form of the conception?

Among other adornments of the Polynesian paradise, the "Kalana i Hau-ola," there grew the *Ulu kapu a Kane*, "the tabued bread-fruit tree," and the *Ohia Hemolele*, "the sacred apple-tree." The priests of the olden time are said to have held that the tabued fruit of these trees were in some manner connected with the trouble and death of Kumu-honua and Lalo-honua, the first man and woman, and hence in the ancient chants the former was called "Kane Laa-uli, Kumu-uli, Kulu-ipo," the fallen chief, he who fell from, by, or on account of the tree, the mourner, &c., or names of similar import.

I have only been able to obtain a portion of a Hawaiian

---

[1] Chaldean Account of Genesis, by G. Smith, pp. 234, 245.

chant which bears upon the subject of those trees and the fall of man, as connected with the eating of their fruit; and I am inclined to think it far more ancient than the comments of the priests on the occurrence therein referred to. It may be rendered in English, viz.:—

> "O Kane-Laa-'uli, uli, uli,
> Dead by the feast, feast, feast,
> Dead by the oath, by the law, law, law,
> Truly, thus indeed, dead, dead, dead.
>> O ! vanish the stars !
>> O ! vanish the light !
>> In company with
>> The moon, moon, moon,
>> And cursed be my hand,
>> Cut off be my course !
> E Kane-Laa-'uli, uli, uli,
> E Kane-Laa-huli, huli, huli,
> E Kane-Laa-make, make, make,
> Dead are you, you, you,
> By Kane thy god, god, god,
> Dead by the law, law, law,
> Truly, thus indeed, dead, dead, dead,
> O Kane-Laa-'uli, uli, uli,
> O Kane disobeying the gods, gods, gods,
> O Kane (returned) to dust, dust, dust."

The text reads:—

> *O Kane Laa-'uli, uli, uli,*
> *I make i ahaina, 'ina, 'ina,*
> *I make i hoohiki, i kanawai, wai, wai,*
> *Oia nae, no ka make, make, make.*
>> *O hele ka hoku,*
>> *O hele ka malama,*
>> *Ka kakai pu ae no,*
>> *Me ka Mahina, 'hina, 'hina !*
>> *A Laa kuu lima la !*
>> *Kaapahu kuu hele e !*
> *E Kane-Laa-'uli, uli, uli,*
> *E Kane-Laa-huli, huli, huli,*
> *E Kane-Laa-make, make, make,*
> *O make oe, oe, oe,*
> *Ia Kane Kou Akua, 'kua, 'kua,*

I make kanawai, 'wai, 'wai,
Oia nae no ke make, make, make,
O Kane-Laa-'uli, 'uli, 'uli.
O Kane aaia, ia, ia,
O Kane i ka wai-lepo-leoo, lepo." [1]

The tradition of the creation above referred to, and the enumeration of various animals of the reptile kind, speaks of the *Moopelo* as an astute and lying animal, and that he was also known in the ancient chants by the name of *Ilioha*. In the very chant quoted on pp. 74, 75, after relating the creation of the first man and woman, and giving some eight different names or appellatives whereby they were known, and all referring to their happy and powerful state before the fall, occurs the following allusion to some catastrophe in which the said reptile or "Moo" was concerned, and after which the previous names of the first human pair, expressive of joy and power, were changed to names expressive of misfortune and remorse or grief. The lines of the chant referred to read:

" *Ka Ilioha kupu-ino ku iluna oka moku,*
Loaa na Lii Ku-Honua,
O Polo-Haina ka wahine la e,
He mau Alii kapu a Kane.
    O Polo-Haina, ka wahine
    O Ulia-wale, ke kane,
    O Laa'i ka wahine,
    O Laa'-hee-wale ke kane,
    O Laa'-make ka wahine,
    O Laa'-uli, ke kane,
    O Kanikau, ka wahine
    O Kani-kuo, ke kane,
    O Noho-u, ka wahine,
    O Noho-mihi, ke kane,
    O Huki-ku, ka wahine,

---

[1] This is one of the expressions used to designate the moist earth, from which man was made. Hence *Ua hele i ka wai lepo-lepo* became one of the many poetical or sacerdotal phrases to designate that a person had died—" he has gone to the moist earth, or to the muddy water," soil: from which he was made; or, as we say, returned to dust, from which he sprang.

O Piliwale, ke kane la e,
'Piliwale laua la e."

Which may be rendered in English :—

> " The Ilioha, mischief-maker, stands on the land ;
> He has caught the chief Ku-Honua,
> And Polo-Haina, the woman,
> The Tabu chiefs of Kane," &c., &c.

Here follow the new names of " Fallen," " Tree-eater," "Tree-upset," "Mourner," "Lamentation," "Repenting," &c.; and it is, moreover, curious to observe that, whereas in enumerating the names of the first pair before their misfortune, the chant places the husband's name before that of the wife, in the list of names after the fall the names of the wife precede those of the husband, who becomes, as it were, an intensified echo of the former. The tradition adds, that the first pair lived in " Kalana i Hauola," until they were driven out from there by *Ka-aaia-nukea-nui a Kane,* " the large white bird of Kane."

This is all that Hawaiian folk-lore, so far as I have been able to collect it, tells us of the forbidden fruit in Paradise, and of the disobedience and fall of the first of mankind. It is but little, but is remarkable for its agreement with the Hebrew legend of the same event, and with the Chaldean allusions thereto, as collected by Mr. George Smith.

I know not how far any reference of similar import may have been preserved among the traditions and chants of the south-westerly groups of Polynesia; but in one of the sacrificial hymns of the Marquesas, when human victims were offered, frequent allusions were made to " the red apples eaten in Vavau," *Keika kua kaikai ia i Vevau,* and to " the tabued apples of Atea," *te keika tapu no Atea,* as the cause of death, wars, pestilence, famine, and other calamities, only to be averted or atoned for by the sacrifice of human victims. The close connection between the Hawaiian and Marquesan legends indicates a-common origin, and that that origin can be no other than that from which the Chaldean and Hebrew legends of sacred trees, disobedience, and fall also sprang.

There are still two other Hawaiian legends that also bear upon the subject of the fall of man and the introduction of death in the world: the legend of "Wela-ahi-lani," and that of "Kumu-honua." According to those legends, using one to supplement the other, at the time when the gods created the stars, they also created a multitude of angels or spirits, *i Kini Akua,* who were not created like man, but were made from the spittle of the gods, *i kuha ia,* to be their servants or messengers. These spirits, or a number of them, disobeyed and revolted because they were denied the Awa, which means that they were not permitted to be worshipped; Awa being a sacrificial offering and sign of worship. These evil spirits did not prevail, however, but were conquered by Kane and thrust down into uttermost darkness, *ilalo-loa i ka Po;* and the chief of these spirits was called by some *Kanaloa,* by others, *Milu,* the ruler of "Po," *Akua ino, kupu ino,* the evil spirit.[1] The legend further tells that when Kane, Ku, and Lono were creating the first man from the earth, Kanaloa also was present, and, in imitation of Kane, attempted to make another man out of the earth. When his clay model was ready, he

---

[1] Other legends, however, state that the veritable and primordial lord of the Hawaiian Inferno was called *Manua.* The Inferno itself bore a number of names, such as *Po-pau-ole, Po-'kua-kini, Po-kini-kini, Po-papa-ia-owa, Po-ia-Milu.* "Milu," according to the legends, was but a chief of superior wickedness on earth who was thrust down into "Po," but who was really both inferior and posterior to "Manua." This Inferno, this "Po" with many names, one of which, remarkably enough, was *he Po-lua-ahi,* "the pit of fire," was not an entirely dark place. There was light of some kind, and there was fire. Like the classical Tartarus, it could be visited by gifted mortals, and the spirits of the dead could be brought away from there to the light and life of the upper world. Hawaiian legends relate several instances of such descents and returns to and from "Po." *Mokulehua* brought his wife *Pueo* back from there by the help of his god "Kanikaniaula." *Maluae* brought his son *Kaalii* from there with the help of "Kane" and "Kanaloa." *Hiku* or *Iku* brought up the spirit of the woman *Kawelu* and restored her to life; and several other instances.

called to it to become alive, but no life came to it. Then Kanaloa became very angry, and said to Kane, "I will take your man, and he shall die;" and so it happened; and hence the first man got another name, *Kumu-uli,* which means "a fallen chief," *he Lii kahuli.*

That the Marquesan *Tanaoa* and the Hawaiian *Kanaloa* embody the same original conception of evil, I consider pretty evident. With the Marquesans the idea is treated in the abstract. With them "Tanaoa" is the primary condition of darkness, chaos, confusion, elevated into a divinity battling with Atea, the god of light and order. With the Hawaiians "Kanaloa" is the same idea in the concrete, a personified spirit of evil, the origin of death, the prince of "Po," the Hawaiian chaos, and yet a revolted, disobedient spirit, who was conquered and punished by Kane.[1] In most of the southern groups of Polynesia, though nearly defaced and greatly distorted, the original idea still shines out in the fact that they consider *Tangaloa,* or, contracted, *Taaroa,* as the demiurgos of the world, and the father of gods and men, and is there worshipped as the supreme God, taking precedence of *Tane, Tu, Oro, Roo,* or *Lono,* and others.[2]

That this perversion of the original idea among the southern groups was subsequent in time to the separation of the Hawaiians and Marquesans from the rest of the Polynesian family in the Pacific, I infer from the fact that the introduction and worship of "Kanaloa," as one of the great gods in the Hawaiian group, can only be traced back to the time of the immigration from the southern groups

[1] In "Voyage aux Isles du Grand Ocean," par M. Moerenhout, vol. i. p. 568, he says, "On ne trouve, nulle part, de vestiges des deux principes, ni de ces combats entre les ténèbres et la lumière, la vie et la mort." If lost among Tahitian legends, the Marquesan and Hawaiian have plainly retained those "vestiges."

[2] Some idea may be formed of the supreme consideration in which this god was held on Tahiti from the fact, as M. de Bovis relates, that no worship was offered to him, and, with the single exception of the small island of Tapuenanu, there was not in all the group a single morae erected in his honour. Having created gods and demigods, he was above the consideration of the concerns of mortals.

some eight hundred years ago, and that in the more ancient chants he is never mentioned in conjunction with "Kane," "Ku," and "Lono," and that, even in later Hawaiian worship and mythology, he never took precedence of "Kane."

This Hawaiian myth of "Kanaloa" as a fallen angel antagonistic to the great gods, and the spirit of evil and death in the world, bears a wonderful relation to the Chaldean myth of the seven spirits which rebelled against Anu, and spread consternation in heaven and destruction on earth, but were finally conquered by Bel, the son of Hea. · See "Chaldean Account of Genesis," by G. Smith, p. 107.

The Hebrew legends are more vague and indefinite as to the existence of an evil principle. The serpent of Genesis, the Satan of Job, the Hillel of Isaiah, the dragon of the Revelations—all point, however, to the same underlying idea, that the first cause of sin, death, evil, and calamities was to be found in disobedience and revolt from God. They appear as disconnected scenes of a once grand drama, that in olden times riveted the attention of mankind, and of which, strange to say, the clearest synopsis and the most coherent recollection are, so far, to be found in Polynesian traditions. It is probably in vain to inquire with whom the legend of an evil spirit and his operations in heaven and on earth had its origin. Notwithstanding the apparent unity of design and remarkable coincidences in many points, yet the differences in detail, colouring, and presentation are too great to suppose the legend borrowed by one from either of the others. It probably descended to the Chaldeans, Polynesians, and Hebrews alike from some source or people anterior to themselves, of whom history now is silent.

On the events in the world and the generations of mankind, from the creation of the first man to the time of the

Flood, Polynesian legends are almost as barren as those of the Chaldees or Hebrews. The latter counted ten generations or dynasties from the first man to, and inclusive of, Noah or Xisuthrus, and in this corresponded with the ten Egyptian reigns of the dynasty of gods, from Ptha to Hor II. The Hebrew account mentions three sons of Adam, of which the first killed the second, and mankind was propagated from the first and third up to the time of the Flood; but while the line of Seth, from Adam to Noah, counts ten generations, the line of Cain stops short at the eighth generation.

The Polynesian legends, as we have seen, both in the Tongas and New Zealand, make reference to the killing of the younger by the older of the sons of the first man. The Hawaiian legend is fuller, and, while referring to the same fratricide, gives a complete genealogy of both the older and youngest branches from the first man to the time of the Flood.

I have three different Hawaiian genealogies, going back, with more or less agreement among themselves, to the first created man. One is the genealogy of *Kumuhonua*, connected with the legend frequently referred to. This gives thirteen generations from " Kumuhonua," the first man, to " Nuu " or " Kahinalii," both inclusive, on the line of *Laka*, the oldest son of " Kumuhonua." It also gives thirteen generations, during the same period, on the line of *Ka Pili*, the youngest and third son of " Kumuhonua." The second genealogy is called that of *Kumu-uli*, and was of greatest authority among the highest chiefs down to the latest times, and it was tabu to teach it to common people. This genealogy counts fourteen generations from *Huli-honua*, the first man, to " Nuu " or " Nana Nuu," both inclusive, on the line of " Laka," the son of the first man. The third genealogy, which, properly speaking, is that of *Paao*, the high-priest who came with *Pili* from Tahiti about twenty-five generations ago, and was a reformer of the Hawaiian priesthood, and among whose descendants it has been preserved, counts only twelve generations from "Kumuhonua" to "Nuu," on the line of "Ka-Pili," the youngest son.

These three genealogies were from ancient times considered as of equal authority and independent of each other, the "Kumuhonua" and "Paao" genealogies obtaining principally among the priests and chiefs on Hawaii, and the "Kumuuli" genealogy being specially claimed by the chiefs of Kauai and Oahu as their authority; yet during this early period, from the first man to the Flood, the names of the different generations on the "Kumuhonua" and "Kumuuli" in the line of "Laka" are identical, except where the latter exceeds the former by one; and the names on the "Kumuhonua" and "Paao" in the line of "Ka-Pili" are also identical, except where the former exceeds the latter by one. It is fair to infer, therefore, that there was some common bond of union, some sacred deposit from primeval times, which kept the record of these names intact from the interpolations, changes, and variations which in subsequent times more or less affected the number and order of names of generations in post-diluvian periods.

But though the Polynesian differ from the Chaldeo-Hebraico-Egyptian account of the number of antediluvian gods, kings, and patriarchs, it coincides with the Hebrew in the number of sons of the first man; in the murder of the second son by the first; in the enormous length of days attributed to each generation; in the translation to heaven of not only one, as the Hebrew text gives it, but of two worthy individuals, whose pious lives had merited such favour; and, finally, in the very name of the hero of the Flood and that of his wife—*Nuu* and *Lili-Noe*—which evidently point to the Hebrew and Arabic *Nuh* or *Noah*.

In many of the Polynesian groups, there still exist legends of a flood in which the majority of mankind perished, while only a few escaped. Many of these legends are apparently only later editions and corrupted versions of a once common theme, or attempts to localise the catastrophe and its incidents on this or that group.

In the Fiji group, where so much of Polynesian ancient lore was deposited during their sejour on that group, several versions of an ancient tradition of the Flood have been collected by the Rev. Thomas Williams, of which he gives the following synopsis in his work called "Fiji and the Fijians," p. 196. He says of the Fijians—

"They speak of a deluge which, according to some of their accounts, was partial, but in others is stated to have been universal. The cause of this great flood was the killing of Turukawa—a favourite bird belonging to Ndengei—by two mischievous lads, the grandsons of the god. These, instead of apologising for their offence, added insolent language to the outrage, and fortifying, with the assistance of their friends, the town in which they lived, defied Ndengei to do his worst. It is said that although the angry god took three months to collect his forces, he was unable to subdue the rebels, and, disbanding his army, resolved on more efficient revenge. At his command the dark clouds gathered and burst, pouring streams on the devoted earth. Towns, hills, mountains were successively submerged; but the rebels, secure in the superior height of their own dwelling-place, looked on without concern. But when, at last, the terrible surges invaded their fortress, they cried for direction to a god who, according to one account, instructed them to form a float of the fruit of the shaddock; according to another, sent two canoes for their use; or, says a third, taught them how to build a canoe, and thus secure their own safety. All agree that the highest places were covered, and the remnant of the human race saved in some kind of vessel, which was at last left by the subsiding waters on Mbenga; hence the Mbengans draw their claim to stand first in Fijian rank. The number saved—eight—exactly accords with the "few" of the Scripture record. By this flood it is said that two tribes of the human family became extinct. One consisted entirely of women, and the other were distinguished by the appendage of a tail like that of a dog. The highest point of the island of Koro is associated with the history of the Flood. Its name is *Ngginggi-tangithi-Koro,* which conveys the idea of a little bird sitting there and lamenting the drowned island. In this bird the Christians recognise Noah's dove on its second flight from the ark. I have heard a native, after listening to the incident as given by Moses, chant "*Na qiqi sa tagici Koro ni yali,*"—"The Qiqui laments over Koro, because it is lost."

At Raiatea, Society group, the legend runs that one day *Rua-Haku,* the Lord Rua, the Ocean God, was asleep at the bottom of the sea, when a fisherman came along that way with his hook and line. The hook got entangled in the hair of the god, and the fisherman, thinking he had caught a fine fish on his hook, pulled up so vigorously as to bring the god to the surface. Enraged at being thus disturbed in his sleep, the god threatened instant destruction to the unlucky fisherman; but the latter, having implored the god's pardon, was told to repair to a coral bank or islet called *Toa-marama* for shelter, while the god vented his displeasure on the rest of the world. The fisherman did as he was told, and took a friend, a hog, a dog, and a couple of hens with him to the islet. After that the ocean commenced rising, and continued rising until all the land was covered with water and all the people had perished. Then the waters retired, and the fisherman returned to his former home. Other versions of the event exist at Tahiti, but equally distorted.[1]

[1] M. Moerenhout, in his "Voyage aux Isles de Grand Ocean," vol. i. p. 571, says that the Polynesian legends represent the ocean as overflowing its bed, and rising up to the highest mountains, "sans que, nulle part, il soit question des eaux pluviales." M. Moerenhout apparently did not know the Marquesan and Hawaiian legends, to which I will refer directly.

Of the Marquesan legends bearing on this subject, I have only had access to the " Chant of the Deluge," *te-tai-toko*, in Mr. Lawson's collection.[1] It takes higher ground than the half-remembered and corrupted versions current among the southern groups, and is a remarkable specimen of native poetry, as well as of strict fidelity to the original narrative, so far as that may be ascertained from the Chaldean and Hebrew accounts. Mr. Lawson has given an English translation, but it is so very literal and rugged, that I prefer to give a prose synopsis of the chant in order to convey its contents to the reader.

The chant opens by saying that the Lord Ocean, *Fatu-Moana*, was going to overflow and pass over the dry earth, but that a respite of seven days was granted. It then speaks of the animals who were to be reserved from the Flood. Then speaks of a house to be built high above the waters; a house with stories, with chambers, with openings for light, stored with provisions for the preservation of the various animals. The animals then are fastened with ropes, tied up in couples, and, with one man before and one behind, marched off to this big, deep house of wood. Then the family enter, consisting of four women and four men. The men's names are given " *Fetu-moana*," apparently the father and master of the family, *Fetu-tau-ani*, *Fetu-amo-amo*, and *Ia-fetu-tini*. A turtle is then sacrificed; the family retires to rest amidst the din, confusion, and crowding of the confined animals. Then the storm bursts over them; the rain is pouring fearfully, and gloom prevails; all on earth is displaced and mixed up by the waters.

The second part opens with a description of the waters retreating, and mountain summits and ridges reappearing, the grounding of the house, and the command of the Lord Ocean for the dry land to appear. The head of the family, encouraged by the sight, promises to sacrifice to the Lord Ocean seven holy and precious things and seven sucklings. Then a bird, called *te teetina o Tanaoa*—from

[1] See Appendix, No. IV.

its name apparently of a dark colour—is sent out over the
sea of Hawaii, but after a while returns to the vessel. The
wind sets in from the north. On a second attempt the
same bird alights on the sand of the shore, but is recalled
to the vessel. Then another bird, called *te Teetina o Moepo*,
is sent out over the sea of Hawaii. It lands on the dry
land, and returns with young shoots or branches it had
gathered. The land is now dry, and the great ridges of
Hawaii and of *Matahou* are fit to dwell on. In the third
part reference is made to the debarkation of men and
animals.

In the Hawaiian group there are several versions of the
Flood. Some indicate the decay and corruption of the
original legend in a similar manner to the Fiji and Raiatea
legends above referred to ; but one legend approaches
nearly to the Marquesan, though greatly shortened in
details as I obtained it. It relates that in the time
of *Nuu* or *Nana*[1]*-Nuu*, as he is also called, the Flood
—*Kai-a-Kahinalii*—came upon the earth and destroyed
all living beings; that "Nuu," by command of his god,
built a large vessel with a house on top of it, which
was called and is referred to in the chants as *He Waa-
Halau-Alii o ka Moku*, "the royal vessel," in which he and
his family, consisting of his wife *Lili-Nae*, his three sons,
and their wives, were saved. When the Flood subsided,
" Kane," " Ku," and " Lono " entered the " Waa-Halau " of
" Nuu," and told him to go out. He did so, and found
himself on the top of Mauna-kea (the highest mountain on
the island of Hawaii), and he called a cave there after the
name of his wife, and the cave remains there to this day,
as the legend says, in testimony of the fact. Other versions of the legend say that " Nuu " landed and dwelt in
Kahiki-honua-kele, a large and extensive country. I have
already given the remainder of the legend on page 44, tell-
ing how " Nuu," by mistake, after debarking, offered his

---

[1] Also pronounced *Lana*, *l* and *n* being interchangeable. It means
"floating."

offerings to the moon instead of to "Kane," and the conse-
quences. From "Nuu," the legend says, the world was
again repeopled.

I have only been able to obtain one Hawaiian chant, or
rather portion of a chant, bearing on the subject of the
Flood. Its idiom, language, and allusions indicate it to be
of great antiquity. It is, properly speaking, only the
introduction to the ancient chant of the Flood, and seems
to represent the dismay and consternation of the descendants of "Laka," the eldest son of the first man, at the
coming of the Flood, with an appeal to "Lono" to save
them. The Hawaiian text reads :—

> *Ei ka ai,[1] e ke Akua,*
> *E Kahuli,[2]*
> *E Kahela.[3]*
> *E ka wahine moe iluna ka alo,*
> *O Moe-a-Hanuna,[3]*
> *O Milikaa,[3]*
> *O ka Lepo-Ahulu,[4]*
> *O Pahu-Kini,*
> *O Pahu-lau,*
> *O Kulana-a-Pahu,*
> *O Ola-ka-hua-nui,*
> *O Ka papai-a-Laka,*
> *O Manuu ke eu,*
> *O ka paepae nui, ala i ka moku la, e.*
> *E ala !*
>> *E ala ! e ka ua !*
>> *E ka la,*
>> *E ka ohu-kolo i uka,*
>> *E ka ohu-kolo i kai !*
>> *Kai nuu— kai ee,*
>> *Kai pipili[5] a Iku ;*

---

[1] *Ai*, "food," when addressed to
a god, means the sacrifice, the offering, the gods being supposed to con-
sume what was offered them and de-
light in it.

[2] *Kahuli*, one of the many names
of the first created man.

[3] I am unable at present to refer
these names to any known antediluvian personages. Conjecture in that
case might mislead.

[4] *Lepo-Ahulu*, also one of the many
names of the first man.

[5] *Pipili*, properly means "topsy-
turvy," "helter-skelter." I have
rendered it "boisterous," as appli-
cable to the sea or ocean.

La ! e ua Puni !
O huahua kai,
O ka ale i, o ka ale moe,
O ka ale hakoikoi,
I kahiki,
A hiki a ola,
No nei make ia oe la e Lono.
E kaukau nou e Lono,
E Lono i-ka-Po,[1]
E Lono i-ka-Hekili,
E Lono i-ka-Uwila,
E Lono i-ka-Ua-loko,
E Lono i-ka-Oili maka akua nei la,
·E Lono, e Lono, maka-hia-lele ;
A lele oe i ke kai uli,[2]
A lele oe i ke kai kona,
I kai koolau,
I One-uli, i One-kea,
I mahina, uli, i mahina-kea.
O Pipipi, O Unauna,
O Alealea ;[3] *o hee ;*
O Naka, Kualakai,[4]
O Kama, O Opihi-kau-pali,
O Kulele poo,
O helelei ke oho.[5]
O Waa-Halau-Alii o ka moku,
Kahi i waiho ai na hua olelo a Pii,[6]
O Kama a Poepoe ka wahine i ka ipu-wai.[7]

---

[1] *I-ka-Po,* "from the time of universal night, chaos," one of the ancient titles of the three great gods, "Kane," "Ku," and "Lono." The following lines give the various epithets of Lono, and plainly enough indicate that in the ancient Hawaiian creed he was the god of the atmosphere and its phenomena.

[2] *Kai-uli.* I have rendered it "the Northern Sea," because the following antithesis of "the Southern Sea" and "the Eastern Sea" required it so ; and also in view of the designation of the North mentioned on page 16.

[3] These three names designate different species of shell-fish.

[4] Two other kinds of fishes.

[5] A poetical expression. *Oho* means the hair of the head, and also the leaves of the cocoa-nut tree. The phrase "*O hina ke oho,*" or "*O helelei ke oho,*" conveys the sense of a severe storm which tears the leaves from the cocoa-nut trees.

[6] I am unable, from any legend, chant, or tradition that has come to my knowledge, to explain what this line refers to beyond what the words themselves convey. It would seem, however, from this and the next line, that some account of the antediluvian world was supposed to have been deposited in the Ark, or the *Waa-Halau,* at the time of the Flood.

[7] Probably contracted, or an ancient form of *Ipu-wai-au-au,* "an epithet

The above text may be rendered in English as follows:

> " Here is the food, O God,
>> O Kahuli,
>> O Kahela,
>> O the woman sleeping face upward,
>> O Mae-a-Hanuna,
>> O Milikaa.
>
> O ka Lepo-Ahulu,
> O Pahu-kini,
> O Pahu-lau,
> O Kulana-a-Pahu,
> O Ola-ka-hua-nui,
> O Kapapai a Laka,[1]
> O Manuu, the mischievous,
> O the great supporter, awaken the world.
> O wake up.
>> O wake up, here is the rain,
>> Here is daylight,
>> Here the mists driving inland, ·
>> Here the mists driving seaward,
>> The swelling sea, the rising sea,
>> The boisterous sea of Iku.
>> It has enclosed (us).
>> O the foaming sea,
>> O the rising billows, O the falling billows,
>> O the overwhelming billows,
>> In Kahiki.
>> Salvation comes
>> From this death by you, O Lono.
> An altar for you, O Lono.
> O Lono of the night,
> O Lono of the thunder,
> O Lono of the lightning,
> O Lono of the heavy rain,
> O Lono of the terrible, divine face,
> O Lono, O Lono with the restless eyes,
> Ah, fly to the northern sea,
> Ah, fly to the southern sea,

---

applied to those who kept the genealogies of the chiefs, because they managed to wash the characters of the chiefs so far as their pedigree was concerned."— *Vide* "Andrews's Hawaiian Dictionary," *sub voce.*

[1] *Laka* was the oldest son of Kumuhonua, the first man, and the phrase "*Ka papai a Laka*" is a poetical expression equivalent to "the descendants, the family of Laka."

To the eastern sea,
To the dark shore, to the white shore,
To the dark moon, to the bright moon.
    O Pipipi, O Unauna,
    O Alealea ; O glide away ;
    O Naka, Kualakai,
    O Kama, O Opihi, sticking to the rocks,
    O fly beneath the sand,
    The leaves are falling.
O the Waa-Halau-Alii o ka Moku
Where were deposited the words of Pii,
O Kama-a-Poepoe, the woman of the water-bowl."

    •   •   :   •   •   •   •   •

Were the original legend of the Flood to be reconstructed from Polynesian sources alone, it will be seen at a glance how striking its conformity would be to the Hebrew version of said legend, as well as to the Chaldean in parts. Beside the general correspondence in outline, however, there are minor touches of conformity, such as the truce or respite of seven days before the Flood should come; the fastening of the animals in couples, to be stowed away in the ark; the sending forth the raven, or dark-coloured bird at the first, instead of the dove, as in the Chaldee account; the setting in of the north wind to assist in drying up the earth, not mentioned in the Chaldee; the reference to "the words of Pii," corresponding to the writings of Xisythrus in the Chaldee account of Berasus, deposited in the city of Sippara, but not referred to in Genesis; sacrifice offered before entering the ark or vessel, not referred to in Scripture, but probably indicated in the Chaldee account and the Izdubar legends,[1] which make it extremely improbable that the Polynesian legend was borrowed or copied from either the one or the other. And thus, though closely akin, I think it may justly be ranked as another independent version of that great cataclysm which at some remote period spread desolation over the present Mesopotamian basin.

<hr/>

The Chaldean Account of Genesis, by George Smith, p. 266, &c.

We know that the story of the Flood spread from " Ur of the Chaldees" to the shores of the Mediterranean, and doubtless different versions of it obtained among the intervening nations of Aramians and Hittites, though their accounts of it are now lost to us. It is, therefore, extremely probable that similar versions, variously coloured, found their way southward to Arabia, and eastward to Persia and the early homes of the Arian nations; the more so, as from the earliest times the ancient Chaldea was designated as the *Kiprat-Arbat,* "the four nations," or *Arba-lisun,* " the four tongues," which Mr. G. Rawlinson, in his "Five Great Monarchies of the Ancient Eastern World," vol. i. p. 55, intimates to have consisted of the Cushite, Turanian, Semitic, and Arian elements, among whom the Cushites preponderated in influence. I have just shown that the Polynesian version of the Flood was probably not derived from either Chaldee or Hebrew originals, at least such as we now have them; nor, viewing the state of the Arian legends relating to the Flood, is there the slightest likelihood that it was derived from that quarter. Unfortunately, we have no well-preserved account of the Flood from the Cushite-Arabian quarter; but I am inclined to consider the Polynesian version as originally representing the early traditions on this subject among the Cushite-pre-Joklanite Arabs, whose sway and whose culture extended over India and the Archipelago, and in so far concurrent in time, equal in authenticity, and equally deserving of consideration, with the Chaldee and Hebrew accounts.

———

Of the Hebrew legend of the Tower of Babel I have found no trace among the traditions of the Polynesian tribes, properly so called, in the East Pacific; but in the Fiji group, where so many shreds of Polynesian folk-lore have been stowed away that have been forgotten elsewhere, there is a legend that—

"Near Na-Savu, Veuua Levu, the natives point out the site where, in former ages, men built a vast tower, being eager for astronomic information, and especially anxious to decide the difficult question as to whether the moon was inhabited. To effect their purpose they cast up a high mound, and erected thereon a great building of timber. The tower had already risen far skyward, and the ambitious hopes of its industrious builders seemed near fulfilment, when the lower fastenings suddenly broke asunder, and scattered the workmen over every part of Fiji."[1]

Except the genealogical record, Hawaiian traditions give but a small account of the worthies who flourished immediately after the Flood. We are told that Nuu's three sons were *Nalu-Akea*, *Nalu-Hoohua*, and *Nalu-Manamana*, and that in the tenth generation from Nuu arose one *Lua-Nuu*, or "the second Nuu," known also in the legends as *Kanehoalani*, *Ku-Pule*, and other names. The legend adds that by command of his God he was the first to introduce circumcision to be practised among all his descendants. He left his native home, and moved a long way off until he reached a land called *Honua-ilalo*, "the southern country," and hence he got the name *Lalo-Kona*, and his wife was called *Honua-Po-ilalo*. He was the father of *Ku-Nawao* by his slave-woman *Ahu*, and of *Kalani Menehune* by his wife *Mee-Hiwa*. Another legend says that the God "Kane" ordered Lua-Nuu to go up on a mountain and perform a sacrifice there. Lua-Nuu looked among the mountains of *Kahiki-ku*, but none of them appeared suitable for the purpose. Then Lua-Nuu inquired of God where he might find a proper place, and God replied to him: "Go travel to the eastward, and where you find a sharp, peaked hill projecting precipitously into the ocean, that is the hill for the sacrifice." Then Lua-

---

[1] Fiji and the Fijians, by Rev. Mr. Williams, p. 199.

Nuu and his son, *Kupulu-pulu-a-Nuu,* and his servant, *Pili-Lua-Nuu,* started off in their boat to the eastward; and in remembrance of this event the Hawaiians called the mountain back of Kualoa, Koolau, Oahu, after one of Lua-Nuu's names—"Kanehoalani"—and the smaller hills in front of it were named after "Kupulu-pulu" and "Pili-Lua-Nuu." By a strange coincidence, Lua-Nuu is the tenth descendant from "Nuu," by both the oldest and youngest of Nuu's sons, "Nalu-Akea" and "Nalu-Mana-mana," of whom the former is represented to have been the progenitor of the *Kouaka maoli,* the people living on the mainland of Kane—*Aina Kumu-paa a Kane*—and the latter to have been the progenitor of the white people— *he poe keoko maoli.* Here again the national conscious-ness of a mixed origin of race reveals itself in a legendary, half-mythical form, similar to the creation legend, where the body of the first man was made of red earth and the head of white clay.

This tenth descendant from the hero of the Flood, this "Lua-Nuu" or "Kane-hoa-lani," does again forcibly recall the Hebrew legend of the tenth from Noah—the Abram who travelled into Egypt; the Abraham of the promise, the originator, by Divine command, of the practice of cir-cumcision; the father of the slave-woman's child Ishmael, as well as of the legitimate Isaac—the man who in blind obedience would have sacrificed his own child. To make the correspondence more complete, this *Lua-Nuu,* through his grandson *Kini-lau-a-mano,* became the ancestor of the twelve children of the latter, and the original founder of the *Mene-hune* people, from whom this legend makes the Polynesian family descend.

Here again the Marquesan legends come to the support of the Hawaiian traditions. They tell us that *Toho the Take,* the first of that national name, was the grandson of *Apana,* to whom the introduction of circumcision is ascribed; that "Toho" was the younger of the twins born to *I-aaka,* the son of "Apana;" and the Marquesan account

of the children of " Toho " is even more conformable to the
Hebrew legend than the Hawaiian account of the children
of " Kini-lau-a-mano," inasmuch as the latter enumerates
only the twelve sons, whereas the former mentions not
only the twelve sons, but also the thirteenth child, the
daughter.

After this period of " Kini-lau-a-mano's " or " Toho's "
twelve sons, the similarity between Polynesian and Hebrew-
Chaldean legends becomes very scarce and not well defined.
There are references to *Kana-loa* and *Kane-Apua*, his
brother, a pair of prophets or high-priests, who overthrew
the power of King *Waha-nui*, and who walked about the
world causing water to flow from rocks, and similar wonderful exploits, which, in the light of the foregoing resem-
blances, may bear reference to Moses and Aaron.[1]   In the

[1] S. M. Kamakau, the Hawaiian
archæologist, to whom we are indebted
for the preservation of so many of
the ancient legends, relates the following as part of an ancient legend :—
"*Kealii-Wahanui*, king of the country called *Honua-i-lalo*, oppressed
the *Lahui-Menehune* (the Menehune
people). Their God, *Kane*, sent *Kane-
Apua* and *Kanaloa*, the elder brother,
to bring the people away, and take
them to the land which *Kane* had
given them, and which was called *Ka
aina Momona-a-Kane*, or, with another name, *Ka One Lauena a Kane*,
and also *Ka Aina i Ka Haupo a
Kane*. The people were then told to
observe the four *Ku* days in the beginning of the month as *Kapu Hoano*
(sacred or holy days), in remembrance
of this event, because they thus
'arose'—*Ku*—to depart from that
land. Their offerings on the occasion
were swine and goats. The narrator
of the legend explains that formerly
there were goats without horns, called
Malailua, on the slopes of the Mauna-
loa mountain in Hawaii, and that
they were found there up to the time
of Kamehameha I. The legend further relates that, after leaving the

land of *Honua-i-lalo*, the people came
to the *Kai-ula-a-Kane* (the Red Sea of
Kane) ; that they were pursued by
Ke Alii Wahanui ; that *Kane-Apua*
and *Kanaloa* prayed to *Lono*, and
that they then waded across the sea,
travelled through desert lands, and
finally reached the *Aina-Lauena-a-
Kane.*"

On first receiving this legend, I
was inclined to doubt its genuineness,
and to consider it as a paraphrase or
adaptation of the Biblical account by
some semi-civilised or semi-Christian-
ised Hawaiian, after the discovery of
this group by Captain Cook. But a
larger and better acquaintance with
Hawaiian folklore has shown me
that, though the details of the legend, as narrated by the Christian and
civilised Kamakau, may possibly in
some degree, and unconsciously to
him, perhaps, have received a Biblical
colouring, yet the main facts of the
legend, with the identical names of
places and persons, are referred to
more or less distinctly in other legends
of undoubted antiquity. I am compelled, therefore, to class the legend
among the other Chaldæo-Arabico-
Hebraic mementoes which the Poly-

famous Hawaiian legend of *Hiaka-i-ka-poli-o-Pele*, it is said that when "Hiaka" went to the island of Kauai to recover and restore to life the body of *Lohiau*, the lover of her sister "Pele," she arrived at the foot of the Kalalau mountain shortly before sunset, and being told by her friends at Haena that there would not be daylight suffi- ·cient to climb the *Pali* (mountain) and get the body out of the cave in which it was hidden, she prayed to her gods to keep the sun stationary, *i ka muli o Hea*, "over the brook, pool, or estuary of Hea," until she had accomplished her object. The prayer was heard, the sun stood still, the mountain was climbed, the guardians of the cave van- quished, and the body recovered. What previous legend, if any, had been culled and applied to furnish this episode of the Hiaka legend, I cannot say. If the Hebrew legend of Joshua, or a Cushite version, gave rise to it, it only brings down the community of legends a little later in time. And so would the allusion in the legend of *Naula- a-Maihea*, the Oahu prophet who left Oahu for Kauai, was upset in his canoe, was swallowed by a whale, and thrown up alive on the beach of Wailua, Kanai, unless the legend of Jonah, with which it corresponds in a measure, as well as the previous legend of Joshua and the sun, were Hebrew anachronisms, compiled and adapted in later times from long antecedent materials, of which the Polynesian refer- ences are but broken and distorted echoes, bits of legendary mosaic, displaced from their original surroundings, and made to fit with later associations.

In the legend of "Aukele-nui-a-Iku," previously re- ferred to, especially in the opening parts of it—being the youngest but one of twelve children; being the pet and

nesians brought with them from their ancient homesteads in the West. And it is possible that the legend was pre- served in after times by the priest- hood, as offering a rational explana- tion of the institution of the Kapu- days of *Ku*. Another feature attests the genuine antiquity of the legend, viz., that no other gods are referred to than to those primordial ones of Hawaiian theogony—*Kane*, *Ku*, and *Lono*, the latter of whom is clearly recognised as the god of the atmo- sphere, of air and of water, the *Lononoho-i-ka-wai* of the Creatio chants.

favourite of his father, and consequently bitterly hated by his brothers; being thrown into a pit by them, and left to die; being delivered from the pit by his next eldest brother; his adventures and successes in foreign lands; and, finally, his journey to the place where " the water of life," *Ka wai ola-loa a Kane,* was kept; his obtaining it, and therewith resuscitating his brothers, who had been killed and drowned some years before—there is a most striking resemblance to the Hebrew legend of Joseph and his brethren. In the beginning of the Hawaiian legend the scene is laid in that ancient, well-remembered, and often-quoted home of ·the Polynesians, the *Kua-i-helani* of song and saga, situated in *Kahiki-ku,* and bordering on the ocean.

This is about all that I have been able to collect of the most striking coincidences and similarity between Polynesian and Hebrew-Chaldean legends. The correspondence seems almost too great to be ascribed to the accidental development of the same train of ideas in the minds of people apparently so widely separated in time and distance as the Hawaiians and the Israelites. Two hypotheses may with some plausibility be suggested to account for this remarkable resemblance of folklore. One is, that during the time of the Spanish galleon trade, in the sixteenth and seventeenth centuries A.C., between the Spanish main and Manilla, some shipwrecked people (Spaniards or Portuguese)—of whose arrival at these Hawaiian islands there can now be no doubt—had obtained sufficient influence to introduce these scraps of Bible history into the legendary lore of this people. The other hypothesis is, that at some remote period a body of the scattered Israelites had arrived either at these islands direct, or in Malaysia, before the exodus of the Polynesian family, and thus imparted a knowledge of their doctrines, of the early life of their ancestors, and of some of their peculiar customs, and that, having been absorbed by the people among whom they found a refuge, this is all that remains to at-

test their presence—intellectual tombstones over a lost
and forgotten race, yet sufficient, after twenty-six centuries of silence, to solve in some measure the ethnic
puzzle of "the lost tribes of Israel."

On the first hypothesis I would remark, that if the shipwrecked foreigners were educated men, or only possessed
of such scriptural knowledge as was then imparted to the
commonalty of laymen, it is morally impossible to conceive that a Spaniard of the sixteenth century should con-
fine his instruction to some of the leading events of the
Old Testament, and be totally silent upon the Christian
dispensation, and the cruciolatry, mariolatry, and hagi-
olatry of that day. And it is equally impossible to conceive that the Hawaiian listeners, chiefs, priests, or commoners, should have retained and incorporated so much of
the former in their own folklore, and yet have utterly
rejected or forgotten every item bearing upon the latter.
Besides, even were this possible, it fails to account for the
fact that so many of these legends, wholly or in part, more
or less distorted, are to be met with among the southern
groups of Polynesia, where the Spaniards never went, with
the exception of Mendana's voyage, when, however, no men
were left at the Marquesas to propagate bits of Bible history from either Old or New Testament.

In regard to the other hypothesis, the Israelitish impact
on Polynesian folklore, it is certainly more plausible, and
cannot be so curtly disposed of as the Spanish theory.
The assertors may not be able to prove that any portion
of the "lost tribes of Israel" ever arrived at the Hawaiian
group, or at the Asiatic Archipelago, during the occupation and before the exodus of the Polynesian family; but
they may boldly stand on the established facts, and logically
infer the cause from the results, and thus throw the onus
upon us to show that the results do not warrant the inference, and to account in some other way for their appearance.

I have already shown, in the foregoing pages, in what
the Polynesian and Hebrew and Chaldean legends differ

from and agree with each other, and have ventured my opinion that, so far from being copies the one from the other, they are, in fact, independent and original versions of a once common legend, or series of legends, held alike by Cushite, Semite, Turanian, and Arian, up to a certain time, when the divergences of national life and other causes brought other subjects, peculiar to each, prominently in the foreground; and that as these divergences hardened into system and creed, that grand old heirloom of a common past became overlaid and coloured by the particular social and religious atmosphere through which it has passed up to the surface of the present time.

But beside this general reason for refusing to adopt the Israelitish theory, that the Polynesian legends were introduced by fugitive or emigrant Hebrews from the subverted kingdoms of Israel or Judah, there is the more special reason to be added, that on those grand episodes of Hebrew national life—the Egyptian bondage, the exodus,[1] the law on Sinai, the conquest of Canaan, the organisation and splendour of Solomon's empire, his temple and his wisdom, become proverbial among the nations of the East subsequent to his time, and the dismemberment and fall of that empire—that on all these, to a Hebrew momentous and never-to-be-forgotten subjects, the Polynesian legends are absolutely silent. Had the former legends, whose correspondence I have noted, been derived from Hebrew sources, it is perfectly inconceivable that the latter legends should not also have been imparted, and some traces of them remained in the Polynesian folklore.

Among the customs, usages, rites of worship, modes of thought, prevalent among the Polynesians, much may be found that still further indicates their connection, ethnic and social, with the races who met and mingled at the early dawn of history in the Mesopotamian basin.

[1] See note to p. 99, touching the legend of *Kane-Apua* and his brother *Kanaloa.*

Circumcision.

The custom of circumcising every male child was an almost universal custom among the Polynesian tribes. It was generally performed by the priests, and was accompanied with religious ceremonies. In some places, however, as in New Zealand and the Southern Marquesas, the practice had become obsolete, or, for reasons now unknown and forgotten, prohibited. In the Hawaiian group its origin was ascribed to "Lua Nuu," the tenth in descent from the period of the Flood (*vide* p. 128), thus not only indicating its extreme antiquity, but also its correlation to the Hebrew legend of Abraham. Another Hawaiian legend ascribes its introduction to *Paumakua*, a famous navigator, and noted ancestor of Hawaiian chiefs, who flourished about twenty-eight generations ago, or in the early part of the eleventh century of our era. But "Paumakua" belonged to the period of the South Polynesian incursions in the Hawaiian group, and probably only renewed or enforced the ancient practice.

In tracing back the custom of circumcision, we find it practised by the Tagals and other pre-Malay tribes in the Asiatic Archipelago. It was the custom in Egypt [1] from the earliest times; also of Cushite-Arabia,[2] and Phœnicia, or rather Palestine.[3] It does not appear to have obtained

---

[1] In Sir Gardner Wilkinson's notes to Mr. Rawlinson's Herodotus, book ii. chap. 37, I read that "its (circumcision) institution in Egypt reaches to the most remote antiquity; we find it existing at the earliest period of which any monuments remain, more than 2400 years before our era, and there is no reason to doubt that it dated still earlier. . . . It was a distinctive mark between the Egyptians and their enemies; and in later times, when Egypt contained many foreign settlers, it was looked upon as a distinctive sign between the orthodox Egyptian and the stranger."

[3] " Circumcision established in Ye-

men from remotest antiquity."— "Manual of Ancient History of the East," by Lenormant and Chevallier, vol. ii. p. 318.

[2] Herodotus, book ii. chap. 104, says: "Phœnicians and the Syrians of Palestine;" but in the notes to Mr. Rawlinson's edition signed "G. W.," it is shown that "circumcision was not practised by the Philistines . . . nor by the generality of the Phœnicians." In Egypt the custom was common, "at least as early as the fourth dynasty, and probably earlier." It was also observed in Ethiopia and Abyssinia.

among the Chaldeans, the Arian nations, or the Hebrew congeners of the Semitic stock. In the transmission of customs, however, from one people to another, whose origin and purposes are lost and forgotten through the lapse of ages, the observance of circumcision among the Kaffirs of South Africa may supply a link to establish the extension of Cushite-Arabian influence, through commerce and colonisation, in that direction.

Sir G. Wilkinson, in his notes to Rawlinson's edition of Herodotus, *loc. cit.*, argues that the Hebrews did not borrow circumcision from Egypt after the exodus, because its institution with them dated back to Abraham, and, having fallen into desuetude, was merely renewed or reinforced by Moses. But the remarkable parallelism of the Hawaiian legend of Lua-Nuu with the Hebrew legend of Abraham, and the institution of circumcision connected with each, doubtless indicate a common origin for both legends—a Cushite-Arabian origin, in a land where circumcision was practised "from remotest antiquity," as well as in Egypt. Considering, moreover, that Abraham did not adopt circumcision until after his visit to, and return from, Egypt, on the occasion of the birth of his son Ishmael by the Egyptian woman Hagar, there is certainly some ground for holding that a custom—unknown to the Semitic tribes of whose lineage Abraham claimed to be, unknown or not practised by the Chaldean branch of the Cushite family where he and his father before him were born and bred—was borrowed or adopted by him from the Arabian or Egyptian Cushites, with whom he came in contact after leaving the uncircumcised Chaldeans of Ur and the uncircumcised Semites of Haran. Taken together with the numerous other instances of correlation of Polynesian and Cushite folklore, this custom and accompanying legend is but another argument for the long and intimate connection between the Cushite Arabs and the Polynesian ancestors, while the latter were still living on the shores of the Erythnean, or, somewhat later, occupying the Sunda isles, the *Saba-ii, Sava-ii,* "the volcanic Saba" of Polynesian cosmogony.

Manner of Burial.

Two modes of burial, if so they may be called, obtained among the Polynesians. In the Marquesan and Tahiti groups, deceased people of consequence were exposed on raised platforms until natural decomposition and the action of the air had reduced the corpse to a skeleton. This custom was also practised by some of the Dyakh tribes in Borneo, and at the island of Pulo Nias, and may at some time have obtained greater prevalence in the Asiatic Archipelago, but I have found no traces of it in Hindostan or beyond. In the Hawaiian group this mode of burial was not practised. There the older and more general manner of disposing of the dead was to embalm the body, or rather cover it with a glutinous wash made from the Ti-root,[1] which effectually sealed up the pores of the skin and excluded the air. The body was then deposited in a sitting posture in a cáve on the mountain-side, or on some natural shelf or niche on the side of a precipice. These burial-caves seem to have been either private family property, or the property of the commune living on the land where they were situated. Offerings were frequently carried there, and prayers performed by the relatives of the deceased. Tradition says that the first man, Kumuhonua, was buried on the top of a high mountain, and his descendants were all buried around him until the place was filled.

In analogy with the above custom we find that the burial-places in the Hedjaz, in Southern Syria, in Egypt, and Nubia were generally on or near the summit of mountains, and in natural caves on their sides ; and among the various races which crowded each other on the plains of ancient Chaldea, where mountain-sides or natural caves were not available, the preservation of the dead by interment in artificial tombs was equally practised. In no

[1] *Dracæna terminalis.*

part of Polynesia, so far as I can learn, is there any indication that cremation was ever practised. Interment, no doubt, was the earliest custom. It preceded cremation in Greece and in Europe generally,[1] and the Hindoo custom of burning the corpses did probably not spread either west or east until after the Polynesians had left the mainland of Asia, nor did it obtain in the Indian Archi-

[1] According to the researches of J. Grimm ("Ueber das Verbrennen der Leichen"), all the Arian peoples, with one exception, practised cremation at their funerals from time immemorial, in place of interment. The Indians, Greeks, Romans, Gauls, ancient Germans, Lithuanians, and Slavs, during heathen times, burned their dead with ceremonies which present evident traces of resemblance, notwithstanding their diversity. The Iranians alone at an early time abandoned this ancient custom on account of the radical difference which arose in their religious creed. The Hebrews and Arabs never practised cremation. (*Vide* A. Pictet, "Orig. Ind. Europ.," vol. ii. p. 504.) Is it fully established that the schism of the Iranians was subsequent to the separation and migrations of the Greeks, Romans, &c., &c., from the Arian stock? M. Pictet adds, on p. 505, *loc. cit.:* "Cette coutume, comme l'observe Grimm, a dû prendre naissance aux temps primitifs de la vie pastorale, avant l'etablissement de demeures fixes, parce qu'elle permettait d'emporter avec soi la cendre vénérée des morts." If so, why did it not obtain among the Turanian peoples, than whom none were more pastoral or nomadic? But on page 529, vol. ii., of the work just quoted, M. Pictet says: "D'après tous le developpements qui précèdent, il semble évident que l'usage de brûler les morts doit avoir existé déjà chez les Aryas primitifs; mais il est à présumer que la coutume plus simple de l'inhumation a tenu chez eux une certaine place, comme chez la plupart de leurs descendants. On la voit même prescrite, dans quelques cas, par les lois de plusieurs peuples. Ainsi, d'après Manu (v. 68) un enfant au-dessous de deux ans doit être inhumé, et il en était de même chez les Romains (Juven. Sat. 15, v. 139), suivant Pline (7, 16), avant la dentition. Au temps de Cécrops, l'incinération était peu pratiquée, et l'inhumation parait avoir prédominé chez les Romains les plus anciens (Cicér. Leg. 22, 26; Plin. 7, 54). Numa défendit de brûler son corps, ce qui indique la simultanéité des deux usages, confirmée 300 ans plus tard par la loi des Douze tables. Dans toute l'Europe du Nord, on trouve l'inhumation comme la coutume la plus ancienne, celle qui appartenait à ce qu'on appelle l'âge de la pierre, et ce n'est qu'à l'âge du bronze que les urnes cinéraires font leur apparition dans les tombeaux. On en conclut, non sans vraisemblance, qu'elles sont l'indice de l'arrivée en Europe des premières immigrations ariennes, se mêtant à une race antérieure que nous ne connaissons plus que par les restes de l'âge de la pierre. Ce que l'on peut conjecturer, déjà pour les anciens Aryas, c'est que l'incinération, qui exigeait toujours un certain appareil, était réservée pour les chefs et les hommes considérables, tandis que l'inhumation était le lot de la multitude." This but confirms what I said above, that interment was of older practice than cremation, even among the Arians, and may have descended to the Polynesians from them as well as from the Cushites.

pelago while the Polynesians yet were the masters there. It is practised to some extent among the Dyaks, but only exceptionally, whereas interment is the most prevalent mode.

In connection with the funeral rites of the Polynesians, it may be observed that the practice of immolating one or more of the wives of a deceased chief, which obtained in Tonga and the Fiji islands, was not adhered to in the Hawaiian group, nor generally among the other groups; but it was *de rigueur* that more or less of the friends of the deceased should accompany him or her in death, in manifestation of their love and attachment. Those who thus died were called *Moe-pu*, "companions in sleep." The act, however, was purely voluntary, and generally performed by starving, sometimes by strangling. In Hawaii, when a chief died, according to rank and circumstances, from one to forty human victims were in later times sacrificed at the Heiau (temple) in honour to the deceased. In some places, as in New Zealand, slaves were killed to accompany and attend on their masters. A somewhat similar custom obtains also among the Dyaks and Battas, where slaves are slain on the graves of the deceased.

I have no means at hand to ascertain if this custom of immolating wives, friends, and slaves in honour of the dead was ever practised among the Cushite peoples, and transmitted by them to the forefathers of the Battas, Dyaks, and their Polynesian cousins; but it certainly obtained among the Arian branches before their dispersion.[1] It prevailed among the Gauls, Scandinavians, Lithuanians, and Slavs. With some the sacrifice of the wife was voluntary and optional, but with all the sacrifice of clients and slaves was compulsory. Among the Vedic Hindoos the immolation of the wife was not compulsory, though she was expected to make a semblance of accompanying her husband on the funeral pyre.[2] Thus, if the

---

[1] "Origines Ind. Europ.," par A. Pictet, vol. ii. p. 527.
[2] Ibid., p. 526.

custom did not come to the Polynesians from their Cushite teachers and civilisers, it was one of those early national traits of Arian descent which no subsequent Cushite training could efface.

Of Castes.

It is undeniable that a system of caste, a peculiar and exclusive division of society, obtained throughout Polynesia at the time when its groups were first visited by Europeans. Though the arrangement of these classes of society differed somewhat in different groups, yet a threefold division may be considered as the most ancient—chiefs, commoners or freemen, and slaves, or, as expressed in Hawaiian, *na Lii, na Makaainana,* and *na Kauwa.* In Tahiti, *Arii, Raatira, Manahune.* In Tonga, *Eiki, Matabule, Mua,* and *Tua.* In Samoa, *Alii, Tulafale, Songa.* In Rarotonga, *Ariki, Rangatira, Unga.* In New Zealand there were but two classes, the *Rangatira,* the freemen, and the *Taurekareka,* or slaves. In Marquesas, *Hakaiki, Tuapoi.* The priesthood does not seem originally to have been a separate class or caste among the Polynesians, but to have been a prerogative, right, or duty of the chiefs and heads of families. In course of time it became hereditary in certain families, as in Hawaii. In New Zealand, where the peculiarly distinctive title and functions of chieftainship had become extinct, yet the priests were styled *Ariki,* indicating the former connection between the chiefship and the priesthood. In Tahiti the priests were generally relations of the chief families, but socially never more than the delegates of the presiding chief for religious purposes.[1]

---

[1] See "Etat de la Societé Taitienne a l'arrivée des Européens," par M. de Bovis, in "Revue Coloniale," 1855. In this, in many regards, thoughtful and well-written essay, M. de Bovis considers that the Tahitian group was peopled by at least three different swarms of immigrants; that the Manahune, being the first, was conquered by the Raatira, who, in their turn were subdued by the Arii. He does not think that the Arii and Raatira arrived together at the group, and that the distance between the

That this division of society was older than the arrival of the Polynesians in the Pacific, and was brought with them from their former habitats in the west, may safely be inferred from the universality of the custom among all the principal groups; and on each the institution is as old as the people, and goes back to the earliest times of their remembrance.

In the west, then, among the Polynesian congeners in the Asiatic Archipelago, and beyond, let us look for the origin of this political organisation of society.

Throughout the Indian Archipelago, whatever modifications may have supervened from conquest, change of religion, and other causes, the essential groundwork of pre-Malay society was a division into chiefs, landholders, subjects by tenure, but free in persons, and slaves, whom war or other social causes reduced to that condition. With the introduction of Brahmanism in the Archipelago, its elaborate system of caste does not seem to have fallen in congenial soil or to have materially modified the ancient division of society. That division is then older than the Hindoo or Malay supremacy in that Archipelago. It is one of the remnants of the lod Cushite, Chaldeo-Arabian training and civilisation, which, twenty to thirty centuries after its power had vanished elsewhere and its very name been forgotten, has so strangely been preserved in Polynesian folklore and in Polynesian customs. At first sight it may appear so, to judge from the condition of society in the latter centuries of Polynesian life, when ages of oppression and deepening barbarism had succeeded in sharply defining and cruelly

two castes was too great for them to have had a common origin (pp. 240, &c.)

It is very probable that the Tahitian group was peopled at different times by the arrival of Polynesian emigrants. But whether those emigrants came from Fiji *via* Samoa, or from Fiji direct, on the expulsion of the Polynesians from that group, they cer-

tainly brought with them the same orders of society which prevailed in their former homes.

M. de Bovis further intimates that the crisp, frizzled hair, and lean, lank bodies, found in some of the Polynesian tribes, as well as the number of Malay words, derive from a later immigration of Malays into Polynesia.

enforcing the lines of separation between different classes of society. In this way, on some of the groups, as on Hawaii, the priestly order obtained exclusive privileges, and became a tabued caste, whose dicta even the highest chiefs only disregarded at their peril. But behind this later corruption and degradation the national legends give us glimpses of the earlier condition of society, when, as above stated, it exhibited a less artificial and more primitive form. We look in vain to the older Cushite-Sabæan or Cushite-Chaldean systems of caste; we look in vain to the later Brahminical system for a prototype of the original Polynesian classification of men.[1] It is certainly older than the latter, and, if not older than the former, it is different in principle and origin, though somewhat modified perhaps by contact with it. Failing in these directions to find an analogy or an original of Polynesian classification, I find it in the early Arian condition of society, previous to the irruption in India, previous to the migrations of the Indo-European branches, when, having already become aggressive, the nation or its various tribes naturally enough were divided into the warrior class, subsequently the nobles, those who fought the battles of the tribe or nation, and the cultivators, herdsmen, artisans, and general mass of the people who provided for the wants of the former.[2] To these two primary classes became in time added the slave class, whom the fortune of war or social laws had reduced to slavery. And that such was the early Arian condition of society may be inferred also from the classification obtaining among the Scandinavian branch of the Arian stock at its first appearance in historic light,[3] which was that of chiefs,

[1] "The basis of the social organisation of the Sabæan kingdom was the system of caste, unknown to the Shemites, an essentially Cushite institution, which, wherever it is found, is easily proved to have originated with that race. We have seen it flourishing at Babylon. The Arians of India, who adopted it, borrowed it from the Cushite populations who preceded them in the basins of the Indus and Ganges, and whom they conquered, namely, the Sudras and Kausikas."—Manual of the Ancient History of the East, by Lenormant and Chevallier, vol. ii. p. 317.

[2] *Vide* Max Müller's Essay on "Caste" in "Chips from a German Workshop," vol. ii.

[3] About 400 B.C.

freemen, and slaves; the chiefs performing the functions of priesthood down to Christian times,[1] and the freemen consisting of the husbandmen and the body of the people generally, who were free to follow this or that chief, and whose consent was necessary to all public enterprises. This branch, moreover, taking a northern route in its migration through the wilds of Scythia and Russia, was less, if at all, affected by contact with the Cushite civilisation, which so deeply tinged the Indo-European branches who took a more southerly route.

As the Arian organisation was then, before the dispersion of the race, north, west, and south, so the Polynesian has remained with slight modifications until comparatively modern times. Like interment of the dead, it was an Arian heirloom from a pristine, pre-vedic age, which Cushite culture and contact did not eradicate. If the seeds of stringent exclusiveness and priestly supremacy were sown by Cushite intercourse, they took long ages to develop, and in most of the tribes never bore fruit at all.

It is true that a Hawaiian legend relates that *Kahiko*, an ancestor of the people, had three sons, *Wakea*, *Lihau-ula*, and *Makuu;* that the chiefs, *Alii*, sprang from the first; the priests, *Kahuna*, from the second; and the husbandmen, *Makaainana*, from the last, thus indicating a possible origin of the classification of the people. But this legend, besides being contradicted by other legends of probably older date, which mention only two sons of "Kahiko," and that "Lihau-ula" was older brother of "Wakea," and was not a priest, but a warrior chief whom "Wakea" conquered in battle, is evidently a composition of later date, when the priesthood had become a tabued institution and caste, and sought a sanction for itself, and a *raison d'être* in the ancient folklore.[2]

---

[1] "The early kings of the various Grecian states, like those of Rome, were uniformly priests likewise."— G. Rawlinson's Herodotus, vol. iii. 161, n. 2.

[2] In later Hawaiian times the priesthood, *Oihaˆnu Kahuna*, consisted of ten branches or colleges. He who was master of or proficient in all was called a high priest, *Kahuna*

The Tabu.

Throughout Polynesia the *Tapu* or *Kapu* system of promulgating and enforcing religious or political laws, was equally known, equally developed, and equally practised. It was a body of negative commandments—"Thou shalt *not*" do this, that, or the other thing under penalty, binding on the consciences of the people. The meaning of the word is "sacred, prohibited, set apart," whether referring to religious or civil matters. The religious tabus relating to rites, observances, public worship, and the maintenance of the gods and their priests, were well known, comparatively fixed in their character, and the people brought up from childhood in the knowledge and observance of them. But the civil tabus were as uncertain and capricious as the mind of the chief, priest, or individual who imposed them on others, or on himself and his family.

However much the Kapu system may in after ages have been abused, it no doubt was originally a common law of the entire Polynesian family for the protection of

Nui. The names of these branches of learning or colleges were—1st, *Anaana;* 2d, *Hoopiopio;* 3d, *Hoounauna;* these three were connected with the practice of sorcery, by prayer and signs, &c., for the death or injury of another; 4th, *Hookomokomo;* 5th, *Poi-Uhane;* connected with divination by causing spirits of the dead to enter the body of a person and possess it; 6th, *Lapaaumaoli,* medicine and surgery generally; 7th, *Kuhikuhi-puuone,* pertaining to the building of temples, dwellings, &c., their location, propriety of time, and favourable or unfavourable conditions, materials, &c.; 8th, *Oneone-i-honua;* 9th, *Kilo-kilo;* 10th, *Nana-uli,* different degrees and classes of soothsayers, diviners, and prophets. Each one of these ten was again subdivided in classes and occupations of detail connected with the religious rites and sacrifices.

8

The priesthood was governed by rules and regulations of its own stringent oaths were exacted before admission, and severe penalties upon infraction. A number of gods were invoked by the different classes and subdivisions of the priesthood; but the principal god, who seems to have been the presiding and tutelar deity of the entire body of priests, was called *Uli.* As I have found no god in the archaic Hawaiian theogonies, nor those of the other Polynesian groups, bearing the name of *Uli,* I am inclined to believe that it was at first a sacerdotal epithet, degenerating into a soubriquet, and finally becoming a distinct personification; its first sense being equivalent to that of *Hiwa,* "sacred, dark-coloured, blue or black," and as such applied to one of the great principal gods.

H

persons and things, an appeal to the gods for punishment of offenders, where human vigilance failed to detect them, or human power fell short of reaching them.

The universality of the "Kapu" within the Polynesian area, without referring to the positive declarations of particular legends, makes it beyond a doubt that the Polynesians brought it with them from their former abodes in the west, and there traces are yet found of it. In Timor a system of interdict, called *Pomali*,[1] was practised, which by competent travellers is said to very strongly resemble the Polynesian "Kapu;" and among the Dyaks of Borneo a similar custom of interdict is said to have obtained, and was there called *Pamali*.[1] Among the Cingalese and southern Hindoos, the word *Kapu*, which is the name of the scarlet string worn round the arm or wrist, to indicate that the wearer is engaged in a sacred cause, and should not be interrupted,[2]—singularly enough, though with somewhat altered sense, recalls the name and purpose of the Polynesian interdict. When we consider that the Ceylonese never adopted Brahmanism, and that their earliest civilisation and religious notions were moulded, if not created, by the Cushite Arabs, whose intercourse with, and hold over, the Dravidian and other peoples in southern India and the islands, was long and intimate, it is reasonable, in conjunction with other facts, to seek a common origin for the Polynesian and the Cingalese word in some Cushite term of religious import, now forgotten and as yet undiscovered.

Tattooing.

This custom has been so widely diffused among the various nations of antiquity as to afford no reliable guide in ethnic inquiries; yet now and then certain traits connected with it challenge attention by their striking similarity to those of other peoples, and their apparent conformity to a

---

[1] Malay Archipelago, by R. A. Wallace, p. 203.

[2] Oriental Illustrations, by Joseph Roberts, p. 133.

once common rule. It is well known to be universally practised among the Polynesian tribes, varying only in style, in pattern, and fulness; and variations occur even among different subdivisions of the same tribe. This also was a custom brought with them from the west. According to M. Domeny de Rienzi, it is practised on the Island of Savu, south-east of Timor, and among the Dyaks of Borneo and other tribes in the Asiatic Archipel.[1] In Leitch Ritchie's "History of the Indian Empire," vol. ii. p. 428, Art. "New Zealand," occurs the following paragraph :— "Tattooing is fast going out of fashion with cannibalism; but it appears to have been but little practised at any time by the females, who have merely three short lines drawn from the under-lip. This is precisely the case with the Coptic women."

Holy Waters.

Among the many Polynesian customs which they brought with them on entering the Pacific, and which serve as links long lost or overlooked in the ethnic chain that binds them to the Cushite and Arian races, may be mentioned the preparation and use of sacred or holy waters. From New Zealand to Hawaii the custom prevailed, and its efficacy was believed in. The origin and explanation of the custom is thus given in the Hawaiian "Kumuhonua" legend :— "The Ocean, *ka moana nui a Kane,* which surrounds the earth, was made salt by *Kane,* so that its waters should not stink, and to keep it thus in a healthy and uninfected state is the special occupation of *Kane.* In imitation of *Kane,* therefore, the priests prepared waters of purification, prayer, and sanctification, *Wai-hui-kala, Wai-lupa-lupa,* and *ke kai-olena,* for the public ceremonials, for private consola-tion, and to drive away demons and diseases. Such holy waters were called by the general name of *ka wai kapu a Kane."* [2] From the sprinkling of a new-born child to the

---

[1] Oceanie, par M. M. G. L. Domeny de Rienzi, vol. i. p. 65.

[2] In some ancient prayers in my possession, these waters are also called

washing of the dying, its application was constant and multifarious. The baptismal ceremony—*E Riri*—of the New Zealanders, related by Dieffenbach,[1] with the accompanying prayers invoking the gods *Tu* and *Rongo* (the Hawaiian Ku and Lono), is a valuable and remarkable remnant of the ancient culte.[2] The use of these holy waters was of the highest antiquity, and universal throughout Polynesia. It was a necessary adjunct in private and public worship, a *vade mecum* in life, a *viaticum* in death; and even now, fifty years after the introduction of Christianity in these Hawaiian islands, there are few of the older people who would forego its use to alleviate pain and remove disease.

A custom so universal, so deeprooted, must have existed previous to the arrival of the Polynesians in the Pacific. I have not the means of knowing to what extent, if at all, its use has been retained among the Polynesian cousins in the Malay Archipelago, but it certainly had its origin farther west.

That holy water—the water of the Ganges, and, perhaps, previously of the Indus—was employed by the Hindoos for almost the same purposes as by the Polynesians is well known, and would at first sight seem to claim priority of consideration when looking for prototypes or analogues of the Polynesian custom. But there is a radical difference between the two, which makes it little likely that the latter owed its origin to the former. The holy water of the Hindoos—the Ganges water—is holy *per se*, and requires no mixture, preparation, or prayers to make it so. The holy water of the Polynesians was expressly prepared and consecrated with prayers in order to obtain that particular efficiency for religious and medical purposes which it was believed to possess. The Polynesian holy water

---

Wai-oha. The word *Oha* in this sense is obsolete in the Hawaiian, but is still retained in the Marquesan dialect, where it means "sacred, adorable."

[1] Travels in New Zealand, by Dieffenbach, p. 28.

[2] See Appendix, No. V

represented the great world-ocean and its purifying processes; the Ganges water represented nothing but itself.

Looking beyond the Indus and the Chaldean Empire, of whose customs in this respect I have seen no detailed information, I find in Ancient Greece a striking correspondence with the Polynesian custom. Holy water, and sprinkling and washing with it, was an indispensable element of the old Greek ritual. In the preparation of the Greek holy water, as well as in the Hawaiian, salt was a necessary ingredient. With the former, sea-water was preferred, when attainable, on account of its saltness; otherwise salt was invariably mixed with the fresh water, and sometimes brimstone added. At the entrance of the Greek temples stood the " Perirrantœrion" or vessel containing the holy water, and no person was permitted to pass beyond or assist at the sacrifices who had not previously washed his hands in it, or been sprinkled with the water it contained. The Greek custom of lustral waters was probably of Arian origin,[1] but the peculiar manner of its preparation, unknown to, or, so far as I can learn, not practised by, their Arian congeners, may possibly be a modification brought about by their connection with the Cushite civilisation, of which the early Phœnicians were such remarkable propagandists; or, perhaps earlier still,

---

[1] In Les Origines Indo-Européennes, par Ad. Pichet, vol. ii. p. 681, I read:

"Les traits essentiels d'une culte, elémentaire des eaux se retrouvent encore presque inaltérés chez les principaux peuples de race Arienne. Dans le Rigvêda, comme dans l'Avesta, elles sont encore invoquées sous leur nom propre, *âpas*, au pluriel et collectivement. On les appelle les mères, les divines ; on dit d'elles qu' elles renferment l'*amrta*, l'ambroisie, et tous les remèdes salutaires ; on leur demande, non-seulement la sauté du corps, mais la purification de l'âme de tout péché. Pour les Iran-iens, les eaux créés par Ormuzd étaient aussi le principal moyen de purification, surtout après avoir été consacrées par la ceremonie du *Zaothra*, ce qui rappelle singulièrement l'eau bénite du catholicism (Spiegel, *Avesta*, ii., xcii.) L'emploi des eaux lustrales dans l'antiquité classique est suffisamment connu. Les Scandinaves considéraient les eaux du ciel comme sacrées ; l'Edda les appelle *heilög vötn*, et *heilawdc* du moyen âge germanique, c'est à dire l'eau de source puisée à minuit, ou avant le lever du soleil, devenait un remède puissant, et acquerait de propriétés magiques (Grimm, *Deut. Myth.* 327).

while skirting the upper borders of Chaldea on their migration through Asia Minor. At any rate, this similarity in a matter of detail of preparation cannot well be considered as a coincidence under pressure of similar circumstances, but was more likely an engraftment in different directions from a common source and a once common religious idea.

The idea of holy water as a co-efficient in religious ceremonies was common to the Oriental nations. The Jews only borrowed their Laver from others. And the metaphysical explanation of the Hawaiians is perhaps as ancient a conception of the action of the sun on the ocean as any on record.

Cities of Refuge.

Some stress has been laid on the peculiar institution called "cities of refuge," Hawaiian, *Puu-honua*, which was found to have obtained among the Polynesians, especially the Hawaiians, and which has been quoted as another instance of Hebraic influence upon the customs and culture of the Hawaiians. Cities of refuge, however, were not an institution peculiar to the Hebrews, and originating with them. They existed in the time of ancient Greece. We read of the temple of Ceres at Hermione, in Argolis, which was a similar institution; and there were numerous others, both there and elsewhere, where Cushite influence had modified the customs and moulded the culte of the people on its own pattern.

The Division of the Year, &c.

The Polynesians divided the year into seasons, months, and days. The seasons—*Tau* or *Kau*—of the year were generally two, the rainy or winter season, and the dry or summer season, varying according to the particular situation of the group, either north or south of the equator. The commencement of the seasons, however, were regulated by the rising of the *Makarii* stars, the Pleiades, at the time of the setting of the sun. Thus, in the Society group, the year was divided in *Makarii-i-nia*, Pleiades above the horizon, and *Makarii-i-raro*, Pleiades below— the first from November to May, the latter from May to November. In the Hawaiian group the year was also divided in two seasons—*Hooilo*, the rainy season, from about 20th November to 20th May; and *Kau*, the dry season, from 20th May to 20th November.[1] In the Samoan, *Tau* or *Tau-sanga* meant originally a period of six months, and afterwards was employed to express the full year, or twelvemonth, as in the Tonga group. There are traces also on the Society group of the year having been divided in three seasons, as at one time was done by the ancient Egyptians, Arabs, and Greeks, though the arrangement of the months within each season seems to me to have been arbitrary, and probably local.

In regard to the division of the year by months, the Polynesians counted by twelve and by thirteen months, the former obtaining in the Tonga, Samoan, and Hawaiian groups, the latter in the Marquesas and Society groups. Each month consisted of thirty days. It is known that the Hawaiians, who counted twelve months of thirty days each, intercalated five days at the end of the month *Welehu*, about the 20th December, which were tabu-days, dedicated to the festival of the god *Lono;* after which the

---

[1] Mr. R. G. Haliburton, of Halifax, N.S., has shown that the primitive year of the Pleiades was a pre-historical tradition, spread amongst almost all races of mankind in both the new and old hemispheres, and alike in the north and south. The leading characteristics of that year being that it began on the 19th day of *Athyr*, or November, when the Pleiades, or their containing constellation, the Bull—the great *Tau* of the Egyptians, the *Taurus* of the Latins, the *Thor* of the Scandinavians, and the *Atlyr* or *Arthur* of the ancient Britons— was on the meridian at midnight. *Vide* Life and Work at the Great Pyramid, 1865, by C. Piazzi Smyth, vol. i. chap. xii. p. 330.

In the Hawaiian group the red star in the constellation is called *Kao*—the star Antares, in the horns of the Bull —was also called *Makalii*. That the ancient Hawaiians should have called the constellation of the Bull—Taurus —by the very name which was one of the earliest appellations for that animal, while the Arian stock was yet unsundered, is one of those quiet but surprising witnesses to the Western origin and Arian connection of the Polynesian family, which rise in judgment against modern theorists of Papuan, Malay, Mexican, or other proclivities.

New Year began with the first day of the month *Makalii* which day, being the first of the year, was called *Makahiki* (equivalent to "commencement-day"), and afterwards became the conventional term for a year in the Hawaiian, Marquesas, and Society groups.[1] There is evidence that the Marquesans at one time counted the year by ten lunar months, and called it a *Puni*—a circle, a round, a revolution—but how they managed either this or the year of thirteen months to correspond with the division by seasons, or with the sidereal year, I am not informed. It is probable that in Tahiti the month *Te-eri* was occasionally, perhaps alternately, dropped from the calendar.[2]

That a computation by lunar months preceded the other is evident from the very names given to different days in the month, but both computations were certainly far older than the arrival of the Polynesians in the Pacific. They brought those names and those computations with them.

The absolute Hawaiian expression of *Ana-hulu* indicates a primary but subsequently disused division of the month

---

[1] Rev. S. Dibble, in his History of the Sandwich Islands, Lahainaluna, 1843, p. 108, says : "Those who took the most care in measuring time measured it by means both of the moon and the fixed stars. They divided the year into twelve months, and each month into thirty days. They had a distinct name for each of the days of the month, as has been shown on a former page, and commenced their numbering on the first day that the new moon appeared in the west. This course made it necessary to drop a day about once in two months, and thus reduce their year into twelve lunations instead of three hundred and sixty days. This being about eleven days less than the sidereal year, they discovered the discrepancy, and corrected their reckoning by the stars. In practice, therefore, the year varied, being sometimes twelve, sometimes thirteen lunar months. So also they sometimes numbered twenty-nine, and sometimes thirty days in a month." Mr. Dibble omits to mention that the "correction" of their reckoning "by the stars" was made by the intercalation I have referred to. It thus appears that the Hawaiians employed two modes of reckoning—by lunar cycles, whereby the monthly feasts, or Kapu-days, were regulated; and the sidereal cycle, by which the close of the year, and the annual feast of Lono, was regulated.

[2] The alternation of twenty-nine and thirty days in the Hawaiian months, referred to by Mr. Dibble in the above note, though certainly not in general usage among the Hawaiians, yet, as one of the several modes of computing time which they brought with them from their primitive abodes, forcibly reminds one of the Hebrew and Assyrian division in months of alternate twenty-nine and thirty days.

into periods of ten days, corresponding to the increase, the full, and the decline of the moon, analogous to the Greek *Dechœmera* and the Egyptian *Se-su ;* and the institution of the Hawaiian *Kapu* or sacred-days at intervals of ten days seems to favour such a conclusion, for I look upon the fourth monthly Kapu-day,—that of *Kane* on the 27th of the month,—as of subsequent introduction, following so closely, as it does, upon the Kapu-day of *Kaloa-ku-kahi,* the 24th.[1] Though obsolete now in common parlance, the term *Ana-hulu* is of frequent occurrence in the ancient legends and songs as a measure of time comprising ten days.

The Hawaiian day was divided in three general parts, like that of the early Greeks and Latins,[2]—morning, noon, and afternoon—*Kakahi-aka,* breaking the shadows, *scil.* of night; *Awakea,* for *Ao-akea,* the plain, full day; and *Auina-la,* the decline of the day. The lapse of the night, however, was noted by five stations, if I may say so, and four intervals of time, viz.: (1.) *Kihi,* at 6 P.M., or about sunset; (2.) *Pili,* between sunset and midnight; (3.) *Kau,* indicating midnight; (4.) *Pilipuka,* between midnight and

---

[1] S. M. Kamakau, in one of his articles on ancient Hawaiian beliefs, refers to an old legend, according to which "the creation commenced on the 26th (27th ?) of the month, on the day called *Kane,* and was continued during the days called *Lono, Mauli, Muku, Hilo,* and *Hoaka.* In six days the creation was done. The seventh day, the day called *Ku,* became the first Kapu-day—*La-Kapu.* The first and the last of these seven days in every month have been kept Kapu ever since by all generations of Hawaiians." The seven days of creation and rest (*Kapu*) may be a dim recollection of the Hebrew-Chaldean version of the creation ; but the application of the first day as a Kapu-day to *Kane* is evidently a priestly commentary, and of later origin. Practically the Hawaiians, and none of the other Polynesians, so far as I know, never had a week of seven days. On comparing the Tahitian and Hawaiian calendars, and finding the *Kanaloa* (*Taaroa* and *Kaloa*) days in the same position on both, I am strongly inclined to believe that when in after ages the South Polynesian element obtained ascendancy in Hawaii, its principal god *Taaroa, Tangaroa,* and the days dedicated to him, were interpolated on the Hawaiian calendar, and the *Kane*-day and its festival or Kapu was made to follow after that of *Taaroa,* a being whom the Hawaiians did not recognise as a divinity in their earlier creed, nor until after that invasion of South Polynesians, of which I shall have more to say hereafter.

[2] Ἡὠς, Μεσον-'Ημας, and Δειλη ; Mane, Meridies, Suprema.

sunrise, or about 3 A.M.; (5.) *Kihipuka,* corresponding to sunrise, or about 6 A.M. According to M. D. de Rienzi a similar division of day and night seems to have been current of old in Jawa.

To this may be added that the Polynesians also counted time by the nights—*Po.* "To-morrow" was *A-po-po,* lit. the night's night. "Yesterday" was *Po-i-nehe-nei,* the past night. *Po-akahi, Po-alua,* the first, the second day. *Po* was the collective term for the twenty-four hours, and *Ao* or daylight was but the complement of the full *Po.* This method of reckoning by nights ascends to the hoariest antiquity. The unbroken Arians counted by nights, and the custom prevailed late into historic times among the Hindoos, the Iranians, the Gauls, the Cymri, the Saxons, and Scandinavians.[1] The Hebrews commenced time with the evening of the first day: whether the idea came to them from Chaldea or from Egypt, I cannot say. The Babylonians believed that the world had been created at the autumnal equinox.[2]

There has been so little light thrown upon the ancient computations of time among the pre-Malay inhabitants of the Indian Archipelago—those blood-relations of the Polynesians—that I am again unable to refer to them as a connecting link between the latter and their more western congeners; but the lunar computations of both Arians and Cushites; the division of seasons by both; the method of determining the sidereal year by the Pleiades; the method of intercalating the twelve months of thirty days with five days, which obtained in Egypt and in Persia and among the Vedic Arians, though the latter intercalated an entire month of thirty days after every quinquennial cycle;[3] the division of the month in thirds of ten days each, as in Egypt and ancient Greece,

---

[1] Origines Ind.-Europ., par A. Pictet, vol. ii. p. 588.

[2] Manual of Ancient History of the East, by Lenormant and Chevallier, vol. i. p. 451.

[3] Origines Ind.-Europ., par A. Pictet, vol. ii. p. 608.

and which possibly was the basis of the ancient Javanese subdivision of the week into five days, before Brahmanism introduced the week of seven days;[1] the division of the day into three portions and the night into four; the counting the length of time by nights and not by days; all these cumulative parallelisms, I think, will go far to confirm the western origin of the Polynesians, and their intimate connection in pre-historic times with the Arian and Cushite peoples. They cannot all be fortuitous coincidences, and must, therefore, justly be considered as remnants of a once common civilisation, which the isolation of two thousand years or more has not been able entirely to efface, though partially obscured.[2]

I think it proper in connection with this subject to refer to an article in the "Ethnological Society's (London) Transactions," vol. ii. p. 173, "On the Antiquity of Man from the Evidence of Language," by J. Crawfurd, a gentleman whose researches and knowledge regarding the Indian Archipelago and its various peoples were undoubtedly great and valuable. He says that "the terms employed in

---

[1] Speaking of the rural calendar of Jawa, which was in vogue before the introduction of Brahmanism, M. D. de Rienzi, in Oceanie, vol. i. p. 167, says : "Le calendrier rural est de 360 jours. Il se divise en douze mois ou douze saisons, d'une longueur inegale, et est terminé par des jours intercalaires."

[2] It appears that there was considerable diversity between the different sections of the Hawaiian group in counting the months and the days. In several respects the Kauai and Oahu calendar differed from that which was generally followed on Hawaii and Maui. I obtained my information from Hon. S. M. Kamakau, an intelligent and educated Hawaiian, born and brought up while the heathen regime still prevailed. On the other hand David Malo, an equally intelligent and educated Ha-

waiian, who, some twenty-five years ago, composed a work on "Hawaiian Antiquities," mentions that the ancient year closed with the month of *Ikuwa*, about 20th of November, whereas Kamakau gives it as ending with the month of *Welehu*, or about 20th December, and the new year commencing with the month *Makalii*. Both of these authorities agree, however, that the public sacrifices and Kapu-days were only observed during eight months of the year, and discontinued during the months of *Ikuwa*, *Welehu*, *Makalii*, and *Kaelo*, when, in the month of *Kaulua*, they recommenced again.

It is probable that D. Malo refers to the sidereal year regulated by the Pleiades, and according to which the seasons were divided, and that Kamakau refers to the solar year regulated by the winter or December solstice.

the computation of time, according to their poverty or maturity, afford material evidence of the antiquity of man." He quotes Australians who have no terms for solar day, month, or year. He refers to the same poverty in the ruder languages of Africa and America, and then says: "The principal nations of the Phillipine Islands had made considerable progress when first seen by Europeans; yet their languages have no native name for solar day, month, or year, for these have been taken from the more advanced Malayan nations. The language of Madagascar has no names for month or for year, and has taken both from the Malay; and it is remarkable that the Malayan term for year has even reached the rude inhabitants of the islands of the Pacific."

"Interdum dormitat Homerus;" it will be seen from the foregoing pages that, as regards the "rude inhabitants of the islands of the Pacific," Mr. Crawfurd's remarks are not borne out by actual facts, nor yet by philological evidence. The principal Polynesian groups, as above shown, had not only names for year, month, and seasons, but had also distinct names for every month and every day in a month. Nor are these names of Malay origin. The Malay word for year is *Taun* or *Tahun*. In all the Polynesian dialects the primary and original meaning of *Tau* is "a season," "a period of time." In the Tonga group it has the further sense of "the produce of a season," and, derivatively, "a year." In the Samoan group, beside the primary sense of "season," it has the definite meaning of "a period of six months," and conventionally that of "a year." In the Society group it simply means "a season." In the Hawaiian group, when not applied to the summer season, it retains the original sense of an indefinite "period of time," "a lifetime," "an age," and is never applied to a year; its duration may be more or less than a year, according to circumstances and the context. Thus in all the Polynesian dialects it retains the primary abstract sense, whereas in the Malay it has only the derivative concrete meaning.

The Polynesian also retains what I consider the original form of the word, while the suffix *n* in the Malay betrays a later corruption. Had the Polynesians received the word from the Malays, its form, by the invariable rules of the former language, would have been *Tauna* or *Kahuna*. The Polynesian names for month are *Masina* or *Mahina*, *Malama*, and *Avae*, and there are certainly no trace of Malay in them; they are identical with the current names of the moon, and indicate the early computation by lunar months.

In proof that the Polynesians were not beholden to the Malays for the names of year, season, month, or days, but had a nomenclature particularly their own, the following tables may suffice:—

NAMES OF MONTHS.

	Hawaiian.	Samoan.	Tonga.	Society Islands, Huahine.	Marquesas, Fatuhiwa.
1	Makalii	Utuwa-mua	Liha-mua	Avarehu	Kuhua
2	Kaelo	Utuwa-muli	Liha-mui	Faaahu	Katuna
3	Kaulua	Faaafu	Wai-mua	Pipiri	Ehuo
4	Nana	Lo	Wai-mui	Taaoa	Nanaua
5	Welo	Aunuau	Hilinga-gele-gele	Aununu	Oaumanu
6	Ikiiki	Oloamanu	Tanu-manga	Apaapa	Awea
7	Kaaona	Palolo-mua	Uluenga	Paroro-mua	Ehua
8	Hinaieleele	Palolo-muli	Hilinga-mea	Paroro-muri	Weo
9	Hilinehu [1]	Mulifa	Fuca-afu-mate	Muriaha	Uaoa
10	Hilinama [1]	Lotuanga	Fuca-afu-moui	Hiaia	Uahaameau
11	Ikuwa	Taumafamua	Uluagi-mate	Tema	Pohe
12	Welehu	Toe-tauafa		Te-eri	Napea
13				Te-tae	Makau

[1] Also called "Mahoe-mua" and "Mahoe-hope."

NAMES OF THE DAYS IN THE MONTH.

	Hawaiian.	Society Islands.	Marquesan.
1	Hilo	Hiro-hiti	Ku-nui
2	Hoaka	Hoata	Ku-hawa
3	Kukahi	Hami-ami-mua	Hoaka
4	Ku-lua	Hami-ami-roto	Maheamakahi
5	Ku-kolu	Hami-ami-muri	Maheamawaena
6	Ku-pau	Ore-ore-mua	Koekoe-kahi
7	Ole-ku-kahi	Ole-ore-muri	Koekoe-waena
8	Ole-ku-lua	Tamatea	Poipoi-haapao
9	Ole-ku-kolu	Huna	Huna
10	Ole-ku-pau	Ari	A'i
11	Huna	Maharu	Huka
12	Mohalu	Hua	Meha'u
13	Hua	Maitu	Hua
14	Akua	Hotu	Akua
15	Hoku	Mara'i	Huku-nui
16	Mahealani	Turu-tea	Huku-manae
17	Kulu	Raau-mua	Ku'u
18	Laau-ku-kahi	Raau-roto	Aniwa
19	Laau-ku-lua	Raau-muri	Makahi
20	Laau-pau	Ore-ore-mua	Kaau
21	Ole-ku-kahi	Ore-ore-roto	Kaekae-kahi
22	Ole-ku-lua	Ore-ore-muri	Waena
23	Ole-pau	Taaroa-mua	Haapao
24	Kaloa-ku-kahi	Taaroa-roto	Hanaokahi
25	Kaloa-ku-lua	Taaroa-muri	Wawena
26	Kaloa-pau	Tane	Haapaa
27	Kane	Ro'o-nui	Puhiwa
28	Lono	Ro'o-maori	Kane
29	Mauli	Mutu	Ona-nui
30	Muku	Teriere	Onamate

The names of the Tahitian and Hawaiian seasons have been mentioned. The solstices were observed and named in Tahiti. The December solstice was called *Rua-maoro* or *Rua-roa;* the June solstice, *Rua-poto.* The Hawaiians called the northern limit of the sun in the ecliptic *ke Ala-nui polohiwa a Kane,* " the black shining road of Kane ;" and the southern limit was called *ke Ala-nui polohiwa a Kanaloa,* " the black shining road of Kanaloa;" and the equator was named *ke Ala-ula a ke kuukuu,* " the bright road of the spider;" and also *ke Ala i ka piko o Wakea,* " the road to the navel of Wakea," equivalent to " the centre of the world." [1]

Whatever the origin of these names, and the knowledge which underlies them, they certainly owe nothing to Malay instruction.

Superstition.

As a matter of course, and not otherwise to be expected, the Polynesian folklore abounds with superstitious notions and usages. Their belief in, and reverent and affectionate regard for, their deceased ancestors,[2] the *Au-makua* of Hawaii, the benevolent ones who protected their descendants, the *Oro-matua* of Tahiti, the malevolent ones who were to be propitiated by prayer and offerings.[3] Their

---

[1] The ancient Hawaiians knew and named the five earliest known planets, which were called collectively *na Hoku aea,* " the wandering stars," in contradistinction to the " fixed stars," *na Hoku paa.* Their names were according to Hoapili—

Mercury, *Kaawela,* also *Hoku-ula.*
Mars, *Holoholopinau.*
Venus, *Naholoholo.*
Jupiter, *Hoomanalonalo,* also *Iao* and *Ikaika.*
Saturn, *Makulu.*

Mr. Dibble (History of Sandwich Islands, p. 107) says that "Hoapili was so much in the habit of observing these that he could at any moment tell the position of each ; and that he had heard from others that there was

one more travelling star, but he had never recognised it, and was acquainted with only these five. The more distinguished fixed stars and clusters had their distinct names, and the people were in the habit of observing them so much, that they judged of the hour of the night about as accurately as of the hour of the day."

[2] The ancient inhabitants of Yemen, Arabia, canonised and worshipped their ancestors.—Manual of the Ancient History of the East, by Lenormant and Chevallier, vol. ii.

[3] In Wajou, the principal territory of the Buguis in Celebes, the president or head of the chiefs is styled the Arumatua.

belief in ghosts and apparitions, whether benignant or malicious; their implicit faith in all manner of witchcraft, enchantments, sortilege, signs, and omens;[1] their practices of incantation, objurgation, and divination—all these various modes of superstition, more or less current among every race of people, appear to have been a very early inheritance of the Polynesians; but the difficulty is to trace them to their proper sources, either Cushite or Arian, for so many of them seem to have been shared by both alike. Some of them, however, can philologically be referred to an Arian root, and among them I would mention—

Haw. *Lapu*, "ghost, apparition, spectre." They were good or bad according to the known personal character of the deceased, whom they were supposed to represent. *Lapu-ia*, "to be possessed of a spirit, to be haunted." I have only found this word with this application in the Hawaiian. Etymologically it refers to the verb *Lapu-lapu* (Haw.), "to collect together in little heaps, to pick up, as small sticks for fuel;" to *Rapu* (N. Zeal.), "to search for;" to *Rapu* (Tahit.), "to scratch, squeeze, pinch, stir up, be in confusion;" *Napu*, "to be confused, nonplussed;" to *Ravu* (Fiji), "to smite, smash, kill." This *Lapu* and its cognate verbs refer themselves without much difficulty to the *Rbhu* or *Rabhu* of Vedic mythology, spirits or inferior deities of a benevolent character, and to the Sanskrit root, verb *Rabh*, "to seize, to take," with its Indo-European congeners, such as *Rabies* (Lat.), "rage, madness;" *Rhaib* (Welsh), "fascination;" *Rheibes*, "sorcerer," *et al.*[1]

Another word of the same class is the Hawaiian *Mana*, "supernatural power, an attribute of the gods, glory, might, intelligence, worship;" *Hoomana*, "to worship, adore;" *Hoo-mana-mana*, "to bewitch, enchant." Samoan, *Mana*, "supernatural power;" *Tuu-mana*, "to curse, to rejoice in another's misfortunes." Tahitian, *Mana*, "strength, power,

[1] See Appendix, No. VI.
[2] *Vide* Orig. Ind.-Europ., par A.

Pritet, vol. ii. p. 637, and Burfey's
Sanskrit Dictionary, *sub voce.*

influence." Tonga, *mana*, "thunder, omen, sign." Fiji, *mana*, "an omen, wonder, miracle," a word used at the closing of a prayer or address to the gods, equivalent to "Amen, so be it." The word connects itself etymologically with the Sanskrit *mantra*, "prayer, magic formula, incantation, charm;" the Zend *manthra*, "incantation against diseases;" the Greek μαντις, "a prophet, soothsayer;" the Latin *moneo*, "to remind, instruct, predict;" *monstrum*, "whatever is strange and unnatural, a prodigy, a marvel;" the Irish *manadh*, "incantation, divination, omen;" *manai*, "sorceries, juggling," all which primarily refer themselves to the old Arian root *man*, "to think, to wish, to mind, to know," and also indicate the early and common application of the word to designate what was marvellous or supernatural, an application dating back to the Arian unity."[1]

Human Sacrifices.

The custom of sacrificing human victims goes back to so old a date among the Polynesian family, that it is almost in vain to attempt to define a time for its introduction. However accustomed and callous the Polynesian may have become to human sacrifices, as a means to avert public danger, to appease the gods, or to satisfy the caprices of priests and rulers, yet there may be found in the ancient legends palpable indications that there was a time before that, when human sacrifices were not only not of common occurrence, and an established rule, but were absolutely prohibited. *Kapu ke kanaka na Kane*, "sacred is the man to Kane,"—for whom and by whom he was made—was the oldest Polynesian doctrine handed down by tradition, however much it may have been disregarded in after times. The universality of the custom among the leading Polynesian tribes would seem to indicate that it was one of many evil practices brought with them from the Indian Archipelago. But wherever the custom came from, the

[1] *Vide* Orig. Ind.-Europ., par A. Pictet, *loc. cit.*

maxim above referred to remained in the national folklore as a standing, though ineffectual, protest against it, showing plainly that at one time, in the far indistinct past, the cruel practice was contrary to the national creed and national mode of thought.   With this maxim, then, pointing to a condition of purer creed and simpler manners, how far must we ascend in the past ages and past connections of Polynesian life ere we reach that state of society in which human sacrifices were prohibited, abhorred, and unusual?   We do not find it among the Cushite instructors of the Polynesian ancestors, at least not at the period when the latter may be considered as the pupils of the former.   We must then ascend the Arian line of connection to find the source whence the maxim originated. Speaking on the subject of sacrifices among the Arian people before their separation, M. A. Pictet says: " La comparaison des termes qui se rapportent aux sacrifices semble montrer qu'ils consistaient surtout en libations, mais que l'on immolait aussi certains animaux.   Rien n'indique, par contre, que l'effroyable coutume des sacrifices humains, pratiquée plus tard aux temps de barbarie, ait attristé le culte des ancêtres de notre race."[1]   In ancient Greece sacrifices were of the fruits of the earth, and it was originally forbidden to immolate victims, under pains of death.   Afterwards animals were sacrificed. Human sacrifice was accounted so barbarous an act by the ancient Greeks, that Lycaon was feigned by the poets to have been turned into a wolf for offering such a sacrifice to Jupiter.   In latter times this custom became more common.[2]

Cannibalism.

Though the custom of cannibalism among some of the Polynesian tribes, as well as among the Battas of Sumatra and the eastern Dyaks of Borneo, would seem to justify

[1] Origines Ind.-Europ., vol. ii. p. 702.   [2] Harwood's Grecian Antiquities, pp. 146-51.

the inference of a community of origin; yet I am strongly inclined to believe that it was not a common national trait at the time of the unity of the Polynesian race in the Indian Archipelago, and as such brought with the wandering Polynesians into the Pacific, but rather of comparatively later date, originating during their sejour among and contact with the man eating Fijians, on their first arrival in the Pacific. It is true that among the Marquesans and New Zealanders the custom prevailed extensively, and they claimed a fabulous antiquity for its origin; but among the Tongans the practice was exceptional with some of their warriors in war-time, and then as a matter of bravado, and avowedly in imitation of their Fijian neighbours; and among the Society Islanders and the Hawaiians the custom never obtained. With these two branches of the Polynesian family, though the practice of cannibalism was not unknown, yet it was looked upon with horror as an exceptional depravity of a few wicked and˙outlawed persons, who in the ancient legends were loaded with infamy and exterminated as monsters.[1] There is no reference in the legends of either the Hawaiian or the Society group to a time when cannibalism was a national practice that was afterwards discontinued. The very fact that on occasions of human sacrifices, both on Hawaii and at Tahiti, the left eye of the victim was offered to the presiding chief, who made a semblance to eat it, *but did not*, was a virtual protest against the custom as being neither original nor universal with the Polynesian family, and was merely a seeming concession to a horrid fashion that had

[1] Rev. Mr. Dibble, in his History of the Sandwich Islands, 1843, p. 133, &c., refers to the tradition of the cannibal chief Kalo-aikanaka at Halemanu, Oahu, Hawaiian group. The tradition was well known in Dibble's time, and is also referred to by Messrs. Tyerman and Bennett, agents of the London Mission Society. But Dibble expressly states that "the practice was not common, and it is due to the Hawaiians to say that those few instances that did exist were looked upon by most of the people with horror and detestation." The extermination of the Halemanu chief and his accomplices, and the infam.y to which his memory was consigned in the national traditions, ought to be sufficient refutation of the accusation brought against the Hawaiians.

been adopted by other tribes of the family during their contact and combats with the Fijians.

As regards cannibalism among the Battas and Dyaks, the practice among the two peoples differs so widely in occasion, mode of procedure, and other matters, as to preclude the idea of a community of origin, and therefore probably arose separately in each of them from local causes and circumstances now unknown; the more so, as it is not known to have been practised by the other pre-Malay tribes of kindred blood, either on the same islands or in more isolated places.

I think it fair, therefore, to conclude that this horrible practice was not an original heirloom brought with the Polynesians from their primitive homes in the Far West, but was adopted subsequently by a few of their tribes under conditions and circumstances now unknown; and the non-observance and indignant reprobation of the same by two such leading members of the Polynesian family, as the Tahitian and Hawaiian, and, I would fain believe, the Samoan, ought in justice and equity redeem the race from the stigma so lavishly thrown upon it as a whole.[1]

On a previous page I have referred to a Hawaiian legend which narrates that a certain chief, called *Hawa-ii-loa* or *Kekowa-o-Hawa-ii*, was the first who discovered and settled on the island of Hawaii of the Hawaiian group, and that he called it after his own name. The legend further adds that at that time this group consisted of only the two larger islands, Hawaii and Maui, the other islands having as yet not emerged from the ocean. I referred to the legend to show, by the traditional evidence of the Polynesians, that they came into the Pacific from the Far West, and that by whatever route they came they claimed some continent or large islands in the West as their birthplace.

But though the legend unequivocally confirms the proposition of the Western origin of the Polynesians, it is by

---

[1] *Vide* Appendix, No. VII.

no means conclusive that either Hawaii, Sawaii, or Habai in the Pacific was the terminus of that celebrated voyage of discovery; and for reasons to be found in the legend itself, I am induced to believe that the departure of that voyage was from some part of the coast of the Erythræan Sea, in Southern Arabia, and that its terminus was at Jawa in the Sunda group.

First, the legend expressly makes *Hawaii-loa* the seventeenth generation after the Flood, and the fourth only after that mythical and legendary Twelveship with which the traditional life of so many Eastern peoples begins. He is said to have been born and lived on the eastern coast of *Kapa-kapa-ua-a-Kane*, "the land where his forefathers dwelt before him," which land was also called *ka Aina-kai-Mele-mele-a-Kane*, or "the land of the yellow, or handsome sea." But this land bore also the name *Hawa-ii-kua-uli-kai-oo*, or "Hawaii with the verdant hills and the dotted sea." Under previous considerations, does not the latter epithet coincide with the Erythræan Sea, called by the older Greeks "the sacred wave," and "the coralled bed?" From analogy and the general idiomacy of the Polynesian language, it becomes highly probable that *Kapa-kapa-ua* is an old intensitive, duplicated form of the Cushite *Zaba*, and this derivation would harmonise the old Arabian traditions, which place Paradise in the south-west part of Arabia, with the Hawaiian tradition, which states that after the expulsion from *Kalana-i-Hau-ola*, the descendants of the first man went eastward and occupied the coasts of *Kapa-kapa-ua*. Now, from numerous other parts of this and other legends, we learn that *Kapa-kapa-ua* was a subdivision of the large continent generally called *Kahiki-ku*, or Eastern Kahiki, and from other references we infer that it was situated in the western part of that continent, and that to the south of it was a large land or continent called *Ku-i-lalo* or *Honua-ku-i-lalo*, "the southern land," renowned for its warlike and savage people, while to the west was another large land or continent called *Kahiki-moe*, "the

Western Kahiki." If we now refer to some of the ancient and obsolete Hawaiian names for the North, we find two that arrest our attention in connection with this inquiry. The reader may remember that among the Hawaiian names for the North were *Ulu-nui* and *Mele-mele*, and that originally they were names of lands situated to the northward of some former habitat of the Polynesian family, or of those from whom they received their culture, their myths, and a goodly portion of their legends. Now the land of *Mele-mele* forcibly connects itself with "the Sea of Mele-mele" above referred to, and indicates another land or country or kingdom situated on the shores of the same sea, but to the north of the birthplace of Hawaii-loa. Viewed under that light, and assuming the south-eastern coast of Arabia to be the *Kapa-kapa-ua* of the legend, the name of the other northern land, *Ulu-nui*, cannot possibly have any other explanation than that of *Ur*, the city and kingdom of *Uruch* in ancient Chaldea, at the head of the Persian Gulf.

From this coast Hawaii-loa set sail, and steered to the eastward, crossing the ocean called *Moana-kai-maokioki*, or "the spotted, many-coloured sea," and also called *Moana-kai-popolo*, "the blue or dark-green sea." Considering his point of departure, that ocean must have been the Indian Ocean, and the two large islands which he discovered can be no other than Sumatra and Java. He called the one after his own name, *Hawa-ii*, and the other after that of his son *Maui*. But I have previously shown that the Polynesian *Hawa-ii*, *Sawa-ii*, *Habai*, and the Malaysian *Jawa*, *Djawa*, *Ciawa* and *Zapa-ge* are all referable for their protonom to the Arabian *Zaba*, the centre and pride of the Cushite Empire, whose commerce, colonies, and conquests extended from Madagascar to the Moluccas. With these premises it is difficult to conceive that these two islands could have been any of the Polynesian groups, or that whatever might have been the western site of that original *Kapa-kapa-ua*, the navigator of those days could have crossed the Pacific Ocean in an easterly direction within the belt of the trade-winds, and not have encountered any of its numerous islands and Atoll groups before reaching either of the three groups bearing the name of Hawaii. And if this, by some singular combination of fortuitous circumstances, could have been done once, it is hardly credible that it could have been repeated often. Yet the legend makes no mention of any such landfall, and Hawaii-loa is represented as having made several voyages afterwards between *Kapa-kapa-ua* and *Hawa-ii*, as well as other voyages to "the extreme south," *i ka mole o ka honua*, and to some other Western land, not *Kapa-kapa-ua*, where dwelt a "people with turned-up eyes," *Lahui maka-lilio*, and travelling over this land to the northward and westward, he came to the country called *Kua-hewa-hewa;* a very large country or continent. Returning from this country, he is said to have brought with him two white men, *poe keokeo kane*, whom he married on his return home to Hawaiian women.

It would be interesting to know who these people with turned-up eyes or drawn-up eyes, living on a continent to the west of the Sunda Isles, may have been. They certainly were not Chinese, Japanese, or any of the Mongol families of men. At first view the legend would seem to give strength to the opinion that Hawaii-loa actually had discovered and settled on the Hawaiian group; for, knowing no other oblique-eyed people than the Chinese and their varieties, they could not have been reached by a westerly voyage unless the point of departure had been somewhere in the Pacific. But it is fair to question whether the Chinese and their varieties were the only oblique-eyed people in the world. With the Sunda Isles as a point of departure, and a westerly course, the coast of Africa is the natural landfall. What people inhabited that coast in times so far back as those of Hawaii-loa? Denon, in his "Voyage en Egypte," describing from the ancient paintings in the temples and tombs of Egypt, says: "The female forms resembled figures of beautiful women of the present day; round and voluptuous; a small nose, the eyes long, half-shut, and *turned up at the outer angle*,[1] like those of all persons whose sight is habitually fatigued by the burning heat of the sun, or the dazzling whiteness of snow; the cheeks round and rather thick, lips full, mouth large, but cheerful and smiling." With the exception of the "turned-up eyes," a Polynesian beauty might have sat for the picture.

In some of Dr. Livingstone's letters, published in the Proceedings of the Royal Geographical Society, November 8, 1869, speaking of the people of Rua, on the west side of Lake Tanganyika, he says that they are said to live in rock-excavations, that "the people are very dark, well made, and *outer angle of eyes slanting upwards*."

Here, then, we have the testimony of the ancient Egyptians themselves, that "turned-up eyes" was not an individual specialty or deformity, but so common a characteristic of their people—the women at least—as to be preserved and faithfully copied on their pictorial records. As the women of ancient Egypt enjoyed a degree of social and political consideration, of which their modern Oriental sisters are sadly deprived, it is improbable that any painter of that time would have dared to thus caricature his countrywomen. The trait, then, was a national one, and it is so designated in the Hawaiian legend.

As regards the other people "with outer angle of eyes slanting upward," though now living in the centre of Africa, no man acquainted with the migrations of peoples and the changes of empire would venture, without positive proof in confirmation, to assert that at some period in the past unrecorded history of Africa they did not occupy the eastern coast from Abyssinia southward, and thus have been the people of whom the legend speaks. *Lahui maka-lilio*, "people with eyes turned up or drawn up," were, then, anciently found on the African coast, and could be

---

[1] The exact Hawaiian expression, *Maka-lilio*.

reached by a westerly voyage from the Sunda Isles: and thus the Hawaiian legend becomes consistent with itself, and with historical facts independent of it.

Historically considered, I am inclined to think that the legend of Hawaii-loa represents the adventures and achievements of several persons, partly pure Cushites, partly Cushite-Polynesians, which, as ages elapsed, and the individuality of the actor retreated in the background, while the echo of his deeds was caught up by successive generations, were finally ascribed to some central figure who thus became the traditional hero not only of his own time, but also of times anterior as well as posterior to his actual existence. While the one set of legends shows the voyages and intercourse of the early Cushites with the countries and archipels about the Indian Ocean, the other set of legends shows the intercourse and voyages of the earlier Polynesians between the groups of the Pacific. But to find the former set of legends in the possession of the latter race of people argues a connection, political and social, if not ethnic, and to some extent probably both, so intimate, yet so far antecedent, that the latter had really come to identify themselves with the former, and appropriate to their own proper heroes the legends brought them by the others. In much later times the same process was repeated, when the Hawaiian group was overrun by princely adventurers from the South Polynesian groups, who incorporated their own legends and their own version of common legends on the Hawaiian folklore, and interpolated their own heroes on the Hawaiian genealogies.

While, therefore, the presence of the Cushite element in the Polynesian race, in its legends, culture, and creeds, and to no inconsiderable extent in its blood, and at all times an element of supremacy, cannot be ignored in estimating the origin of this race; yet the Arian, mostly pre-Vedic, affinities of the language, with certain Zend proclivities in the phonetic values of some letters in the majority of the Polynesian dialects, are a stubborn fact, pointing either to an absolute ethnic relationship, or to a period of subjection sufficiently prolonged to completely change or materially modify the older tongue of the Polynesian progenitors, whatever that may have been. But still a third element bespeaks its presence with potent and incontrovertible force—the dark colour and the black eyes—and points to an intimate connection, or rather complete fusion with the brown or Dravidian race; whether in or out of India history and tradition are equally silent.

The order in which these elements contributed to the formation of the Polynesian race is not so patent, nor yet at this distance of time, hardly possible to define. Neither history nor tradition records any invasion or immigration into India by the Arian race before the Vedic-Arians crossed the Sarasvati and came in immediate and permanent contact with the brown Dravidian race. And yet the occupation of Hapta-Hindu was an invasion of India, and must have been effected by an entire displacement of the pre-existing Dravidians between the Sutlej and the Indus. The echoes of that event had long died out before the Vedic hymns were composed or the laws of Menu compiled. May not then some other hordes of the Arian family, and more akin to the Iranian division, have passed into India along its western coast from Beluchistan, through Cutch and Guzzerat, and mingling earlier with the Dravidian tribes on the way, and with less religious venom, have changed their colour while they retained their language, as their Vedic brethren did after they commenced settling on the banks of the Ganges? How long they remained in these new habitats, when or by whom displaced, how or by what route arrived at the Indian Archipelago, their struggles with, their conquest and expulsion of the Papuans, are all blank leaves in their history. A few local names, common to the west of India and some parts of Polynesia, would seem to indicate that the stream of migration had set southward through Western Deccan. To what extent, if any, they had come in contact with Cushite culture, commerce, and colonies, before they arrived in the Sunda Isles, no traces are left to indicate with any reliable precision.

But here, if not before, they became subject to the direct enterprise and influence of the Arabian Cushites, who here as elsewhere established their supremacy, introduced their institutions, customs, and creed, and mixing freely with the subject race, identified themselves so thoroughly with it as to substitute their own cosmogony, genealogies, and legends for whatever memories and whatever notions may have previously been entertained. In some such way alone, it seems to me, can we explain the composite character of the Polynesian race. We find the remains of Cushite culture, and creed; we find the Cushite-Arabian type abundantly cropping out;[1] we find the dark colour of the Dravidian race, varying from lightest olive to darkest brown; we find the language fundamentally Arian, but of a form far older than the•oldest written remains. These phenomena must have a natural solution, based upon historical sequences, and, under correction from those of greater knowledge, I have presented mine.

I will now refer to the opinion entertained by many authors, that the Polynesian language is an offshoot from and a corrupted dialect of the now widespread Malay, and that the Polynesian tribes are simply colonists from the Malay stock. The first explorers in this direction of ethnic inquiry, finding that a large number of Polynesian words bore a family likeness to the Malay language, naturally enough concluded that the former was a descendant or an importation from the latter; and the marked contrast in which the Papuan race stood to both Malay and Polynesian probably strengthened the illusion of an ethnic connection between the two latter peoples. When, afterwards, such philologists as Fr. Bopp discovered and established the connection between what he called "the Malayo-

---

[1] The Asiatic Ethiopians or Cushites were, according to Herodotus (vii. 70), of a dark complexion, but with straight hair, not curly like the African Ethiopians. Rawlinson compares them in tint—dark red, brown, or copper colour—to the modern Gallas and Abyssinians, as well as the Cha'b and Montefik Arabs and the Belooches.—The Five Great Monarchies of the Ancient Eastern World, G. Rawlinson, vol. i. p. 52. London, 1871.

Polynesian and the Indo-European" tongues, the conclusion seemed unanswerable that the Malays had received their Sanskrit words from the Hindus, and the Polynesians from the Malays. In Bopp's time the knowledge of the Polynesian was too imperfect to venture a demurrer, and none was made. All honour to Bopp, however, for establishing the kindred of the Polynesian, as well as the Malay, with the Indo-European family of speech; but the degree of kindred of the two former to the latter, and their relationship between themselves, as intimated by Bopp, may well be called in question at this day. I think that few people who are competent to form an opinion on the subject, and have seen and observed the Malays and Polynesians—not by individual exceptions, but by masses, and at their homes—will now maintain that they are ethnically descended from the same race. They have both, doubtless, passed through the Dravidian crucible, but the Polynesian entered it from the north-west, and the Malay, I think it will yet be found, entered it from the north-east. The Polynesians brought some primordial form of the Arian language with them when they came to India, as their mother-tongue; the Malays, whatever may have been their aboriginal tongue, acquired their connection with, and knowledge of, the Arian in its Sanskrit or Sanskritoid form, during their sejour in India, before they followed the Polynesians into the Indian Archipelago. Thus, while a large number of words are common to both, yet the form of these words in the Polynesian is by far the most archaic, the most conformable to what we may conceive to have been the earlier form of the Arian language, ere it acquired the Vedic-Sanskrit or Zend developments.[1]

Malay and Javanese historians and traditions give themselves no higher origin in the Sunda Isles than the first century of the present era. One account represents them as coming from India, under the leadership of a son

[1] The original elements of the Arian language consisted of open syllables of one consonant, followed by one vowel, or of a single vowel. — M.   Müller, Lectures on the Science of Language, 2d series, p. 192. London, 1864.

of the Rajah Souren, the founder of Bisnagour, and establishing their empire at Palembang, Sumatra.[1] Another account says that they came from the Telinga country, in north-east Deccan, with one Tritestra, or Aji-Saka, and established their empire in Jawa, at the foot of Mount Semiru. He introduced Brahmin culture, customs, and creed. He found the country inhabited by Rakshasas, which in a Brahmin mouth meant the infidel, non-Brahmin, Cushitised inhabitants of India and the islands. With these people several and bitter wars were had before the new settlers established themselves. That these Rakshasas were the Polynesians, who at some previous period had displaced the Papuans, and were now displaced in their turn by the rising Malay power, I think there can be little doubt. It is manifestly wrong, therefore, to class the Polynesians as colonists, or their language as a dialect, of the Malay. There is nothing in the Polynesian language to show that they are later than the Vedic development of the Arian race, probably much older; there is nothing in the Malay to show that they are older than the Sanskrit development of that same race. The one is the genuine stock, the other an engraftment upon it.

In connection with this subject of relation, ethnic or otherwise, between the Malay and Polynesian peoples, I ought not to pass over in silence an essay by Rev. S. J. Whitmee, an English missionary of many years' residence in the Samoan group, and published in the " Contemporary Review," February 1873, pp. 389–407. In this essay Mr. Whitmee, with much justice and correctness, refutes the assertion of so eminent a naturalist and traveller as Mr. A. R. Wallace, who in his " Malay Archipelago," chap. xl., declares that the Polynesian race is merely " a modification of the Papuan race, superinduced by an admixture of Malay or some light-coloured Mongol element, the Papuan, however, largely predominating physically, mentally, and

---

[1] "Monde Maritime," par G. A. Walkenaer. About 1159-60 A.C. the Palembang chiefs invaded Jawa, and extended their conquests to the peninsula of Malacca, thus called Oudjong-tanah.—*Ibid.*

morally ; but that such admixture probably occurred at
such a remote period as, through the lapse of ages, to have
become a permanent type." But in avoiding the Scylla of
Mr. Wallace and the Papuan theory, Mr. Whitmee has
fallen upon the Charybdis of Bopp and the Malay theorists.
Mr. Whitmee refuses credence to Mr. Wallace's classification of the Polynesians, but he believes him explicitly in
his classification of the Malays. Mr. Wallace sweeps the
almost entire population of the Indian Archipelago into
one ethnic net, and calls his catch the Malay race. The
Malays proper, the Javanese, the Battas, the Dyaks, the
Buguis, the Suluans, the Moluccans and Buruans, the coast
inhabitants and the mountaineers, are all Malays in his
generalisation, and their different languages are but different dialects of the Malay. Such generalisation is hasty,
and cannot but be misleading. As well class the Magyar
and the Sclave, the Finn and the Swede, in the same ethnic
compartments as to crowd the Batta and the Dyak, the Pulo-
Nias man, the Bugui, the Buruan, Saouan, and numerous
other original tribes still surviving in the Archipelago, into
the comparatively modern Malay box. The Malays themselves, with instinctive national consciousness, and, I am
tempted to say, conscientiousness, consider the above tribes
as ethnically different from themselves, and express that
sentiment or consciousness by calling the others *Orang-
Benua*, " men of the country," *i.e.*, " aborigines." Mr. Wallace makes no distinction, except that of degree of civilisation, between these latter, whom the Polynesians resemble
ethnically, and the Malays, whom, if they (the Polynesians) resemble them at all, it is by accident, as a Jew
might resemble a Roman. Misled by Mr. Wallace's generalisation, Mr. Whitmee fails also in making a distinction
between the Malays proper and the pre-Malay inhabitants
of the Archipel. Hence the summary of Malay words,
quoted by Mr. Whitmee as having " Polynesian equivalents
very closely resembling them," is not a correct showing in
the sense that Mr. Whitmee intends it. Leaving out the
numerals, of the thirty-six remaining words in the list of

Mr. Whitmee, only eleven are Malay words proper, while twenty-five belong to the language of those very pre-Malay tribes, with which and of which the Polynesians formed an integral part before the intrusion of the Malays; and of those other eleven Malay words with " Polynesian equivalents," nine are such equivalents for the very reason that they are Arian words adopted by the Malay.

Mr. Wallace, in the work above quoted, asserts that the Polynesian has a greater physical, mental, and moral reresemblance to the Papuan than to the Malay. Mr. Whitmee, in the essay referred to, asserts the greater physical, mental, and moral resemblance of the Polynesian to the Malay. Each one argues a kindred of race according to his views. Both cannot possibly be right; and, from my reading of Polynesian characteristics and Polynesian folklore, they are both wrong. Great similarity of character may be found in peoples of widely different origin, and great dissimilarity of appearance in peoples of known community of race. What can be more similar in character than the Papuan, as described by Mr. Wallace, and the Marquesan of to-day? And yet the latter is probably a fairer and nearer approach to the primitive Arian type among its descendants in the East than the Celt among its descendants in the West. What can be more dissimilar in appearance than the light-haired, blue-eyed, high-statured Scandinavian, and the black-haired, dark-eyed, low-statured Bas-Breton? And yet their community of race is now undisputed. There is, then, something deeper, older, more expressive as a criterion of the consanguinity of peoples than the character, which may be the result of social conditions during long previous ages—tyranny, oppression, debasement, or the reverse; or of appearance, which may be the result of physical and local conditions and surroundings, operating for ages in a given direction, inland or maritime, alpine or lowland, forest or prairie, fertile or desert, sunny or cold, border people subject to outside influences and mixtures, or people in the interior or in isolated situations. This something, this criterion, I hold to be the language of a people.

It is true that languages perish and languages decay; but the decay and the extinction are always *pari passu* with the decay and extinction of the particular people to whom such or such language was the aboriginal mother-tongue. The Gauls, whom Brennus led and whom Cæsar conquered, perished with their language during the five centuries of Roman occupation. The Cushite race and the Cushite language disappeared together from Arabia and the Mesopotamian basin, and Semites filled their places. But the languages preserved of both these peoples prove that the former were of kindred race with the Romans, and that the latter were of alien race to the Semites.

And so, when the English language shall have superseded the Polynesian in the Pacific groups, the pure Polynesian, as an ethnic branch of the Arian tree, will have vanished from the scene, whether civilised or savage, and be succeeded by an Anglo-Polynesian people, drawing largely at first from the vanishing stock, but gradually becoming quite distinct in character and appearance. And yet the Polynesian language, preserved in books and more or less interspersed in the vernacular of the new people, will attest the originally ethnic kindred of the old stock to the new, and tell the future inquirer how the Polynesian, after various Dravidian and Cushite detours, returned to the primitive Arian type through a fusion with one or more of its Indo-European descendants.[1]

The Numeral System.

In further confirmation of the Polynesian relation to the Arian stock, at a very early period, the numeral systems of both will furnish rather decisive testimony. It is now pretty well established that the more ancient and rude a people is or was, the more limited is or was its

---

[1] See Appendix, No. VIII.

numeral system. The Australian aborigines to this day do not count beyond three or four. The Dravidian languages exhibit signs, by the composition of their higher numbers, that at one time the range of their numerals was equally limited. The Polynesian language gives undoubted evidence that at one time the people who spoke it did not count beyond four, and that its ideas of higher numbers were expressed by multiples of four. Judging from the Hawaiian dialect, which has preserved so much of the archaic idiomacy of the language, the Polynesians and their pre-Malay congeners in the Indian Archipel evidently counted "one, two, three, four," and that amount called kau-na [1] was their tally, when the process was repeated again.

That the same quaternary system obtained in the Arian family, in early times, is evident not only from the marked relationship between the four first Arian and Polynesian numbers, but the method of counting by fours as a tally still obtains among some of the Arian descendants in Europe. To the personal knowledge of the writer, on the Baltic coast of Sweden small fish, specially herring, are counted by fours, each four being called a *kast*.

The following table will show the relation I am seeking to establish. It is selected from Arian and Polynesian branches; but there is this to be observed, that while the latter in all probability exhibit the archaic form of the language, the former exhibit a comparatively later and more or less modified form of the same.

---

[1] Professor Fr. Bopp, in his excellent work, "Ueber die Verwandtschaft der Malayisch-Polynesischen Sprachen mit den Indisch-Europäischen" (Berlin, 1841), proposes that the Hawaiian *kau-na* is derived from, or abbreviation of, the Javanese Basa-Krima form *sa-kavan* or simply *kavan*, meaning "four," and suggests it to be a corruption (Verstümmelung) of the Sanskrit *catvar*, "four." The Polynesian *kau-na*, however, is a contraction of *kau-ana*, the participial ending *ana* rendering it a substantive; and the root-word *kau* remains in the Tonga dialect as a collective noun, indicating "a collection," "a gathering together," "a body of somethings," and in that sense is also used as a plural article and a prefix. It is more likely, therefore, that this Polynesian *kau* and *kau-na* is the root of, or closely related to, another Javanese word *kavan*, meaning "a herd, a flock," than that it is a descendant from the Sanskrit *cat-var*, through the Javanese *kavan*, four.

	1.	2.	3.	4.	5.	6.	7.	8.	9.	10.
Samoan	Tasi.	Lua.	Tolu.	Fa.	Lima.	Ono.	Fitu.	Valu.	Iva.	Senga-fulu.[1]
Hawaiian	Kahi.	Lua.	Kolu.	Ha.	Lima.	Ono.	Hiku.	Walu.	Iwa.	Umi.
Marquesan	Tahi.	Ua.	To'u.	Fa.	Ima.	Ono.	Fitu.	Va'u.	Iva.	Onohu'u.
Mangaia	Tahi.	Rua.	Toru.	Fa.	Rima.	Ono.	Hitu.	Varu.	Iva.	Raungahuru.
Waihu (Easter Is.)	Tahi.	Aite.	Toru.	Haa.	Agoka.	Hono.	Hitu.	Varu.	Hiva.	Anahuru.
Paumotu	Arari.	Rua.[2]	Ageti.	Aope.	Rima.[3]	Ahene.	Ahito.	Ahiava.	Anipa.	Horihori.
Tahiti	Tahi.	Rua.	Toru.	Ha.	Rima.	Ono.[4]	Hitu.	Varu.	Iva.	Ahuru.
Rapa	Ta'i.	Bua.	Toru.	Aa.	Rima.	Ono.	Itu.	Varu.	Iva.	Ngauru.
Rorotonga	Tai.	Bua.	Toru.	A.	Rima.	Ono.	Iru.	Varu.	Iva.	Ngauru.
Tonga	Taha.	Ua.	Tolu.	Fa.	Nima.	Ono.	Fitu.	Valu.	Hiva.	Hongafulu.[5]
New Zealand	Tahi.	Rua.	Toru.	Wha.	Rima.[6]	Ono.	Whitu.	Waru.	Iwa.	Ngahuru.
Niue (Savage Is.)	Taha.	Ua.	Tolu.	Fa.	Lima.	Ono.	Fitu.	Valu.	Iva.	Hongafulu.
Fakaafo (Union)	Tasi.	Lua.	Tolu.	Fa.	Lima.	On.	Fitu.	Valu.	Iva.	Sefulu.
Rotuma	Ta.	Rua.	Thol.	Hak.	Lium.	Ono.	Hith.	Vol.	Siar.	Sanghul.
Niwa (New Heb.)	Tasi.	Rua.	Toru.	Fa.	Rima.	Hono.	Fitu.	Varu.	Iva.	Tangafuru.
Isle of Cocos	Tasi.	Lua.	Tolu.	Tea.	Lima.	Onam.	Fitu.	Valu.	Iva.	Ongafulu.
Batta	Sada.	Duo.	Tolu.	Opak.	Lima.	Anam.	Paitu.	Walu.	Sia.	Sapulu.
Lampong	Sai.	Rua.	Tolu.	Ampa.	Lima.	Gennep.	Pitu.	Valu.	Siwa.	Puhu.
Sunda	Hidji.	Duwa.	Tilu.	Opak.	Limo.	Nanam.	Tudju.	Dalapen.	Salapan.	Sapulu.
Javanese	Siji.	Loru.	Tulu.	Papak.	Lima.	Unu.[7]	Pitu.	Valo.	Sanga.	Sapulo.
Pulo-Nias	Sara.	Dua.	Tula.	Ufa.	Rima.	Anam.	Fitu.	Walu.	Suwa.	Fulu.
Dyak-Idaan	Uni.	Dui.	Toru.	Ampat.	Limo.	Anam.	Fitu.	Hasia.	Siu.	Sapulu.
„ *Lamih*	Sa.	Duo.	Tale.	Pat.	Liimak.	Nam.	Tuo.	Walo.	Siam.	Mapud.
„ *Lamuh*	Ji.	Dua.	Telo.	Pat.	Lema.	Nam.	Tusuh.	Sayah.	Petan.	Sapuloh.
„ *Lokipot*	Se.	Upfe.	Telow.	Pat.	Rima.	Anong.	Tujok.	Murai.	Paih.	Polow.
„ *Sambas*	Mengarit.	Dua.	Taru.	Apat.	Lima.	Jahawen.	Iju.	Mahih.	Piri.	Sapuloh.
„ *Pontianak*	Iju.	Dua.	Telo.	Ampa.	Lima.	Onong.	Uju.	Hanja.	Ileteam.	
Bugui (Borneo)	Sedi.	Duwa.	Tolu.	Opak.	Lima.	Mna.	Pitu.	Aruwa.	Assera.	Sopulu.
„ (Written)	Sadi.	Dua.	Telu.	Mpa.	Lima.		Pitu.	Harua.	Hasaera.	Sapulu.

	1	2	3	4	5	6	7	8	9	10
Ceram-Ahtiago [10]..	Esa.	Elua.	Entol.	Enhata.	Enlima.	Ennoi.	Enhit.	Enwol.	Ensiwa.	Fotusa.
,, Wahai	Sali.	Lua.	Tolo.	Ati.	Nima.	Onam.	Fitu.	Alu.	Sia.	Husa.
Saru	Ise.	Rue.	Tolu.	Apa.	Lumi.	Una.	Pitu.	Aru.	Saio.	Singauru.
Moses Island	Kau.	Bua.	Tolu.	Wali.	Rima.	Eno.	Vitu.	Jalu.	Siwa.	Sangapulu.
Tagal	Isa.	Dalua.	Tatle.	Ampat.	Lima.	Anim.	Pito.	Walo.	Siam.	Polo.
Papango....	Isa-metong.	Adua.	A-tlo.	Apat.	Lima.	Anam.	Pitu.	Valo.	Siam.	Apolo.
Mindanao....	Isa.	Dava.	Tulu.	Apat.	Lima.	Anam.	Pitu.	Valu.	Siau.	Sanpulu.
Malgasse....	Isa.[11]	Bua.	Tolu.	Efa.[12]	Liman.[13]	One.[14]	Hitu.	Valu.	Siwa.	Fulu.
Malay....	Satu.	Dua.	Tiga.	Ampat.	Lima.	Anam.	Tujo.	Delapan.	Sambilan.	Sapuloh.

	1	2	3	4	5	6	7	8	9	10
Sanskrit....	Eka.	Dvi.	Tri.	Catvar.	Panch.	Shash.	Sapt.	Aght.	Nava.	Das.
Persian....	Yek.	Du.	Sih.	Kehar.	Penge.	Ses.	Heft.	Hest.	Nuh.	Deh.
Hindustanee....	Eik.	Duy.	Thr.	Tzar.	Penge.	Tzo.	Tatu.	Aatza.	Nouy.	Dass.
Zingara....	Yec.	Due.	Trin.	Stor.	Peng.	Sho.	Afta.	Oitu.	Enneah.	Desh.
Sclavonian....	Yediuo.	Dova.	Tri.	Chetoiriyo.	Pamie.	Seate.	Sedme.	Osme.	Devante.	Desamte.
Latin....	Unus.	Duo.	Tres.	Quatuor.	Quinque.	Sex.	Septem.	Octo.	Novem.	Decem.
Greek....	'Eis.	Dyo.	Treis.	Tettara.[15]	Pente.	'Ex.	'Epta.	Oktô.	Ennea.	Deka.
Welsh....	Un.	Dau.	Tri.	Pedwar.	Pump.	Ohwech.	Saith.	Wyth.	Naw.	Deg.
Anglo-Saxon....	An.	Twa.	Thri.	Feover.	Fif.	Six.	Seofon.	Eatha.	Nigon.	Tyn.
Gothic....		Tvai.		Fidvar.	Fimf.		Sibun.	Athan.	Ninn.	Tig.[16]

1 Or Sefulu. 2 Or Piti. 3 Or Pae. 4 Or Fene, Hene. 5 Or Angafulu. 6 Or Ringa. 7 Or Ano. 8 In Ternati, Yagi. 9 Waiapo.
10 In Crawfurd's Dissertation, vol. i. p. 226, of "Grammar and Dictionary of Malay Language," he gives the following a Ceramese ("Sirang") numbers, but does not give He also give mba, 8 K'or 1 Or Elatr 'd :—1 Takura, 2 Dua, 3 Tolo, 4 Pat, 5 Lim, 6 Onan, 7 Titura, 8 Dalapante, Tambora on the island of Sumbawa:—1 Seena, 2 Kalae, 3 Nib, 4 Kude-in, and Hene. 15 Or Ool. Pessyres. 16 Or Tiguns.

Sambuiante, 10 Patusa. H... the locality whence obtained
Kutel-in, 6 Bata-in, 7 Kur... es the following numbers for '
11 Or Rek, also Trai. 12 ... 1eho, 9 Iali, 10 Sarone. a. 13 Or Diiny. 14 Or Eni..a

Believing, with Professor Bopp, that the origin as well as the cause of resemblance, or of difference, in the first numeral of the different branches of a kindred tongue, must be sought for in those oldest remnants of a once common speech, the definite and indefinite articles and pronouns; and recognising that within the Arian family at least, with which I have some acquaintance, the primary expressions "the," "this," "that," "a," "an," either simply or combined, were the original equivalents of "one," as a number, the early connection between the Indo-European and Polynesian is not very difficult to establish.

1. The Polynesian *ka, ke, ta, te, ha, he*, refer immediately to a common origin with the Sanskrit *ka* and *sa*, the Greek το, τη, ὁς, ἡ, the Gothic *tha*, the Latin *hi-c, hœ-c, ho-c*, and evince the same dialectical tendencies. Bopp considers the Sanskrit *eka* as composed of *e*, a demonstrative pronoun, and *ka*, an interrogative. But this *eka*, "one," has a near relation, and one applied to the same uses in the Tagal *ica, ca, caca*, meaning "the," "this," "that," and also "one." The Tagal and Malgasse *isa*, "one," refers itself to the Sanskrit *esa*, "this;" and even in Sanskrit the single *sa* remains as a demonstrative article, and the numeral "one" in compound words, as in *sa-kart*, "ein-mal," "once." To this *sa* refers itself, without doubt, the second constituent of the Polynesian *taha*, "one," and is evidently akin to the Gothic obsolete form of *ha* in compound words, such as *ha-ihs*, "one-eyed," *ha-nfs*, "one-handed," *et al.*

That *sa* was in Archaic times a numeral designating "one," and common to the various branches of the Arian stock, is further illustrated by the Javanese *siji*, "one," contracted from ancient *sa-vigi*, which itself is an Arian compound of *sa*, "one," and *viga* (Sanskrit), "a kernel, a seed;" also by the Malay *sa-tu*, contracted from *sa-batu*, "one stone," and of which the North Celebes (Bolanghitan) dialect *so-boto* is a better preserved form. The Basa-Krima points to the same archaism in its *sa-kavan*, "four," lit., "one-four" or "one-kau," and in *sa-dhasa*, "ten," lit., "one-ten." The softening of the broad *a* in *sa* to *i* in *si* of the Polynesian *ta-si*, is perhaps as old as any of the branches of the Arian tongue. It is found in Buru (Cajeli) *si-lei*, "one," Buru (Waiapo) *um-si-un*, "one," in the South Celebes (Salayer) *se-dri*, "one," in the Salibabo *se-mbao*, "one," in the Sula Islands *hi-a*, "one." Instead, therefore, of considering with Professor Bopp that the Hawaiian *ka-hi* and Samoan *ta-si* are attenuated derivations of the Tonga *ta-ha* or an older *ta-sa*, "one," I look upon them as coeval varieties of a once common expression for the numeral "one."

It is possible that the Brahui (Beluchistan) numeral *asit*, "one," in which the *t* is either a Cushite or Dravidian postfix, concreted afterwards, may have a linguistic affinity to the Polynesian *tasi*. If so, the initial *t* must have been dropped; and I have no means of knowing the ancient form of the Brahui word. But this same Brahui *asit* singularly enough recalls to mind the ancient Latin *as*, the generic name for a unit, and the Greek ἐις, αις, "one."

2. The relation of the Polynesian number two to the Indo-European branches is self-evident by a glance at the foregoing table. The same dialectical tendency to change *d* into *l* or *r* is manifest in the Polynesian branch as in the Indo-European.

3. The correspondence between the Indo-European *tri* and the Polynesian *toru*, *tolu*, is not so palpable on the face of it, though the radicals of both are identical. The absence of this form in the Persian, and its substitution by *sih*, would lead to infer that other synonyms may have existed also in the other branches in early times, but are now lost. The Latin form of *ter* in *ternus* indicates clearly the ancient connection.

4. The numeral four, however, corresponds remarkably well in all the varieties of both the Indo-European and Polynesian branches. The *chat*, *quat*, *chit*, *tet*, *pet*, and *fid* forms of the former family bespeak unmistakeable relation with the *pat*, *fat*, *pa*, *fa*, and *ha* forms of the latter family.

Professor Bopp, in the work above referred to, seems to consider the Sanskrit form of the numeral four as the original, archaic form, from which all the others, whether in the Indo-European or Polynesian family, have descended or deteriorated. And not only this number, but also all the preceding ones, and most of the subsequent ones. Not content with establishing their family relation, he exalts the Sanskrit to the position of a parent and an architype, by which the others are to be measured. He says that the Malayan dialects are less corrupted or mutilated (verstümmelt) from this architype, this mother-form, than the Polynesian. He may be right in one sense; for whatever there is in common between the Malay and the Arian, the Malay probably derived from the Sanskrit or the Sanskritoid dialects of upper India; whereas the Polynesian owes nothing to the Sanskrit, properly so called, having left the homestead of the Arian race long ages before the Sanskrit, Zend, or other European sisters had assumed to so large extent those trappings of inflections and those habits of elision, by which these younger branches of the ancient stock now mutually recognise each other, however far apart their lot in after-life was thrown.

But to return to the numeral under consideration. Is it at all credible, simply on philological grounds, that the first conception of the number four by the ancient Arians should have found expression in so long and complicated a word as *chatvar?* Disclaiming any profound knowledge of the Sanskrit, yet I make bold to say that *chatvar* or *chatvaras* is a compound word, and hence comparatively modern, when treating of archaic forms of speech. I take it to be composed of *chat*, or its dialectical variations in *quat, pet, pat, tet, fid*, original expressions of the conception four, and *var*, expressing a revolution, a cycle, a total, a tally. With that *chat*, and *pat*, the Polynesian *pa, fa*, and *ha*, stand in intimate relation; but inasmuch as the latter never shared in the final consonant which distinguishes the articulation of the word by all the other branches, it is reasonable to infer that the Polynesians had separated from the mother stock before consonantal endings, implying a subsequent compound, had been introduced to give greater variety of meaning and definiteness of expression to words from the same primitive root.[1]

Up to this number four it is thus evident, I think, that the Indo-European and the Polynesian numerals were derived from the same mother-tongue, and that the Polynesian manner of expressing them was the more ancient; but it is also evident that, before the Arian stock had passed beyond the quaternary system of counting, one branch—the Polynesian—had also passed beyond the influences, associations, and conditions under which the remaining branches built up, and gave expression to, the higher numerals from four upwards.

Under what conditions of civilisation, or from what ethnic relations or neighbourhoods, the Polynesian family adopted the higher numerals from four to ten, is a question I have not had sufficient means within my reach—if the means exist at all—satisfactorily and positively to solve. There are several reasons which incline me to believe that they were adopted after the family had left the Arian stock, and while in course of amalgamation with the Dravidian in Upper India, or on the Iranian sea-

---

[1] That the final *t* in *chat, tet, quat,* &c., was not an original radical in the Arian expression for four may, I think, be inferred from its absence in the Anglo-Saxon and Armorican dialects of the Indo-European family; the former having *fe-o-ver,* the latter *pe-var.* That two cognate branches of the same lineage, coming down abreast from the hoariest antiquity, should have differed, and continued to differ, in the pronunciation of the number four, shows to me—especially in view of the entire Polynesian usage, and of the Malgasse, Pulo-Nias, Lampong, Bugui, Tidore, Gi-lolo, Buru, and Savu forms of the pre-Malay dialects—that this final *t* or *d* was not an essential, integral part of the word. I believe it is now generally understood that the Indo-European varieties did not derive one from the other, or all from the Sanskrit; but that they were, so far back as knowledge can trace them, contemporary provincialisms, so to say, of a common tongue, of whose antique, if not original forms of speech, some were preserved with greater fidelity in one dialect, others in others.

board, along the Persian Gulf. With all due deference
for so industrious and capable workers in philological
mines as Bopp and Logan, it is far from obvious that these
higher numerals are either reduplications or combinations
of the lower numerals existing in the Polynesian family
proper, or among its Arian cousins. The universality of
their adoption, from Easter Island to Madagascar, and the
incredibly small difference in pronunciation, all things
considered, amount almost to proof positive that they
were introduced into the language, such as they now are,
by a people of higher civilisation than the Arians possessed when the Polynesians left them, and while the
latter were yet a compact body with small dialectical
tendencies, and those of no well defined development.
And that people, whether in India, Beluchistan, or further
on, was doubtless an early variety of the Dravidian stock,
already civilised, or in course of civilisation, by the all-
pervading Cushites of the ancient Arabian or Chaldean
times.

5. The numeral five, *lima, rima, nima,* is a purely
indigenous Polynesian word, though not without Arian
connections and analogies. As soon as the family passed
beyond the quaternary system of counting, the hand—
lima—became the natural signification and expression for
the totality of the five fingers or of a tally. That this
word appears exclusively in the Polynesian family as a
numeral for five, and not in any of the Indo-European
languages, is to me another proof that the former separated
from the latter before the quinary system was adopted.

The higher Polynesian numerals, six, seven, eight, nine,
point strongly to a Dravidian formation grafted on to the
Polynesian language, but by what branch of the Dravidian
stock the distinctive initial words of those numerals were
employed, I am unable to point out, if they are at all
derived from any Dravidian source. It would seem as if
the Polynesians, after having perfected the quinary system
from their own vocabulary, had adopted the terms of a

foreign vocabulary, already made to hand and more or less corrupted, for the higher numbers.

6. The Polynesian terms for "six," *ono, hono, ene, hene, unu,* and *una,* appear to connect themselves with the South Dravidian forms of the term for "one," such as *on-ru, on-du, un-di,* though they possibly may refer to one of the early Arian synonyms for "one," which the Latins in the West preserved in *unus,* and the Dyak-Idaans of the East retained in *uni* as expressions for "one." By the time the Polynesians adopted the quinary system, they were already beyond the influence and associations of their Arian congeners; and having employed their own, the Arian, language in counting one set of fives, the contents of one hand, they employed a foreign language—that of the Dravidians, with whom at that time they probably were in process of amalgamation—to count the next set of numbers, or at least to contribute greatly to their formation. The Gilolo (Galela) and Tidore *moi* and *remoi,* "one," strongly point to the North Dravidian (kol) formation of *moi,* "one." Whether the Polynesian *mua,* "the first," and *muli,* "the last," refer themselves, as Bopp is inclined to prefer, to the Sanskrit *mula,* "root, beginning," or to the Dravidian numeral formation in *mo, mu,* I will not presume to decide. That the Greek has preserved the root of this word in *mounos, monos,* "one," "only," "alone," would seem to strengthen the Arian view of the question. But the Sanskrit *mula* has a well-defined affinity in the Polynesian (Hawaiian) *mole,* "root, foundation, bottom," as well as in the Latin *moles.* Professor Bopp, in the work often referred to, thinks the Polynesian forms of *hene, fene, ene,* for "six," and the Indo-Nesian forms in *anam, nenem,* &c., are corrupted derivations from the Sanskrit (gen.) *sannam,* a modification of *sah-nam* from an original *sas,* "six." This conclusion is etymologically possible, and the analogy of the Latin *senī* (distrib. num.) "six," would be even stronger and more direct to the Polynesian *hene, fene, ene,* could it be proven that the Polynesian is only a corrupted form of

Malay, and the Malay a corrupted form of Sanskrit. But so far all data, historical, traditional, and linguistic, lead in a contrary direction, and thus render Bopp's theory and reasoning untenable, though at the time he wrote those data were not collected.

7. The Polynesian number "seven," *fitu, hiku,* &c., the Indo-Nesian *pitu,* &c., is really more difficult to class than the number six. Professor Bopp, according to his theory, considers the Polynesian forms as a corruption ("Verstüm-melung und Schwächung") of the Sanskrit *sapta,* that the first syllable *sa* has been lost, that the last vowel *a* has been softened to *u* or *o,* and that to accommodate the Polynesian idiom a light vowel as *i* has been inserted between the original *p* and *t* in the last syllable *pta.* This is also etymologically possible, but is it historically so? Professor Buschmann, according to Bopp, *loc. cit.,* con-siders the terms *pitu, fitu, hiku,* as of purely Polynesian origin, and home-made, so to say. He refers the first syllable to a weakening of the Polynesian *pa, fa, ha,* "four," and the second syllable to a contraction of the Polynesian *tolu,* "three," thus assuming that the whole word originally was *fa-tolu,* $4 + 3 = 7$. This reference is ingenious and plausible; the more so as it starts from a quaternary basis, and builds up the higher numbers on that. But, unfortunately for this hypothesis, there is no instance within the whole range of the Polynesian lan-guage, from Madagascar to Easter Island, of any dialectical forms in *fa-tu, fe-tu, fa-tolu, fe-tolu,* or *fi-tolu,* or the same forms commencing with *p* or *h,* or with the initial *h* dropped, as often is the case among the Polynesian dialects. Had the *pitu, fitu,* been of Polynesian origin, some signs of its gradual corruption from an original *fa-tolu* to the present *pitu, fitu, hiku, itu,* could not fail to be found in some one of so many widely scattered and long isolated dialects. Were the word of Polynesian formation, it must have been adopted as the numeral "seven," and the cor-ruption from *fa-tolu* to *fitu* taken place, while the Poly-

nesians yet were a unit, a comparatively compact body, and before their dispersion East and West over the Indian Ocean. I have attempted to show, however, in previous pages, that, at that period of their existence, the Polynesians lived with and among the Dravidian race of India; that, when they separated from their Arian connections, their system of counting was quaternary; that the number "five" was only adopted after such separation, in some intermediate stage, inasmuch as their name for "five," though an Arian word, was not the word adopted to express that number by the remaining unbroken tribes of the Arian family; and that they commenced their numeration of the higher numerals with a decidedly Dravidian word, and in all probability continued the scale upward to "ten" from the same linguistic formation, though I am unable to state the particular Dravidian dialect from which the word in question was borrowed. It has a Dravidian postfix, but whether the radical *pi* is Dravidian or Cushite, I am unable to say; it is not Polynesian.

8. The Polynesian *walu, varu, aru,* "eight," is doubtless a foreign word and incorporated as such in the language. It has no Arian affinities, and cannot well, as Professor Bopp endeavours to do, be decomposed into the same elements as the Malay *delapan.* It has its own *raison d'etre* and connects itself either as an amplification of an ancient Dravidian binary term in *bar, var,* or, which I am more inclined to think, it is identical with the third person plural of the Dravidian pronoun, *aru, avaru varu,* "they." The Dravidian connection with the Polynesians when these higher numerals were introduced in the language is further evidenced by the very exceptions to the general term. Thus the Gilolo (Galela) *itu-pangi,* the Buru (Waiapo) *et-rua,* "eight," refer plainly to the Dravidian (Tamil) *ettu, yettu,* "eight," while the *ru* and *tu* postfixes in all are distinctively Dravidian family marks that should not be hastily set aside in determining the origin of these words.

9. The Polynesian number "nine," *siwa, hiwa, iwa,* with Indo-Nesian varieties in *sia, sio, siau, siam, siwer,* I confess myself unable, from my limited philological resources, to trace satisfactorily to its origin. I cannot entertain the idea of Professor Bopp that *siwa* is a mutilation and corruption of the Malay *sambilan.* It is the same word in Madagascar and in Easter Island, and must have existed in the Polynesian language ages before it came in contact with the Malay. No Polynesian or pre-Malay tribe in the Archipelago comes in any measure near the Malay *sambilan* in its appellation of the number "nine." Even the Sunda dialect, which has been so greatly Malayified, has not adopted the word, but adheres to what was probably the older Malay formation, and calls "nine" *salapan,* as it calls "eight" *dalapan.* The Indo-Nesian synonyms for "nine," Javanese *sanga,* Bugui *hassera,* and the Dyak varieties *petan, paih, piri, iletean,* throw no light, so far as I know, on the language from which they all were derived. There is no apparent reason why the Polynesians, after having adopted "six," "seven," and "eight," from a foreign tongue, should have reverted to their own language for the formation of the number "nine." And yet the change of the first vowel from *i* to *a* in the Savu *saio,* and to *u* in the Pulo-Nias *su-wa,* might lead to the inference that the first syllable represented the ancient Arian *sa, si,* demonstrative pronoun, and number one, while the second syllable *wa* was an abbreviation of the already adopted *walu;* the more so, as in Mindanao and the Solo Archipel nine is *si-au,* and in the Sangvir Islands it is *ka-si-au,* showing a lapse of the middle *l* not uncommon in some dialects like the Marquesan. And this inference requires additional weight from the Teor *si-wer,* where the liquid is retained, though the final *u* is omitted. The word would then represent 1, 8, or $1 + 8 = 9$.

10. The Polynesian "ten," *pulu, fulu, huru,* with varying prefixes of *sa, se, san, sanga, singa, tanga, aua, ono,*

honga, is doubtless a genuine Polynesian word. Its literal and archaic meaning in all the dialects is that of "feathers, hair, wool." When the denary system was adopted, "ten" became a new tally, and was expressed by a word indicating a multitude, as may be seen from its synonym *umi* lit., "the beard."[1] But the Polynesian *puru, fulu, huru* is evidently near kindred to the Sanskrit (Ved.) *pûru*, "much, many, exceeding," though I am not aware that in any of the Indo-European branches it was ever used to express any definite quantity. The concrete sense of "feathers, hair," &c., must be very ancient, however, inasmuch as the denary system must have been adopted before the Polynesians occupied the Indian Archipelago, and while yet subject to, or mingling with, the Dravidian tribes of India, and before the Vedic Arians had crossed the Indus.

As to the prefix *sa, se, sanga, singa, ana, hongo*, &c., I consider the two first as the old Arian numeral "one," thus making the *sa-* or *se-pula* equal to "one ten." *Sanga* and its varieties is composed of the same numeral *sa*, and the Polynesian plural prefix *na*, thus making the word properly written as *sa-nga-pulu;* and in that way the original plural sense of *nga-pulu*, "the feathers," crops out under its later conventional meaning of "ten."

That the quaternary system of counting continued long after the denary system was adopted among the Polynesians is evidenced in the Hawaiian dialect. There "ten fours" were called a *kana-ha* or an *iako* or a *ka'au* = 40; "ten forties" were called a *lau* = 400; ten "lau" were one *mano* = 4000; ten "mano" were one *kini* = 40,000; and ten "kini" were one *lehu* = 400,000, the highest number known to them. The expressions for a single hundred or a single thousand were unknown to the Hawaiians until

[1] In Hawaiian, *umi*, "ten;" *umi-umi*, "beard." Samoan *umi*, "ten fathoms." Tahitian, *umi-umi*, "beard;" *umi*, "ten fathoms." Marquesan, *kumi-kumi*, "beard." Mangarewa, Paumotu, *id.*, Fiji *kumi*, "beard;" *va-kumi*, "bearded." The Ceram *hutu* and *hutu-sa*, "ten," refer themselves to the Tidore and Galela *hutu*, "hair."

the discovery of the group by Cook, and subsequent intercourse with foreigners. Some of these words, like the *pulu*
and *umi* and *hutu*, have preserved their original meanings
alongside of the later conventional and numeral designations. Thus LAU still means "the leaves of trees" in the
Hawaiian, Samoan, Marquesan, New Zealand, and Fiji
dialects; in the Tonga contracted to *lo;* and still retains
the primary sense in composites, as *lau-ulu* (Samoan),
"hair," lit., "the leaves of the head," as *lo-nutu* (Tonga),
"lips," lit., "the leaves of the mouth," *et al.* In the Indo-
nesian dialects, the same word, with the same meaning,
still remains in the Ceram *lau, laun;* Malay *daun,* "leaf,"
and others. Thus LEHU, under varying dialectical forms
of *rehu, reu, lefu, efu,* means "ashes, dust;" in Fiji *levu,*
"large, numerous, great," already a secondary meaning; in
the Amblaw and Javanese *avu,* in Malay *habu,* Sunda
lebu, also mean ashes. In the Hawaiian and other Polynesian dialects, the duplicated form *lehu-lehu* means "many,
numerous, and an indefinite large number." In none of
the Polynesian, however, except the Hawaiian, has this
word assumed the conventional sense of a definite number;
but in Indonesia we find Malgasse *ar-rivu,* 1000; Tagal
libo, id., Malay *sa-ribu, id.,* Sunda *sa-rivu, id.,* Javanese *sévu, id.,* while in the island of Mysol *lafu* only represents "ten." Thus the Hawaiian KINI, beside the definite
number, means "an indefinitely great number, a retinue of
persons, a following;" Marquesan *tini,* "many, innumerable;" Tahitian *po-tini-tini,* "an indefinitely large number;" while in Fiji *tini,* and in Ceram (Camar.) *tinein*
means only "ten." And thus, lastly, MANO, which in
Hawaiian represents 4000, and in Tonga 10,000, has a
primary meaning of "many, numerous, an indefinite multitude."

I think the facts collected, in the foregoing attempt to satisfactorily solve the question of the Polynesian origin, will warrant the conclusion that the various branches of that family, from New Zealand to the Hawaiian group, and from Easter Island to the outlying eastern portion of the Fiji Archipel, are descended from a people that was agnate to, but far older than, the Vedic family of the Arian race; that it entered India before these Vedic Arians; that there it underwent a mixture with the Dravidian race, which, as in the case of the Vedic Arians themselves, has permanently affected its complexion; that there also, in greater or less degree, it became moulded to the Cushite-Arabian civilisation of that time; that, whether driven out of India by force, or voluntarily leaving for colonising purposes, it established itself in the Indian Archipelago at an early period, and spread itself from Sumatra to Timor and Luzon; that here the Cushite influence became paramount to such a degree as to completely engraft its own legends, myths, culte, and partially institutions, upon the folklore and customs of the Polynesians; that it was followed into this archipelago by Brahmanised or Buddhist Ario-Dravidians from the eastern coasts of Deccan, with a probably strong Burmah-Tibetan admixture, who in their turn, but after protracted struggles, obtained the ascendancy, and drove the Polynesians to the mountain ranges and the interior of the larger islands, or compelled them to leave altogether; that no particular time can be assigned for leaving the Indian Archipelago and pushing into the Pacific—it may have occurred centuries before the present era, but was certainly not later than about the first century of it; that the diversity of features and complexion in the Polynesian family—the frequently broad forehead, Roman nose, light olive complexion, wavy and sometimes ruddy hair—attest as much its Arian descent and Cushite connection, as its darker colour, its spreading nostrils, and its black eyes attest its mixture with the Dravidian race;

and, finally, that if the present Hindu is a Vedic descendant, the Polynesian is *à fortiori* a Vedic ancestor.

In estimating the time of arrival of the Polynesian family in the Pacific, I have been guided almost wholly by their own genealogies and traditions. No other history throws any light on their departure, their passage, or their arrival. When once they entered the Pacific, they were lost, as it were, and forgotten. Among the many legends and traditions still existing in the Asiatic Archipelago of large and extensive migrations, occasioned by civil feuds, foreign invasion, or the desolating effects of earthquakes and eruptions, of pestilence and famine, it is impossible to fix upon any one as the one, or the ones, that pushed their fortunes into the Pacific. In the Java and Bugui legends we are told that such or such a prince left with a thousand followers or more to escape oppression, or evil of some kind or other, or to found a new home in a better land: and while not a few of those who found that home on the cis-Papuan side were duly reported in song and saga, not one of those who went beyond the Gilolo passage or Torres Straits, and found that home on the trans-Papuan side, remains upon the memory of those from whom they separated, or of those by whom they were displaced.

But the Polynesian legends and genealogies themselves, bearing upon this point, are extremely obscure, confused, and contradictory, and consequently difficult to bring into chronological order. The generally-received genealogies of most of the leading Polynesian groups lead up to *Wakea*, *Atea*, or *Makea*, and his wife *Papa*, as the earliest progenitors, the first chiefs of their respective groups. Other genealogies, like that of "Kumuhonua," bring the line of Hawaiian chiefs on Hawaiian soil up to *Hawaii-loa*, who is said to have first discovered and settled on these islands while on a fishing excursion, sailing east from his native home. Another, a Tahitian legend, goes also back of *Wakea* to *Tii*, whom it makes the first settler or discoverer of their group, and whom some Hawaiian legends claim as a brother of *Hawaii-loa*. But I have shown that the Hawaii-loa legend is probably the concentration of several originally distinct legends upon one person, and that if he of whom the legend speaks was the first discoverer and settler of the Hawaiian group, his place on the genealogy is a fatal and irreconcilable anachronism. Moreover, according to the legend, the Hawaiian group at the time of its discovery by *Hawaii-loa* consisted only of the two islands of Hawaii and Maui, the other islands of the group not having yet arisen from the sea; yet, before the death of the discoverer, they are not only made to rise up from the ocean, but to become wooded, watered, and fertile, and to have been allotted as the homes and principalities of his other children. The Wakea period is almost equally unsatisfactory and difficult a starting-point in computing the age of the Polynesian race in the Pacific. Between the Hawaiian genealogies alone, which lead back to Wakea from the present time, there is a difference between fifty-seven generations on the shortest, and seventy on the longest, a difference representing a period of about 400 years. There may be lacunas on the shorter line ; I am morally sure that there are interpolations on the longer. The latter would represent the year 230 B.C. as a medium year, the former the year 160 A.C. Yet admitting the high antiquity of the Wakea and Papa legends, it is obvious from the legends themselves that the islands now held by the Polynesian race were already peopled in the time of Wakea, and that too by people of his own race and kindred. When or how that people arrived is now an absolute blank. They may have been waifs, they may have been colonists from the eastern fringe of the Polynesian area in the Asiatic Archipelago, but of their traditions or their descent not a vestige remains. The Wakea period eclipsed or obscured all previous movements or migrations in an easterly direction.

The Wakean era, however, was undoubtedly one of great disturbance, displacement, and change in the ancient Polynesian homesteads. The very fact that so many of the principal tribes have retained his legend, though under different forms, and have attempted to localise him and his wife on their own groups, proves to me that he was anterior to, or at least contemporary with, some great popular movement preceding or attending the first considerable exodus into the Pacific, the memory of which was linked to his name, and thus handed down to posterity. His wars with *Lihaula*, his brother; his wars with *Kaneia-Kumuhonua*, in which he was conquered, driven out of the land and fled over the sea, though he is said to have recovered his kingdom afterwards; his changes in the religious and social institutions of the people, or which have been ascribed to him; all point to an area of unrest, tribal if not ethnic displacement and material modifications among the Polynesian forefathers, but still occurring in some common country, ere the original stream of migration had divided itself over the different Pacific groups where the legend is still preserved.

Now this period of Wakea, counting on the shortest Hawaiian genealogy, corresponds with the commencement of the Malay Empire in the Indian Archipelago. In the year 76 A.D., according to Javanese historians, *Tritestra* invaded Java, and commenced those wars against the Rakshasas, the Polynesio-Cushite pre-Malay inhabitants, which ended in their subjugation, isolation, or expulsion throughout the Archipelago. Eighty years from that time bring us to the period of Wakea, and the same time possibly brought the Malays from Java and Sumatra, where they first set foot, to Timor, Gilolo, and the Philippines.

Taking this epoch, therefore, as the starting-point for the great exodus and general appearance of the Polynesian family in the Pacific, there is an interval of time of 900 to 1000 years in which to people the various islands and groups now held by that family, until we meet with the uncontested Hawaiian traditions which affirm that twenty-eight generations ago that group was already densely peopled by that family.

But twenty-eight generations only represent a period of somewhat less than 900 years, and within that period there is no distinct tradition or remembrance of the active state of the volcanoes on the leeward islands of the Hawaiian group, or of the upheavals and subsidences to which those islands have been subjected. Yet recent discoveries have established the fact that those islands were inhabited before their volcanoes had ceased their action and the land assumed its present form. The legends of *Pele, Hiaka,* and that family of demigods, it is true, would seem to infer the ancient Hawaiian belief that the leeward islands were inhabited while their volcanoes were still active; but the legend of *Pele* itself, in its application to the Hawaiian group, when critically considered, must be subsequent to the great commotion which prevailed among the Polynesian tribes about twenty-six or twenty-eight generations ago, and is rather a mythical attempt in after ages to explain the volcanic phenomena of the group, than an historical datum for their occurrence. The tone of the legend, its several associations, and especially the therein occurring prayer of *Malaehaakoa,* the *Kahu* or guard of *Hiaka,* bespeak its later composition from Southern materials recast in a Hawaiian mould.

It is impossible to judge the age of a lava flow by its appearance. Portions of the lava stream of 1840, flowing from the crater of Kilauea into Puna district, Hawaii, and thence to the sea, a distance of from sixteen to twenty miles, was in 1867 covered with a luxuriant vegetation; while older flows in Puna, of which no memory exists; while the last flow from Mount Hualalai in 1791–92, through Kekaha on the west of Hawaii; and while the flow near Keonioio in Honuaula, island of Maui, called *Hanakaie*, and which is by tradition referred back to the mythological period of *Pele* and her compeers—look as fresh and glossy to-day as if thrown out but yesterday. Geologically speaking, the leeward islands are the oldest of the group, but both on Oahu and on Molokai human remains have been found imbedded in lava flows of undoubted antiquity, and of whose occurrence no vestige of remembrance remains in the Hawaiian folklore.

In 1822 the first wells were dug in the city of Honolulu. They passed through some eight or ten feet of surface loam and underlying volcanic sand, when a coral bed of some eight feet in thickness was encountered and cut through, under which the fresh water was reached. In this coral formation were found embedded a human skull and sundry human bones.[1]

In 1858, in dredging the harbour of Honolulu, island of Oahu, near the new Esplanade, after scooping up and removing the mud and sand at the bottom of the harbour in about twenty feet of water, it was found that underneath this sand and mud was a pan of coral rock which it was necessary to break up and remove in order to obtain the required depth of water. This pan was of an average thickness of two feet, and beneath it was a thick couch of black volcanic sand, such as is found some four or five feet beneath the surface throughout the city, and evidently thrown out by the extinct crater of Punch-bowl-hill in some pre-traditional time. Embedded in this black sand, underneath the coral bed, was found the lower part or pointed end of an ancient spear or *Oo*, about three feet long; and near to it a rounded small stone, the size of a hen's egg and nearly its shape, of a red, close-grained, compact, and heavy lava, such as is not found in the Punch-bowl-hill formation or its vicinity. The broken spear speaks for itself, and shows that man passed over

[1] Hawaiian Club Papers, p. 3; Article, "Early Wells of Honolulu," by James Hunnewell. Boston, October 1868.

that spot by water or by land before the formation of that coral pan which now covers the bottom of the harbour and the adjoining reefs. What purposes the stone had subserved I am not prepared to say, unless it had been used for slings and dropped by the same hand or the same generation that dropped the spear. It bears no geological relation to the black sand around it, to the coral-rock above it, or to the extinct crater one and a quarter mile inland.[1]

In 1859 Mr. R. W. Meyer of Kalae, Molokai, found in the side of a cañon on his estate—some seventy feet below the surface rim of the upper level country, and among a stratum of volcanic mud, Creccia, clay and ashes of several feet in thickness—a human skull, whose every cavity was fully and compactly filled with the volcanic deposit surrounding it, as if it had been cast in a mould, evidently showing that the skull had been filled while the deposit was yet in a fluid state. As that stratum spreads over a considerable tract of land in the neighbourhood, at a varying depth beneath the surface of from ten to four hundred feet, and as the valleys and gulches, which now intersect it in numerous places, were manifestly formed by erosion —perhaps in some measure also by subsequent earthquake shocks—the great age of that human vestige may be reasonably inferred, though impossible to demonstrate within a period of one or five hundred years preceding the coherent traditional accounts of that island.

Hawaiian traditions on Hawaiian soil, though valuable as national reminiscences, more or less obscured by the lapse of time, do not go back with any historical precision much more than twenty-eight generations from the present, or, say 840 years. Within that period the harbour and neighbouring coast-line of Honolulu have remained nearly

---

[1] The writer was present when these articles were dug up from beneath the coral, and deposited them in the Library of Excelsior Lodge, No. 1, I. O. O. F., no public museum existing in Honolulu at the time.

what they now are, nor has any subsidence sufficient to account for the formation of that coral bed beneath the city and its harbour, or of subsequent upheaval, or of any eruption from the Punch-bowl-hill crater, been retained on the memory of those twenty-eight generations.

Among the Hawaiian genealogies now extant, I am, for reasons which will hereafter appear, disposed to consider the *Haloa* or *Hoohokukalani-Nanaulu-Maweke* line as the most reliable. It numbers fifty-six generations from *Wakea* to the present time; twenty-nine from *Wakea* to and including *Maweke*, and twenty-seven from *Maweke* until now. Fifty-six generations, at the recognised term of thirty years to a generation, make 1680 years from now (1870) up to *Wakea*, the recognised progenitor and head of most of the Southern and Eastern Polynesian branches, and brings his era at about A.D. 190, which would in a great measure correspond with the invasion and spread of the Hindu-Malay family in the Asiatic Archipelago. But the first thirteen names on the *Haloa* line, to *Nanaulu*, are now allowed to have been shared, partially if not wholly, with the Marquesan and Tahitian branches of the Polynesian family, possibly also by the Samoan, though I have not now the means of ascertaining. These, then, must have existed elsewhere, and been introduced by the pre-Maweke occupants of the Hawaiian group, which would leave sixteen generations, or about five hundred years, in which to discover and people this group previous to the era of *Maweke* and his contemporaries, the *Paumakua* of Oahu, the *Kuhiailani* of Hawaii, the *Puna* family of chiefs on Kauai, the *Hua* family on Maui, the *Kamauaua* family on Molokai, and others renowned in the legends and songs of the people. By which of these sixteen generations, from *Nanaulu* down to *Maweke*, these islands were settled upon, there is nothing positively to show. The historical presumption, however, would indicate *Nanaulu*, the first of these sixteen, as the epoch of such settlements; and there still exists a Hawaiian tradition concerning his grandson *Pehekeula,* who was a chief on Oahu.

The first thirteen generations just referred to, from *Wakea* to *Nanaulu,* would thus represent the period of arrival and sejour on the Fiji group, and subsequent dispersion over the Pacific. Probably the greater portion of those generations passed away on the Fiji group, for it is otherwise inconceivable how so much of Polynesian language and Polynesian folklore could have been incorporated on the Fijian. And when the expulsion from there took place, several streams of migration issued simultaneously, or nearly so, to the Samoan, Tonga, Tahiti, and other eastward and northward groups. The Marquesas group could be reached from Tahiti in a straight direction, through the trade-winds, and the Hawaiian from the Marquesas, as well as from the Samoan, by taking advantage of the north-east and south-east trade-winds. Whether the expulsion from the Fiji covered one year or fifty years, it does not necessarily follow, as some ethnologists are inclined to hold, that the Polynesians departed *en masse* either to Tonga or the Samoan group; and after an indefinite period of residence there, and when population had become redundant, portions of it again moved eastward to Tahiti; and after another indefinite period, moved northward to the Marquesas, and so on; lastly, to the Hawaiian group. It is natural, and hence more probable, that the Polynesian settlements scattered over the Fiji group were attacked separately and successively, and that each chieftain, as necessity compelled, fled with his family and followers in this or that direction, according as the state of the winds and the season of the year made it most favourable to go. Many such parties, doubtless, made for the same group, and, finding the land already occupied by previous refugees, continued their course to the eastward and northward, until they found some convenient locality, where they finally established themselves permanently. The Polynesian legends would seem to support this latter proposition. While it may be an open question whether the Tahitians came by the way of Samoa or direct from Fiji, Tahitian legends claim that one *Tii* was the first ancestor of Tahitian chiefs on Tahitian soil. Subsequent generations elevated him to the position of a demi-god and grandson of *Taaroa*, the southern god *par excellence* of a later creed. But Hawaiian legends claim this same *Tii* or *Kii*—who was the last of the thirteen from *Wakea* that lived elsewhere than on the Hawaiian group—as the father of *Nanaulu*, with whom Hawaiian aristocracy on Hawaiian soil commences; while his brother *Ulu* remained at the south, and became the ancestor of that enterprising race of chiefs who six hundred years later overran the Pacific, from the Tonga group to the Hawaiian, and who gave rise to an era of commotion and unrest among the Polynesian tribes, the memory whereof is vividly retained in the Hawaiian folklore.

With due reservation, therefore, regarding any light that may hereafter be shed on pre-Wakean voyages and settlements by Polynesians in the Pacific, we arrive at the following leading propositions as chronological signposts—approximately, at least—of Polynesian migrations to and in the Pacific:—

1st. At the close of the first and during the second century of the present era the Polynesians left the Asiatic Archipelago and entered the Pacific, establishing themselves on the Fiji group, and thence spreading to the Samoan, Tonga, and other groups eastward and northward.

2d. During the fifth century A.D. Polynesians settled on the Hawaiian Islands, and remained there, comparatively unknown, until—

3d. The eleventh century A.D., when several parties of fresh emigrants from the Marquesas, Society, and Samoan groups arrived at the Hawaiian islands, and, for the space of five or six generations, revived and maintained an active intercourse with the first-named groups; and—

4th. From the close of the above migratory era, which

may be roughly fixed at the time of *Laa-mai-kahiki* and his children, about twenty-one generations ago, Hawaiian history runs isolated from the other Polynesian groups, until their re-discovery by Captain Cook in 1778.

I have thus attempted to clear the path by which men of more varied knowledge and greater acquirements than myself may travel with increased facility, and restore the Polynesian race to its proper place in the world's history. The ancient folklore at this end of the road unmistakeably points to its former connection with those grand old-world peoples, the Arians and Cushites, of whom until the last century, we hardly knew anything more than the names. It is for the savans of Europe and America to clear the other end of the road, and the more light they can throw upon those ancient races, the more numerous will be the points of affinity between them and the Polynesians.

Hawaiian history, during the first period above referred to, is naturally merged in that of the entire stock which emigrated to the Pacific. Whether the dialectical and other differences which distinguish the Hawaiians from the Southern and Western groups, and each group from the other, existed as already formed tribal characteristics at the time of the migration, or were developed afterwards through dispersion and isolation, there is nothing positive to determine. They are probably owing to both conditions. The same dialectical differences are still recognisable among their pre-Malay congeners in the Asiatic Archipelago, spite of the corrupting influences to which they have been subjected from Malay, Arab, and Chinese intermixture. These differences, then, must have been older than the first dispersion into the Pacific, though they may have been hardened and deepened by subsequent events. I am thus led to infer that at a period, which, for reference sake, I will call the Wakean period, a number of expeditions, impelled by the pressure of the Malay conquests, left their ancient homes on the eastern border of the Asiatic Archipel, and proceeding eastward on both sides of the Papuan Archipel, met on the Fiji group, and thence spread to the eastward, southward, and northward. And such I take it is the tenor of Polynesian folklore when critically studied and properly collated.

In the Northern and Eastern groups the names of places which coincide with, and evidently were called after, local names in their ancient habitats, are to a remarkable extent drawn from the northern portion of the Asiatic Archipelago, the Moluccas, Celebes, Borneo; whereas the South-eastern groups of Polynesia show an equal preference for names drawn from the southern portion of the above Archipel, the Banda islands, Timor, &c., while both streams unite in, and refer to, the more western islands and countries beyond as a common source for their local nomenclature.

In several of the Hawaiian legends respecting Wakea, he is said to have been chief over a country called *O-lolo-i-mehani*. This word is composed of the prefix *O*, the name *lolo*, and the epithet *mehani*. That *lolo* and the reference to it as the western home of Wakea point to that one of the Moluccas which by Spanish, Dutch, and English navigators is variously called *Gi-lolo*, *Ji-lolo*, *Dji-lolo*, and *I-lolo*, I think there is little doubt. The epithet *mehani* is now obsolete, and its meaning forgotten in the Hawaiian dialect, and I think, but am not sure, in the other Polynesian dialects.[1] But in the Amblaw dialect, one of the

---

[1] In Raiatea, of the Society group, there is a mountain called *Mehani*, where the ghosts of the dead were said to go. That mountain, like so many other places in Polynesia, may have been a namesake of some older locality, though its application as a residence for departed spirits might indicate a derivation from the Polynesian (Hawaiian) *hani*, with prefix *mahani*, "to step lightly, to graze, or just to touch, pass quickly through the air, to disappear, vanish." Epithets of places may vary in different ages and under different conditions, and ¡whether the legendary *Mehani* allies itself to the Amblaw or Polynesian signification, there can be no doubt of the identification of the traditional *O-lolo* with the modern *Gi-lolo*.

Bandas, south of Buru, the word still remains, and means "red;" and in Ceram (Ahtiago) *la-hanin*, "red," is evidently the same word. But all the Polynesian tribes invested the red colour with special dignity as a mark of royalty and pre-eminence, and as such it was a most proper epithet for the largest and probably dominant island of the Molucca group.

In the legend of Hawaii-loa and his descendants, *Ka Oupe-Alii*, the grandmother of Wakea's wife *Papa*, is said to have been a princess from *O-lolo-i-mehani*. Other legends of Wakea mention that his father *Kahiko* lived in *O-lalo-waia ;*[1] others again give Wakea a land, which they call *Hihiku*, as his residence ; and Hawaiian commentators on these legends suggest that *O-lolo-i-mehani* was the island of Nukahiwa, Marquesas group, or some place upon it, and that *O-lalo-waia* was some place on Oahu, Hawaiian group, saying that such was one of the ancient names for Oahu, or a portion of it, as *Kana-wai-lua-lani* was an ancient name for the island of Kauai. But a critical comparison of the legends referring to Wakea brings out the fact that he probably never set foot on either Marquesan or Hawaiian soil; and that, the names being given by the earlier settlers, the process is both easy and intelligible by which the priests and bards of aftertimes transferred and localised on their own groups the hero with whose names those places were connected in the ancient legends. In another Hawaiian legend the islands of that group are said to have been created and named by Wakea and Papa. In this cosmogony Wakea is said to have. had illicit intercourse with a woman called *Hina*, and she brought forth the island which Wakea named *Molokai*. In revenge for this unfaithfulness, Papa cohabited with a man called *Lua*, and gave birth to the island of *Oahu ;* and in commemoration of this double adultery, the two islands have ever after preserved the sobriquets arising from their birth, viz., *Molokai-Hina*

[1] See p. 17.

and *Oahu-a-Lua.* Under the crudeness and coarseness of the legend we may discover the lingering reminiscence of a geographical and historical fact, namely, the ancient connection between the *O-lolo* or *Gi-lolo* chief Wakea and the neighbouring island of *Morotai*, after which the Hawaiian Molokai was undoubtedly named. The reference to that island by that name puts the identity of *O-lolo* and *Gi-lolo* beyond much doubt. And the connection of Papa with *Oahu* points to the central and probably once powerful state of *Ouadjon* in Celebes, and recalls the legend which makes Papa a lineal and tabued descendant of *Hawaii-loa*, and claims that Wakea was inferior to her in royal dignity.

In the legend of *Pupuhuluana* the relative position of *O-lolo-i-mehani* is farther indicated. Papa, under her other name of *Haumea*, had caused a fearful drought and famine to devastate not only her own island of Oahu, but also Kauai, Maui, and Hawaii, and she herself had retired to a land frequently mentioned in the legends by the name of *Nuu-meha-lani.* In this distress some people of Oahu fitted out an expedition to procure food from *O-lolo-i-mehani,* "the land of Makalii," *ka aina o Makalii,* which land was to the eastward of Oahu.

With the exception of the allusion already referred to, of *Wakea* having been driven out of his country by a hostile chief, and fleeing over the ocean, and afterwards conquering his enemy and recovering his country, there is no Hawaiian legend that I have become acquainted with which refers to any great migration performed by *Wakea* himself, or by any of his children. Most of the legends which do not treat *Wakea* and *Papa* as gods, or endowed with superhuman powers, assume that they were born and bred on the Hawaiian group; and those who do admit and refer to their foreign origin, yet give no account of their leaving that foreign home for the Pacific, or how they or their descendants arrived here.

Though the Marquesan legends are more explicit than any others upon the migrations of their tribes, and probably the entire Polynesian family, and though one of the migrations preserved in their legends bears the name of *Atea*, there is nothing to connect him with the *Wakea* of the Hawaiian genealogies. It is probable, moreover, that the branch of the Polynesian family to which the Marquesans originally belonged took its departure from *Vevau* or *Wawao*, *i.e.*, Timor, and not from Gilolo, and thus came by Torres Straits and the southern passage into the Pacific. They left the marks of their passage in the still retained names of *Nuu-mea*, near Port de France, in New Caledonia; in *Ua-'ho*, a bay in Lifu, one of the Loyalty isles; in *Uea* or *Ua-ea*, one of those islands; and in a point of land or cape on *Uea*, called *Fae-a-Ue*, "the house of Ua." That name of *Ua*, whoever or whatever he was, meets us again in the Marquesas group, *Ua-pou*, and *Ua-huka* or *Ua-hunga*, according to the harder or softer pronunciation of the natives. A greater acquaintance with the coast-line and the interior of the Papuan groups, and with the people generally, would no doubt greatly increase these vestiges of Polynesian passage and sejour. On the islands of *Vate* and *Mele*, of the New Hebrides, the numeral system is identical with the Polynesian of the earlier dialects, retaining both the *s* and the *r* sounds; and other indications demonstrate the Polynesian presence and, probably, partial absorption in the Papuan race of this group, or, rather, these portions of the group.

The two Marquesan accounts of the wanderings of their people ere they reached their present abodes, while they entirely agree in the earlier and later stages of the journey, materially disagree in the middle portions. Apparently they are the representations or reminiscences of two tribes or branches of the same family, travelling together, or following each other, over the earlier portions of the journey, then separating for several stages, and finally uniting again, or striking the same trail, so to say, until they arrived at the Marquesas group. These itineraries are called by the principal personages whom they represent, or whom the travellers claimed as their ancestors, the *Atea* and the *Tani* migrations. Here are their way-bills :—

ATEA ACCOUNT.			TANI ACCOUNT.		
From *Take-hee-hee* to			From *Take-hee-hee* to		
„	*Ahee-tai*	„	„	*Ahee-take*	„
„	*Ao-nuu*	„	„	*Ao-nuu*	„
„	*Papa-nui*	„	„	*Papa-nui*	„
„	*Take-hee*	„	„	*Take-hee*	„
			„	*Ho-vau*	„
			„	*Nini-oe*	„
			„	*Ao-ewa*	„
„	*Ani-take*	„	„	*Ani-take*	„
			„	*Ho-vau*	„
„	*Hawaii*	„	„	*Vevau*	„
„	*Tu-uma*	„	„	*Tu-uma*	„
„	*Mea-ai*	„	„	*Mea-ai*	„
„	*Fiti-nui*	„	„	*Fiti-nui*	„
„	*Mata-hou*	„	„	*Mata-hou*	„
„	*Tona-nui*	„	„	*Tona-nui*	„
„	*Mau-ewa*	„	„	*Mau-ewa*	„
„	*Pi ina*	„	„	*Pi ina*	„

Thence " over the ocean" to

„	*Ao-maama*	„	*Ao-maama*

Their name for the Marquesas Islands.

The chant or legendary poem which accompanies the *Atea* account appears to be imperfect or partly forgotten. It gives short and passing descriptions of the eight first stations, then passes over *Fiti-nui* in silence, then notices *Mata-hou*, but takes no note of *Tona-nui* and *Mau-ewa*. I have seen no chant explanatory of the *Tani* migration. If any such exists among the Marquesans, it is to be hoped that some resident gentlemen of leisure and archæological predilections may collect and publish them before the priests of the heathen time and the old people generally, from whom they may be collected, have become extinct. From the chants to which I have had access, through the politeness of Professor W. D. Alexander, and which have been collected and carefully translated by Mr. T. C. Lawson, a resident on Hiwaoa or St. Dominica island, the following prosaic and historical *resumé* of the migrations of the *Take*, as the Marquesans are called in the chants, may be presented :—

Take-hee-hee, or *Ahee-tai*, as another legend calls it, was the oldest original home of which the "Takes" had any remembrance. It is described as a mountain-land with a settlement or inhabited district at *Tai ao*, another at *Meini-taha-hua*, and another near the water (lake or river) of *Nuu-teea*. Wars and commotions having arisen among themselves, the people were driven out of this land and migrated to—

Ao-nuu, which is described in the chant as

> *He henua hiwaoa mei Ahee-tai,*
> *He henua hiwahiwa Ao-mai.*

> " A beautiful country far from Ahee-tai,
> A beautiful country is Ao-mai."

While dwelling in *Ao-nuu* a chief ruled over the country whose name was *Faaina*. After him came *Anu-o-Aatuna*. After that the chief *Atea* killed *Umai*, by which civil wars arose, and *Atea* and many other " Takes " were driven out and obliged to seek new homes in other lands. They then migrated to

Papa-nui, which seems to have been reached by sea, for a legend relates that the chief *Tiki-Matohe* and his wife *Hina* left *Aonuu* with their followers and outfit of pigs, fowls, and fruit in a double canoe, and thus, with a favouring wind, arrived at *Papa-nui*. This land is described as a high table-land, surrounded by the sea. It appears also that the *Tani* branch of the family arrived at *Papa-nui* after *Atea*, for one of the chants mentions his cordial reception as one of the same family as *Atea*, and how, for his entertainment, pigs were brought from *Ao-tumi*, and turtle from *Ono-tapu*, and fowls from below *Ii-Hawa* and *Nuu-teea*. The next stopping-place was

Take-hee, which is said to

> *Tu hiwaoa eeke eeke i te hee.*

Here the two branches seem to have separated, the *Tani* legend mentioning five lands not visited, or at least recorded by the *Atea* legend, while the latter makes only two stopping-places between *Take-hee* and *Tu-uma*, where the *Tani* branch seems to have joined it again, or come in upon its track. But while thus separated the *Atea* branch visits *Hawa-ii*, which the legend calls

Tai mamao uta-oa tu te Ii.

" The distant sea or region, far inland stand the volcanoes." The *hupe, kohanui, mio,* and *temanu* trees are said by one chant to have been growing there in abundance. It is also said to have been subject to tremendous hurricanes, followed by famines. Two of the chants give rather particular descriptions of the *Hawa-ii* remembered by the Marquesans. One mentions five headlands or capes, *Fititona-tapu, Pua, Ao, Ao-ena,* and *Ao-oma,* and one mountain which it calls *Mouna-tika-oe.* The other chant, of evidently later origin, mentions a mountain called *Mouna-oa,* which is said to have been raging, burning (*Ii*) on top, and served as a landmark for *Tupaa* when he left Hawa-ii with his family and followers.

The order in which this *Hawa-ii* appears on the Marquesan *carte de voyage,* and other considerations, make it impossible to identify it with the North Pacific Hawaiian group, or even with the *Sawa-ii* of the Samoan group. The constant and emphatic expression of all these legends, that the wanderers came from " below," *mei iao mai,* from the direction towards which the wind was blowing, and were always going " up," *iuna,* in the direction from which the wind was blowing, makes it evident that the Hawa-ii to which they refer must have been situated to the westward or " below " the Fiti, Viti, or Fiji group, from which, with one intermediate station, whose name I am not now able to identify, they proceeded to the Tonga group, *Tonanui,* and thence to the Society group, or *Mau-ewa,* which name I consider to be the same as *Ma-ewa,* a district on the island of Huahine, thence to *Pi ina*, now not known by that name, and thence the wanderers, still going up on the wind, crossed the ocean—*una te tai*—to the Marquesas or *Te Ao-maama*.

That the Marquesans in aftertimes visited the Hawaiian group there can be little doubt, and it is quite probable that the whole or a portion of the early Hawaiian settlers came from or passed through the Marquesas group; but that the *Hawa-ii* of the Marquesan *carte de voyage* is the North Pacific Hawaii is not credible under any proper analysis of the legend. It was, then, to the westward of the Fiji group, and, according to the legend, removed by two stages. But one of these is said in the chant to be "near to Hawa-ii"—

Te Tuuma i Hawa-ii tata ae,

while the situation of the other *Mea-ai* is not indicated.

We thus find ourselves again in face of a western *Hawa-ii*, far west of the Fiji group; but whether it is the same Hawaii to which the Hawaiian legends refer there are no means to decide. Probably it was not. The *Hawa, Sawa,* and *Djawa* name and its composites were not uncommon appellations of island places and districts throughout the Asiatic Archipelago, and some one of these may have been the *Hawa-ii* in question.

Here the *Tani* account of the migrations may offer an indication at least of the direction in which this *Hawa-ii* is to be sought for. Tracing that account backward from *Ao-maama* and beyond the Fiji group, through places identical with the *Atea* account, we find that *Vevau* is the station just previous to *Tuuma*, and not *Hawa-ii*, as the other account calls it. I have already shown that the *Vevau* referred to in the earlier Marquesan legends corresponds, in all probability, to Timor of the Asiatic Archipelago; and thus understood the *Tani* account renders the journey both intelligible and credible. Whether *Hawa-ii* in those ancient times was another name for *Vevau* or Timor, or whether in the *Atea* account it is used as a representative name for the Asiatico-Polynesian area and the eastern and last portion especially, it is now impossible to say.

The current traditional belief among the Southern Marquesans, that they came from *Hawaii*, which in ordinary parlance has become synonymous with "the regions below, the invisible world,"—and the similarly current belief among the Northern Marquesans, that they came from *Vavao*, an island "below," *i.e.*, to westward of, Nukahiwa,—point to the earlier legend and its two migrations, that of *Atea* and that of *Tani*. And dialectical differences between the northern and southern portions of the group confirm the fact of a double origin; whether from two originally distinct tribes, or at two widely separate epochs, I am unable to determine. Mr. Hale, in the "Ethnographical portion of the United States Exploring Expedition," p. 127, inclines to the conclusion that the Marquesans were colonists from Sawaii of the Samoan group. I think it quite probable and very natural that a considerable portion of the Marquesans did come from the Samoa, either direct or *via* the Society group; but the legendary *Hawa-ii* and *Vevau* of the Marquesans lay unquestionably farther west than either the Samoan or the Tonga group.

There is no time, or attempt at specification of time, connected with these Marquesan legends; and the conformity of names in the legends with those on the only Marquesan genealogy which I have seen will not even warrant a conjecture. A better acquaintance with, and a critical comparison of, the Marquesan genealogies still extant might furnish some approximative data for determining the period of these migrations.[1]

1 Mr. Hale of the United States Exploring Expedition under Commodore Wilkes, in the section of Ethnology and Philology, p. 128, quoting from Commodore Porter, states that the chief *Ke-ata-nui* of Nukahiwa was the eighty-eighth generation from *Oataia* (*Atea*) and his wife *Ananoona*, who came from *Vavao* and brought bread-fruit, sugar-cane, and other plants with them. Eighty-eight generations, at thirty years each, make 2640 years back of 1812-14 when Commodore Porter visited the Marquesans. I have little doubt that the *Ke-ata-nui* genealogy was as inflated as the Hawaiian genealogies of the *Ulu-Hema* line, by admixture with Tahitian, Samoan, and possibly Tongan collateral issues.

I am very little acquainted with the Samoan traditions and legendary lore, and am unable, therefore, to state what reference, if any, the ancient legends of that group may make to the Polynesian migrations into the Pacific, the time of their occurring, or whence they started.

The name of the Samoan group, however, affords, in my opinion, some indication of the extraction of the people who named and inhabit it. The group is called by the natives *Samoa*, in the Tonga and other dialects *Hamoa*. The early Spanish visitors to the Molucca islands give the ancient names of Gilolo as "Maurica" and "Bato-chine," and mention the middle part of Gilolo as being called *Gamoca-nora*. The affinity or identity of *Gamoca*, as the Spaniards pronounced it, and *Hamoa* or *Samoa* is intelligible, and no doubt will be unquestioned by Polynesian scholars;[1] but the epithet *nora* I am unable to explain, unless it connects with the Polynesian (Hawaiian) *noa*, meaning "constantly burning, unquenchable as a volcano," and thus referring to the former active state of the volcanoes on Gilolo.

In the absence of positive evidence to the contrary, it is therefore extremely probable that the Samoans came from the Gilolo group and to the north of the Papuan Archipel; and with them, or by the same route, came the Hawaiians,

---

[1] In the account of the United States Exploring Expedition, Com. Wilkes, sect. Ethnology and Philology, Mr. H. Hale, p. 120, proposes that Samoa is a Malay word and adopted by the Navigator Islanders to designate their group; its meaning being "all," *scil.* of that group, and equivalent to the American expression of "Union" when speaking of the United States as a whole, united country. He intimates that it must have been of later adoption, and that the earlier emigrants from the Samoas only knew that group by the name of its largest island, Sawaii. With due deference to so able and careful a writer, I would differ from the Malay extraction and the later adoption of the name. It has been shown, I hope, in previous pages, that the Polynesian owes nothing to the Malay *per se*, least of all the names of its places and islands. As to the later adoption of the name by the Samoans themselves, I think it questionable, inasmuch as the name was known not only to the Tongans, who, however, may be considered as comparative neighbours, but also to the Tahitians and the still farther distant Hawaiians, the latter of whom still designate a land on the island of Maui by the name of Hamoa.

possibly also the Society Islanders; while the Marquesans and the Tongans came by the southern route and Torres Straits, the former from Timor, the latter from Buru. From what has been already said, it is equally probable that some portion of the Fiji group was the primary rendezvous of these two, three, or more streams of migration, and that, whether expelled or leaving voluntarily, a new division took place there according to tribal, dialectical, or other affinities and predilections, some seeking new homes in the north-east, others in the east and south-east. And it has been shown by one genealogy at least that this ethnic movement embraced a period of from seven to thirteen generations previous to the forty-third recognised, and generally considered as authentic, ancestor of the present Hawaiian chief families.

. Of these thirteen names born on most of the Hawaiian genealogies very little is known that throws any historical light on that period. David Malo, a Hawaiian gentleman, educated by the earlier missionaries, states in his " Hawaiian Antiquities," that many well-informed people of the olden time maintained that the six first generations after *Wakea* still lived in *O-lolo-i-mehani.* Be that as it may, it is evident that the *Tahiti* mentioned in these earlier legends,—to and from which *Papa*, Wakea's wife, made so many voyages, where she took other husbands and had other children, from whom the Polynesian Tahitians claim their descent, and where she finally died, —could not have been the Tahiti of the South Pacific, but must be sought for in some of the islands of the Asiatic Archipelago. It is presumable that, when in after ages the intercourse between the Polynesian tribes was renewed, the scenes of those early legends was shifted and modified to suit the requirements of the new area which they then occupied; and thus *O-lolo-i-mehani* became located on Oahu of the Hawaiian group, while the *Tahiti* of the legend was transposed to Tahiti of the Georgian or Society group.

Before proceeding further, as we are entering on peculiarly Hawaiian domain, it may be proper in this place to
insert the various genealogies current among the Hawaiians, so that the reader may understand the force of
our subsequent criticism and attempt at correction. We
will commence with the different genealogies which, starting from the first man, lead down to *Wakea* and *Papa ;*
then those which, starting from *Wakea* and *Papa*, lead
down to the present time.

THE GENEALOGY OF KUMUHONUA.

The letter *k.* means *kame* or husband ; *w.* means *wahine* or wife.

1	Kumuhonua, *k.*	Lalo-Honua, *w.*
2	Laka, or Kolo-i-ke Ao, *k.*	Papa ia Laka, *w.*
	Kulu-Ipo, or Kolo-i-ke Po, or Ahu, *k.*	
	Kapili, or Kaiki-ku-a-Kane, *k.*	
3	Ka Moolewa, *k.*	Olepuu-Honua, *w.*
4	Maluapo, *k.*	Laweao, *w.*
5	Kinilau-a-Mano, *k.*	Upolu, *w.*
6	Halo, *k.*	Kini Ewalu, *w.*
7	Ka Mano Lani, *k.*	Ka Lani-a-Noho, *w.*
8	Ka Maka o ka Lani, *k.*	Ka Moo Lani, *w.*
9	Ka Lei Lani, *k.*	Opua Hiki, *w.*
10	Ka La Lii, *k.*	Ke Ao Melemele, *w.*
11	Haule, *k.*	Loaaio, *w.*
12	Imi Nanea, *k.*	Imi Walea, *w.*
13	Nuu, or Kahinalii, *k.*	

2	Kapili, *k.*	Nohi-nohi-nohele, *w.*
3	Ka Wa Kahiko, *k.*	Luhiluhi Heleae, *w.*
4	Ka Wa Kupua, *k.*	Kahiko-o-Lupa, *w.*
	Kahiko Lei Kau, *w.*	
	Kahiko Lei Ulu, *w.*	
5	Kahiko Lei Honua, *k.*	Nahae-i-Kua, *w.*
	Hakoakoa Lau Leia, *k.*	
	Kupo, *w.*	
6	Ke Ake Nui, *k.*	Ka Ipo Lau Leia-i Heleua, *w.*
		Kalani-Hoóhonua, *w.*
7	Mauli Neweneweloa, *k.*	
	Ke Olai Maolina a kane.	Muo Lani, *w.*

8	Ka Lei Lani, *k.*	Apaiki, *w.*
9	Hauli i Honua, *k.*	Laa-a, *w.*
10	Ka La Lili, *k.*	Ke Ao Melemele, *w.*
11	Lalo-o-Kona, *k.*	Ka Mole Aniani, *w.*
12	Hoo Nanea, *k.*	Hoo-Walea, *w.*
13	Nuu or Kahinalii, *k.*	

13	Nuu, *k.*	Lili-noe, *w.*
14	Nalu Akua, *k.* Nalu Hoohua, *k.* Nalu Manamana, *k.*	Ka Ali Akea, *w.*
15	Naeheehe Lani, *k.*	Kawowo-i-Lani Hikimoe, *w.*
16	Ka Hakui Moku Lei, *k.*	Ke kai Holana, *w.*
17	Ke kai Lei, *k.*	Nalu Lei, *w.*
18	Ka Haku Lani, *k.*	Moeana-i-lalo, *w.*
19	Hele i Kahiki Ku, *k.*	Hooneenee i ka Hikina, *w.*
20	Ka Noelo Hikina, *k.*	Hala Po Loa, *w.*
21	Hele i ka Moo Loa, *k.*	Kawehe'a'ao, *w.*
22	Ke Au Apaapaa, *k.*	Ke Au Laelae, *w.*
23	Lua Nuu, or Kanehoalani, *k.*	

14	Nalu Manamana, *k.*	Manamana-ia-Kuluea, *w.*
15	Ka Io Lani, *k.*	Kawowo-i-Lani, *w.*
16	Hakui Moku, *k.*	Lu-i-ka Po, *w.*
17	Nunu Lani, or Imi Lani, *k.*	Pili Po, *w.*
18	Honua o ka Moku, *k.*	Anahulu ka Po, *w.*
19	Neenee Papu Lani, *k.*	Wehe ka Po, *w.*
20	Hele i kua Hikina, *k.*	Hala ka Po, *w.*
21	Hele Moo Loa, *k.*	Ka Wanaao, *w.*
22	Ke Ao Apaapaa, *k.*	Ke Ao Laelae, *w.*
23	Lua Nuu, or Kanehoalani, *k.*	

23	Lua Nuu, *k.*	Ahu, *w.* Mee Hiwa, Hakulani, Po Malie, *w.*
24	Ku Nawao, *k.* Kalani Mene Hune, *k.* Aholoholo, *k.*	Ka Mole Hikina Kuahine, *w.*
25	Ka Imi Puka Ku, Kinilau-a-Mano, *k.*	Ka Hooluhi Kupaa, *w.*

Ka Hekili Paapaaina, *k.*
Ke Apaapa Nuu, *k.*
Ke Apaapa Lani, *k.*
Nakeke i Lani, *k.*
Kahiki Apaapa Nuu, *k.*
Kahiki Apaapa Lani, *k.*
Nakolokolo Lani, *k.*
Nakeke Honua, *k.*
Ku i ka Ewa Lani, *k.*
Ka Uwai o ka Moku, *k.*
Hoopale Honua, *k.*

26 Newenewe Maolina i Kahiki-ku, *k.*   Nowelo Hikina, *w.*
27 Kaokao Kalani, *k.*   Heha ka Moku, *w.*
28 Aniani Ku, *k.*   Ke kai Pahola, *w.*
29 Aniani Kalani, *k.*   Ka Mee Nui Hikina, *w.*
30 Hawaii Loa, or Ke kowa i Hawaii, *k.*   Hualalai, *w.*
   Kii, *k.*
   Kana Loa, *k.*
   Laa Kapu, *k.*
   Maui-ai-Alii, *k.*
31 Oahu, *w.*   Ku Nui ai a ke Akua, *k.*
   Kauai, *k.*
32 Ku Nui Akea, *k.*   Kahiki Walea, *w.*
33 Ke Lii Alia, *k.*   Kahiki Alii, *w.*
34 Ke Milia, *k.*   Polohainalii, *w.*
35 Ke Lii Ku, or Eleeleualani, *k.* Ka Oupe Alii, *w.*
36 Ku Kalani Ehu, *k.*   Ka Haka ua koko, *w.*
37 *Papa Nui* Hanau Moku, *w.*   *Wakea, k.*

I have another genealogy from *Kumuhonua* to *Papa* and *Wakea*, purporting to be the genealogy followed by the ancient Hawaiian priests of the *Paao* line. That genealogy inserts ten generations between *Newenewe Maolina* and *Hawaii Loa*, Nos. 26 and 30, and thirty-four generations between *Hawaii Loa* and *Papa Nui*, Nos. 30 and 37 on the foregoing list. It is said to have been confirmed and approved by the late chiefess *Iuahine*, wife of *Kaoleioku*, the first born son of *Kamehameha I.*, and grandmother of the present high chiefess, Mrs. Pauahi Bishop; but it is evident at almost the first glance that, even if those ancient priests had correctly preserved the tradition of the number of links in this genealogical chain, yet the naming of them has been an entirely arbitrary operation in far subsequent times,—presenting more the appearance of a geographical list of lands and islands known to the compilers, personified and genealogically arranged, than a proper pedigree of genuine names. It is very probable that this last arrangement of the *Kumuhonua* genealogy was another of those curious interpolations made after that great Southern influx in the Hawaiian group, to which I have alluded in previous pages, and by the *Kahunas* or priests of that period and of those invaders.

The Genealogy of KUMU-ULI.

This genealogy was much praised by the ancient Hawaiian chiefs. It is quoted in the famous chant of *Kualii*, the warrior king of Oahu, and was recited in honour of *Keopuolani*, the wife of Kamehameha I., and who was a tabued scion of the Maui line of kings. It runs thus :—

	Kane.	Ukina-opiopio, *w.*
	Kanaloa.	
	Kauakahi.	
	Maliu.	
1	Hulihonua, *k.*	Keakahulilani, *w.*
	Laka, *k.*	
	Kamooalewa, *k.*	
	Maluakapo, *k.*	
2	Laka, *k.*	Kapapaiakele, *w.*
3	Kamooalewa, *k.*	Olepuukahonua, *w.*
4	Maluapo, *k.*	Lawekeao, *w.*
5	Kinilauamano, *k.*	Ulupalu or Upolu, *w.*
6	Halo, *k.*	Koniewalu, *w.*
7	Kamanonookalani, *k.*	Kalani a noho, *w.*
8	Kamakaoholani, *k.*	Kaehuaokalani, *w.*
9	Keohokalani, *k.*	Kaamookalani, *w.*
10	Kaleiokalani, *k.*	Kaopuahihi, *w.*
11	Kalalii, *k.*	Keaomele, *w.*
12	Haule, *k.*	Loaa, *w.*
13	Nanea, *k.*	Walea, *w.*
14	Nana Nuu, *k.*	Lalohana, *w.*

15	Lalokona.	Lalohoaniani, *w.*
16	Hanuapoiluna, *k.*	Hanuapoilalo, *w.*
17	Pokinikini, *k.*	Polehulehu, *w.*
18	Pomanomano, *k.*	Pohakoikoi, *w.*
19	Kupukupunuu, *k.*	Kupukupulani, *w.*
20	Kamoleokahonua.	Keaaokahonua, *w.*
21	Kapaiaokalani, *k.*	Kanikekaa, *w.*
22	Ohemoku, *k.*	Pinainai, *w.*
23	Mahulu, *k.*	Hiona, *w.*
24	Milipomea, *k.*	Hanahanaiau, *w.*
25	Hookumukapu, *k.*	Hoaono, *w.*
26	Luakahakona, *k.*	Niau, *w.*
27	Kahiko, *k.*	Kupulanakehau, *w.*
28	*Wakea, k.*	*Papa Nui, w.*

The correspondence between the fourteen first generations of this genealogy—with the exception No. 9, *Keoho,*
which in some versions is omitted—with the first thirteen
of the *Kumuhonua* genealogy is, to say the least, remarkable. But the introduction of the four divinities, *Kane,
Kanaloa, Kauakahi,* and *Maliu,* as the natural parents of
the first man *Hulihonua,* and as part and portion of a
human genealogy, is, according to my understanding of
Polynesian folklore, a clear indication that this genealogy
was compiled from pre-existing materials after the influx
of the southern element, about 800 years ago. The *Kumuhonua* legend draws a broad distinction between man and
his Maker, which this legend ignores. Its later origin is,
moreover, evidenced by the introduction of *Kanaloa,* the
great southern god of later times, although, as a compromise or a concession to the primary and comparatively
purer creed of the Hawaiians, he is placed in a secondary
position to *Kane.* After *Nuu, Nana-Nuu,* or *Kahinalii,*
this correspondence ceases, the *Kumu-uli* genealogy leading down to *Wakea,* whereas the other leads down to his
wife *Papa.*

THE GENEALOGY OF OPUKAHONUA.

1 { Opukahonua, k.   Lana, w.
   Lolomu, k.
   Mihi, k.

   { Kananamukumanao, k.
   Ohikimakaloa, w.
2 { Hekilikaaka, k.   Ohikimakaloa, w.
   { Nakolowailani, k.
   Ahulukaaala, w.

3 Mihi, k.   Ahulukaaala, w.
4 Kapuaululana, k.   Holani, w.
5 Kekamaluahaku, k.   Laamea, w.
6 Lanipipili, k.   { Laakeakapu, w.
                    Hinaimanau, w.

   { Lanioaka.
7 { Laakealaakona, k.   Kamaleilani, w.
8 Haulanuiakea, k.   Manau, w.
9 Kahaloalena, k.   Laumaewa, w.
10 Kahalolenaula, k.   { Kanehoalani, w.
                    Hinakului, w.
                    Kaihikapualamea, w.

11 { Kaiwilaniolua.   Kanehoalani, w.
11 { Kapumaweolani.   Haweaoku, w.
11 { Kukonalaa.   Kaenakulani, w.
12 { Kalaniwahine, k.   Malela, w.
 = { Manuiakane.
   Kalanipaumake.
13 { Kamakahiwa, k.   Loi, w.
13 { Makakaile, k.   Paweo, w.
13 { Makakailenuiaola, k. }
14 Kikenui a Ewa, k.   }   Ewa, w.
14 Kalanimanuia, k.   }
15 { Kahiko, k.   Kupulanakehau, w.
15 { Kupulanakehau, w.
15 { Kukalaniehu, k.   Kahakauakoko, w.
15 { Kahakauakoko, w.
16 *Wakea, k.*
16 *Papa, w.*

THE GENEALOGY OF KAPAPAIAKEA.

Quoted in the Chant of Kualii, the King of Oahu.

1 Kapapaiakea, *k.*	Kauhihi, *w.*	**Hinakapeau.**
2 Hinakapeau, *k.*	Ukinohunohu, *w.*	Ukinaopiopi.
3 Ukinaopiopi, *k.*	Moakuanana, *w.*	Kalei.
4 Kalei, *k.*	Keelekoha, *w.*	Kaiakea.
		{ Kamoanaakea.
		{ Hulukeeaea.
5 Kaiakea, *k.*	Kaehokumanawa, *w.*	{ Hauii.
		{ Hauee.
5 Kamoanakea, *k.*	Kauakahikuaana, *w.*	Kanehoalani.
Iwikauikauanui, *k.*	„ „	Hauinuinaholoholo.
5 Hulukeeaea, *k.*	Kahakuakea, *w.*	Hauiikaiapokahi.
6 Hauiikaiapokahi, *k.*	Wahineikapeakapu, *w.*	{ Uliuli.
		{ Maihea.
7 Maihea, *k.*	Kahakapolani, *w.*	{ Kaukeano.
		{ Mehameha.
7 Uliuli, *k.*	Niau, *w.*	Kahiko.
8 Kahiko, *k.*	Kupulanakehau, *w.*	Wakea.
9 *Wakea, k.*	*Papa-nui, w.*	

THE GENEALOGY OF WELAAHILANI.

1 Welaahilani, *k.*	Owe, *w.*	Kahiko.
2 Kahiko-Luamea, *k.*	Kupulanakehau, *w.*	{ Wakea, *k.*
		{ Lihauula, *k.*
		{ Makuu, *k.*
3 *Wakea, k.*	*Papa, w.*	

According to the genealogy called *Kumuulipo,* a woman called *Lailai* was the first person on earth, descended from *Po* or chaos. From her and her husband *Kealiiwahilani,* the rest of mankind were derived. Their son was *Kahiko,* the father of *Wakea.*

According to the tradition called *Puanue,* the creators of heaven and earth, and the progenitors of mankind, were *Kumukanikekaa* and her husband *Paialani.*

Among the various Hawaiian genealogies I consider the *Nanaulu* line as the most reliable and least affected by the interpolations and confusion introduced by the southern element so often referred to. It was extensively, almost exclusively, patronised by the Kauai and Oahu chiefs, and seldom referred to by the Maui,—hardly ever by the Hawaii chiefs. I will, therefore, commence with that and bring it down to the person of the present reigning sovereign Kalakaua. I would premise by saying that there exist two versions of the earlier portion of this genealogy, from *Wakea* to *Kii*, one descending from Wakea's son *Haloa*, the other from his daughter *Hoohokukalani*. The former was the most generally current of later times, but the latter appears to me to be the most archaic as well as the most trustworthy, for reasons which will appear when I come to treat of the *Ulu* line, and as the number of generations is the same on both, though the arrangement is somewhat different, I prefer to follow the latter in this earlier portion down to *Nana-ulu*.

THE NANA-ULU GENEALOGY.

1	Wakea, *k.*	Papa, *w.*	{ Haloa, *k.* { Hoohokukalani, *w.*
2	Hoohokukalani, *w.*	Manouluae, *k.*	Waia, *k.*
3	Waia, *k.*	Huhune, *w.*	Wailoa.
4	Wailoa, *k.*	Hikawaopualanea, *w.*	Kakaihili.
5	Kakaihili, *k.*	Haulani, *w.*	Kia.
6	Kia, *k.*	Kamole, *w.*	Ole.
7	Ole, *k.*	Haii, *w.*	Pupue.
8	Pupue, *k.*	Kamahele, *w.*	Manaku.
9	Manaku, *k.*	Hikohaale, *w.*	Nukahakoa.
10	Nukahakoa, *k.*	Koulamaikalani, *w.*	Luanuu.
11	Luanuu, *k.*	Kawaamaukele, *w.*	Kahiko.
12	Kahiko, *k.*	Kaea, *w.*	Kii.
13	Kii, *k.*	Hinakoula, *w.*	{ Nana-ulu. { Ulu.
14	Nanaulu, *k.*	Ulukou, *w.*	Nanamea.
15	Nanamea, *k.*	Puia, *w.*	Pehekeula.

16 Pehekeula, *k.*	Uluae, *w.*	Pehekemana.
17 Pehekemana, *k.*	Nanahapa, *w.*	Nanamua.
18 Nanamua, *k.*	Nanahope, *w.*	Nanaikeauhaku.
19 Nanaikeauhaku, *k.* Elehu, *w.*		Keaoa.
20 Keaoa, *k.*	Waohala, *w.*	Hekumu.
21 Hekumu, *k.*	Kumukoa, *w.*	Umalei.
22 Umalei, *k.*	Umaumanana, *w.*	Kalai.
23. Kalai, *k.*	Laikapa, *w.*	Malelewaa.
24 Malelewaa, *k.*	Pililohai, *w.*	Hopoe.
25 Hopoe, *k.*	Hauananaia, *w.*	Makalawena.
26 Makalawena, *k.*	Koihouhoua, *w.*	Lelehooma.
27 Lelehooma, *k.*	Hapuu, *w.*	Kekupahaikala.
28 Kekupahaikala, *k.*	Maihikea, *w.* -	Maweke.
29 Maweke, *k.*	Naiolaukea, *w.*	Mulielealii.
30 Mulielealii, *k.*	Wehelani, *w.*	Moikeha.
31 Moikeha, *k.*	Henauulua, *w.*	Hookamalii.
32 Hookamalii, *k.*	Keahiula, *w.*	Kahai.
33 Kahai, *k.*	Keheau, *w.*	Kuolono.
34 Kuolono, *k.*	Kaneakaleleoi, *w.*	Maelo, *w.*
35 Maelo, *w.*	Lauli-a-Laa, *k.*	Laulihewa.
36 Laulihewa, *k.*	Akepamaikalani, *w.*	Kahuoi.
37 Kahuoi, *k.*	Pelea, *w.*	Puaakahuoi.
38 Puaakahuoi, *k.*	Nononui, *w.*	Kukahiaililani.
39 Kukahiaililani, *k.*	Kokalola, *w.*	Mailikukahi.
40 Mailikukahi, *k.*	Kanepukoa, *w.*	{ Kalona-nui. { Kalona-iki.
41 Kalona-nui, *k.*	Kaipuholua, *w.*	Kalamakua.
42 Kalamakua, *k.*	Keleanuinohoanaapiapi, *w.* Laielohelohe.	
43 Laielohelohe, *w.*	Piilani, *k.*	Piikea.
44 Piikea, *w.*	Umi-a-Liloa, *k.*	Kumulae.
45 Kumulae, *k.*	Kunuu-nui-puawalau, *w.* Makua.	
46 Makua, *k.*	Kapohelemai, *w.*	I.
47 I., *k.*	Kawalu, *w.*	Ahu-a-I.
48 Ahu-a-I., *k.*	Kaoui, *w.* .	Kapaihi-a-Ahu.
49 Kapaihi-a-Ahu, *k.*	Umiulaakaahuumanu, *w.* Heulu.	
50 Heulu, *k.*	Ikuaana, *w.*	Keawe-a-Heulu.
51 Keawe-a-Heulu, *k.* Ululani, *w.*		Keohohiwa.
52 Keohohiwa, *w.*	Kepookalani, *k.*	Aikanaka.
53 Aikanaka, *k.*	Kamae, *w.*	Keohokalole.
54 Keohokalole, *w.*	Kapaakea, *k.*	55 *Kalakaua.*

The *Ulu* genealogy was the one most in vogue among Hawaii and Maui chiefs. It divides in two principal branches, the *Puna* and *Hema*, and although, through subsequent intermarriages, every aristocratic family in the land can trace itself up to one or the other, and both; yet, for reasons now not well understood or perhaps forgotten, the Hawaii and Maui chiefs, with peculiar pride and pertinacity, preferred to ascend to *Wakea* on the *Hema* line, while the Kauai and Oahu chiefs clung to the *Puna* line with a pride and affection hardly less than that with which they regarded the *Nana-ulu* line just quoted. I will now insert the *Ulu-Hema* line as currently adopted in the time of *Kamehameha* I., and first published by David Malo in 1838, in his *Moolelo Hawaii*, " Hawaiian History."

THE ULU GENEALOGY.

1 Wakea, *k.*	{ Papa, *w.* { Hoohokukalani, *w.*	{ Hoohokukalani, *w.* { Haloa.
2 Haloa, *k.*	Hinamanouluae, *w.*	Waia.
3 Waia, *k.*	Huhune, *w.*	Hinanalo.
4 Hinanalo, *k.*	Haunuu, *w.*	Nanakehili.
5 Nanakehili, *k.*	Haulani, *w.*	Wailoa.
6 Wailoa, *k.*	Hikawaopuaianea, *w.*	Kio.
7 Kio, *k.*	Kamole, *w.*	Ole.
8 Ole, *k.*	Hai, *w.*	Pupue.
9 Pupue,'*k.*	Kamahele, *w.*	Manaku.
10 Manaku, *k.*	Hikohaale, *w.*	Kahiko.
11 Kahiko, *k.*	Kaea, *w.*	Luanuu.
12 Luanuu, *k.*	Kawaamaukele, *w.*	Kii.
13 Kii, *k.*	Hinakoula, *w.*	{ Ulu. { Nana-ulu.
14 Ulu, *k.*	Kapunuu, *w.*	{ Nana. { Kapulani. { Nanaie.
15 Nanaie, *k.*	Kahaumokuleia, *w.*	Nanailani.
16 Nanailani, *k.*	Hinakinau, *w.*	Waikulani.
17 Waikulani, *k.*	Kekauilani, *w.*	Kuheleimoana.
18 Kuheleimoana, *k.*	Mapunaiaala, *w.*	Konohiki.
19 Konohiki, *k.*	Hikaululena, *w.*	Wawena.

20 Wawena, *k.*	Hinamahuia, *w.*	Akalana.
21 Akalana, *k.*	Hinakawea, *w.*	Maui-mua. Maui-hope. Mauikiikii. Mauiakalana.
22 Mauiakalana, *k.*	Hinakealohaila, *w.*	Nanamaoa.
23 Nanamaoa, *k.*	Hinaikapaikua, *w.*	Nanakulei.
24 Nanakulei, *k.*	Kahaukuhonua, *w.*	Nanakaoko.
25 Nanakaoko, *k.*	Kahihiokalani, *w.*	Heleipawa.
26 Heleipawa, *k.*	Kookookumaikalani,*w.*	Hulumanailani.
27 Hulumanailani, *k.*	Hinamaikalani, *w.*	Aikanaka.
28 Aikanaka, *k.*	{ Hinahanaia Kama- lama, *w.*	{ Puna. Hema.
29 Hema, *k.*	Ulumahahoa, *w.*	Kahai.
30 Kahai, *k.*	Hinauluohia, *w.*	Wahioloa.
31 Wahioloa, *k.*	Koolaukahili, *w.*	Laka.
32 Laka, *k.*	Hikawaelena, *w.*	Luanuu.
33 Luanuu,*k.*	Kapokulaiula, *w.*	Kamea.
34 Kamea, *k.*	Popomaili, *w.*	Pohukaina.
35 Pohukaina, *k.*	Huahuakapalei, *w.*	Hua.
36 Hua, *k.*	Hikimolulolea, *w.*	Pau.
37 Pau, *k.*	Kapohaakia, *w.*	Huanuikalalailai.
38 Huanuikalalailai,*k.*	{ Kapoea, *w.* Molehai, *w.*	Paumakua. Kuhelani.
39 Paumakua, *k.*	Manokalililani, *w.*	Haho.
40 Haho,*k.*	Kauilaianapa, *w.*	Palena.
41 Palena, *k.*	Hikawainui, *w.*	{ Hanalaa-nui. Hanalaa-iki.
42 Hanalaanui, *k.*	Mahuia, *w.*	Lanakawai.
43 Lanakawai, *k.*	Kolohialiiokawai, *w.*	Laau.
44 Laau, *k.*	Kukamolimolialoha,*w.*	Pili.
45 Pili, *k.*	Hinaauaku, *w.*	Koa.
46 Koa, *k.*	Hinaaumai, *w.*	Ole.
47 Ole, *k.*	Hinamailelii, *w.*	Kukohou.
48 Kukohou, *k.*	Hinakeuki, *w.*	Kaniuhi.
49 Kaniuhi, *k.*	Hiliamakani, *w.*	Kanipahu.
50 Kanipahu, *k.*	{ Hualani, *w.* Alaikauakoko, *w.*	Kalahumoku. Kalapana.
51 Kalapana, *k.*	Makeamalamaiha- nae, *w.*	Kahaimoeleaikaaiku- pou.
52 Kahaimoeleaikaai- kupou, *k.*	Kapoakauluhailaa, *w.*	Kalaunuiohua.
53 Kalaunuiohua, *k.*	Kaheke, *w.*	Kuaiwa

54 Kuaiwa, *k.*	Kamuleilani, *w.*	Kohoukapu.
		Hukulani.
		Manauea.
55 Kohoukapu, *k.*	Laakapu, *w.*	Kauholanuimahu.
56 Kauholanuimahu,*k.*Neula, *w.*		Kiha.
57 Kiha, *k.*	Waoilea, *w.*	Liloa.
58 Liloa, *k.*	Pinea, *w.*	Hakau.
	Akahiakuleana, *w.*	Umi.
59 Umi, *k.*	Kulamea, *w.*	Kapunanahuanuiaumi.
	Makaalua, *w.*	Nohowaaumi.
	Kapukini, *w.*	Kealiiokaloa.
		Kapulani.
		Keawenuiaumi.
	Piikea, *w.*	Aihakoko.
		Kumalae.
60 Kealiiokaloa, *k.*	Makuahineapalaka, *w.*Kukailani.	
61 Kukailani, *k.*	Kaohukiokalani, *w.*	Kaikilani.
		Makakaualii.
62 Makakaualii, *k.*	Kapukamola, *w.*	Iwikauikaua.
60 Keawenuiaumi, *k.*	Koihalawai, *w.*	Kanaloakuaana.
61 Kanaloakuaana, *k.*	Kaikilani, *w.*	Kealiiokalani.
		Keakealanikane.
		Kalanioumi.
62 Keakealanikane, *k.*	Kealiiokalani, *w.*	Keakamahana.
63 Iwikauikaua, *k.*	Keakamahana, *w.*	Keakealani.
64 Kanaloakapulehu,*k.*Keakealani, *w.*		Keawe.
Kaneikauaiwilani,*k.*	„ „	Kalanikauleleikaiwi.
65 Keawe, *k.*	Kalanikauleleiaiwi, *w.*	Keeaumoku.
		Kekela.
66 Keeaumoku, *k.*	Kamakaimoku, *w.*	Kalanikupuapaikala-
		ninui.
66 Kekela, *w.*	Haae, *k.*	Kekuiapoiwa.
67 Kalanikupuapai- kalaninui, *k.*	Kekuiapoiwa, *w.*	68 *Kamehameha.*

Such is the genealogy which the bards and priests at the Court of Kamehameha I. recited in his honour. Continuing this line to the present time, from *Keawe's* half-sister, *Kalanikauleleiaiwi*, No. 61, we have

65 Kalanikaulele-iaiwi, *w.*	Lonoikahaupu, *k.*	Keawepoepoe.
66 Keawepoepoe, *k.*	Kanoena, *w.*	Kameeiamoku.
67 Kameeiamoku, *k.*	Kamakaeheikuli, *w.*	Kepookalani.
68 Kepookalani, *k.*	Keohohiwa, *w.*	Aikanaka.
69 Aikanaka, *k.*	Kamae, *w.*	Keohokalole.
70 Keohokalole, *w.*	Kapaakea, *k.*	Kalakaua.
71 Kalakaua, *k.*	Kapiolani, *w.*	

The other line of the *Ulu-Hema* genealogy, dividing at *Hanalaa-iki*, and attributed to the Maui chiefs, runs as follows :—

42 Hanalaa-iki, *k.*	Kapukapu, *w.*	Mauiloa.
43 Mauiloa, *k.*	Kauhua, *w.*	Alau.
44 Alau, *k.*	Moikeaea, *w.*	Kanemokuhealii.
45 Kanemokuhealii, *k.*	Keikauhale, *w.*	Lonomai.
46 Lonomai, *k.*	Kolu, *w.*	Wakalana.
47 Wakalana, *k.*	Kauai, *w.*	Alo.
48 Alo, *k.*	Puhia, *w.*	Kaheka.
49 Kaheka, *k.*	Maiaoula, *w.*	Mapuleo.
50 Mapuleo, *k.*	Kamaiokalani, *w.*	Paukei.
51 Paukei, *k.*	Painalea, *w.*	Luakoa.
52 Luakoa, *k.*	Hinaapoapo.	Kuhimana.
53 Kuhimana, *k.*	Kaumana, *w.*	Kamaluohua.
54 Kamaluohua, *k.*	Kapu, *w.*	Loe.
55 Loe, *k.*	Waohaakuna, *w.*	Kahaokuohua.
56 Kahaokuohua, *k.*	Hikakaiula, *w.*	Kaulahea.
57 Kaulahea, *k.*	Kapohanaaupuni, *w.*	Kakae.
58 Kakae, *k.*	Kapohauola, *w.*	Kahekili.
59 Kahekili, *k.*	Haukanuimaka-maka, *w.*	Kawaokaohele.
60 Kawaokaohele, *k.*	Kepalaoa, *w.*	Piilani.
61 Piilani, *k.*	Laielohelohe, *w.*	Kihapiilani.
62 Kihapiilani, *k.*	Kumaka, *w.*	Kamalalawalu.
63 Kamalalawalu, *k.*	Piilaniwahine, *w.*	Kauhi a Kama.
64 Kauhi a Kama, *k.*	Kapukini, *w.*	Kaulanikaumakao-wakea.
65 Kaulanikaumakao-wakea, *k.*	{ Kaneakauhi, *w.* { Makakuwahine, *w.*	Lonohonuakini.
66 Lonohonuakini, *k.*	Kalanikauanakini-lani, *w.*	Umialiloa. Kaulahea.
67 Kaulahea, *k.*	Papaikaniau, *w.*	Kekaulike.
68 Kekaulike, *k.*	Kekuiapoiwanui, *w.*	Kahekili.

69 Kahekili, *k.* Kauwahine, *w.* Kalanikupule.
70 Kalanikupule, *k.*

the last independent king of Maui, conquered by Kamehameha I. Continuing this line, however, from Umialiloa, the brother of Lonohonuakini, No. 66, we descend to the present generation, as follows:—

66 Umialiloa, *k.*	Kuihewamakawalu,*w.*	Kuimiheua.
67 Kuimiheua I., *k.*	Kalanikueiwalono, *w.*	Niau.
68 Niau, *w.*	Mokulani, *k.*	Ululani.
69 Ululani, *w.*	Keawe a Heulu, *k.*	Keohohiwa.
70 Keohohiwa, *w.*	Kepookalani, *k.*	Aikanaka.
71 Aikanaka, *k.*	Kamae, *w.*	Keohokalole.
72 Keohokalole, *w.*	Kapaahea, *k.*	Kalakaua.
73 *Kalakaua*, *k.*	Kapiolani, *w.*	

The other branch of the *Ulu* genealogy, descending from *Hema's* brother *Puna*, is equally voluminous and equally subject to different versions, between which great discrepàncy occurs. The one quoted by several ancient Hawaiians, *scil.*, Kamakau among others, and recited when rival heralds sang the praises of their chiefs, runs as follows:—

29 Puna-imua, *k.*	Hainalau, *w.*	Ua.
30 Ua, *k.*	Kahilinai, *w.*	Uamaikalani.
31 Uamaikalani, *k.*	Haimakalani, *w.*	Uanini.
32 Uanini, *k.*	Welihaakona, *w.*	Auanini.
33 Auanini, *k.*	Maunakuahaokalani, *w.*	Newalani.
34 Newalani, *k.*	Kahihiikaale, *w.*	Lonohuanewa.
35 Lonohuanewa, *k.*	Loiloa, *w.*	Lonowahilani.
36 Lonowahilani, *k.*	Kahikihaaueue, *w.*	Pau.
37 Pau, *k.*	Kapalakuakalani, *w.*	Paumakua.
38 Paumakua, *k.*	Keananui, *w.*	Moeanaimua.
39 Moeanaimua, *k.*	Alahoe, *w.*	Kumakaha.
40 Kumakaha, *k.*	Moanaaulii, *w.*	Nana.
41 Nana, *k.*	Haakaleikini, *w.*	Luahiwa.
42 Luahiwa, *k.*	Kilohana, *w.*	Ahukai.
43 Ahukai, *k.*	Keakamilo, *w.*	Laa.
44 Laa, *k.*	Kaikulani, *w.*	Laamaikahiki.
45 Laamaikahiki, *k.*	Hoakamaikapuaihelu, *w.*	Lauli-a-Laa.

	Waolena, *w.*	Ahukini-a-Laa.
	Manoopupaipai, *w.*	Kukona-Laa.
46 Lauli-a-Laa, *k.*	Maelo, *w.*	Laulihewa.
47 Laulihewa, *k.*		

This is the same *Laulihewa* as No. 36 on the *Nana-ulu* genealogy. Other versions of this portion of the *Puna* line are considerably shorter, and hence, in my opinion, more correct. I now proceed to give the *Puna* line from *Ahukini-a-Laa*, one of the sons of *Laamaikahiki*, down to the present time, it comprises the descent of *Kaumualii*, the last independent king of the island of Kauai :—

46 Ahukini-a-Laa, *k.*	Hai-a-Kamaio, *w.*	Kamahano.
47 Kamahano, *k.*	Kaaueanuiokalani, *w.*	Luanuu.
48 Luanuu, *k.*	Kalanimoeikawai-kai, *w.*	Kukona.
49 Kukona, *k.*	Laupuapuamaa, *w*	Manokalanipo.
50 Manokalanipo, *k.*	Naekapulani, *w.*	Kaumakamano.
51 Kaumakamano, *k.*	Kapoinukai, *w.*	Kahakuakane.
52 Kahakuakane, *k.*	Manukaikoo, *w.*	Kuwalupaukamoku.
53 Kuwalupaukamo-ku, *k.*	Hameawahaula, *w.*	Kahakumakapaweo.
54 Kahakumakapa-weo, *k.*	Kahakukukaena, *w.*	Kalanikukuma.
55 Kalanikukuma, *k.*	Kapoleikauila, *w.*	Ilihiwalani.
56 Ilihiwalani, *k.*	Kamili, *w.*	Kauihi a Hiwa.
57 Kauihi a Hiwa, *k.*	Kueluakawai, *w.*	Kaneiahaka.
58 Kaneiahaka, *w.*	Kealohi, *k.*	Kapulauki.
59 Kapulauki, *w.*	Kainaaila, *k.*	Kuluina.
60 Kuluina.	Kauakahilau.	Lonoikahaupu.
61 Lonoikahaupu, *k.*	Kamuokaumeheiwa, *w.*	Kaumeheiwa.
62 Kaumeheiwa.	Kaapuwai.	Kamakahelei.
63 Kamakahelei, *w.*	Kaeokulani, *k.*	Kaumualii.
64 Kaumualii, *k.*	Kapuaamohu, *w.*	Kinoike.
65 Kinoike, *w.*	Kuhio, *k.*	Kapiolani.
66 *Kapiolani, w.*	*Kalakaua.*	

The Oahu chiefs, claiming descent under the *Nana-ulu* genealogy, mostly derive from *Kalona-iki*, the son of *Mailikukahi*, No. 40, and the Royal *Kualii* family line runs thus :—

41 Kalona-iki, *k.*	Kikenui-a-Ewa, *w.*	{ Piliwale, *k.*
		{ Kamaleamaka, *k.*
		{ Lo-Lale, *k.*
42 Piliwale, *k.*	Paakanilea, *w.*	Kukaniloko.
43 Kukaniloko, *w.*	Luaia, *k.*	Kalaimanuia.
44 Kalaimanuia, *w.*	Lupekapukeahoma-	Kaihikapu.
	kalii, *k.*	
45 Kaihikapu-a-Man-	Kaunuiakanehoala-	Kakuhihewa.
uia, *k.*	ni, *w.*	
46 Kakuhihewa, *k.*	{ Kahaiaonuiakauai-	{ Kanekapu.
	lana, *w.*	{ Kaihikapu.
	{ Kaakaualani, *w.*	Kauakahinui.
47 Kaihikapu-a-Ka-	Kalua-â-Hoohila, *w.*	Kahoowaha.
kuhihewa, *k.*		
48 Kahoowahaoka-	Kawelolauhuki, *w.*	Kauakahi.
lani, *k.*		
49 Kauakahi-a-Ka-	Mahulua, *w.*	Kualii.
hoowaha, *k.*		
50 Kualii, *k.*	Kalanikahimakei-	Peleioholani.
	alii, *w.*	
	Kukuiaimakalani, *w.*	
51 Peleioholani, *k.*	Lonokahikini, *w.*	Kumahana.
52 Kumahana, *k.*		Kaneoneo.

I am not aware that any lineal descendants of *Pelioho-lani* still survive, but there are numerous scions of the *Kualii* house, through his daughter *Kukuiaimakalani* and granddaughter *Kalanipo*, still alive in the fourth and fifth generation, thus bringing this line down to Nos. 55 and 56, corresponding exactly with the *Kalona-nui* branch of the *Nanaulu* genealogy.

To reconcile these different genealogies is impossible; to reconstruct them by the exercise of a proper criticism and with the light thrown upon them by the legends and chants still preserved—regarding the contemporaneity, intermarriages, wars, &c., of various chiefs on different lines—may be practicable, at least approximatively, and the result of my endeavours in that direction will appear in the following synchronical list of the *Nana-ulu* and *Ulu* lines. A few prefatory remarks, however, on these lines, as recorded on the Hawaiian genealogies, may be necessary for the better understanding of the list and the necessity, on behalf of historical truth, of reducing the *Ulu* line to more moderate proportions, and leaving it in an apparently incomplete condition, compared with the *Nana-ulu.*

There are no legends of much historical value referring to the long line of chiefs from *Nanaulu* to and including *Maweke*, embracing a period of fifteen generations, or about 450 years. Even the family—*Nana*—name had ceased to appear as a component part of the chiefs' names. But it is a significant fact, and of considerable importance, that out of all the genealogies of different Hawaiian chief families now known and recited, not one falls in upon the main line of either *Nanaulu* or *Ulu* above the time of *Maweke* or *Paumakua*, with the exception of the *Puna* and *Hema* divisions of the *Ulu* line. From these two (*Maweke* and *Paumakua*) the bare stems without collateral offshoots run up to *Kii*, and from him to *Wakea*. In their time, then, probably commencing some generations earlier, certainly continuing several generations later, took place that general movement and displacement of Polynesian tribes which sent the Hawaiians southward, and the Southerners northward, in quest of new homes, adventures, or renown, of which the Hawaiian legends are so full and circumstantial. The *Maweke* family, through his numerous sons and grandchildren, was probably the most powerful of the original chief families descended from *Nanaulu*, and were thus able to hold their ground against the intrusion and influence of the southern element, and retain their genealogy intact and unmixed ; while most, if not all the other chief families on the same line, of which scattered notices occur here and there in the legends, were gradually absorbed or superseded by the southern chiefs who claimed descent from *Ulu*, through *Puna* and *Hema*. Whatever legends may have existed, connected with names previous to *Maweke*, they were apparently swallowed up and forgotten in the new era then inaugurated.

The historical value of the *Ulu* line, as recorded on Hawaiian genealogies, in the pre-*Maweke*, pre-*Paumakua* period, is very small and very doubtful. In critically examining the post-*Paumakua* period, numerous opportunities present themselves from time to time to compare the various genealogies which lead up to *Paumakua* among themselves, and with others that lead up to *Maweke*, as well as with the legends connected with the prominent chiefs of either line, thus testing their correctness, and enabling the inquirer to detect and adjust their inaccuracies. The pre-*Paumakua* period furnishes neither so many nor so clear tests for historical criticism. The legends have grown into myths, and the myths have degenerated into fables. Still probabilities are not wanting, though very little can be definitely proven.

It is certain that during the migratory period of which *Maweke* and *Paumakua* are the central figures, the Hawaiian group was visited by expeditions from the Samoan, Society, and Marquesas groups, and that Hawaiian expeditions visited them in return. It thus appears both natural and probable that several different versions of the southern or *Ulu* legends and genealogies were introduced by the immigrant chiefs, their priests and followers, which, as the southern element became dominant and consolidated, were localised and incorporated on the general folklore of the Hawaiian group, and the different genealogies of the leaders of these expeditions were pieced together into one connected whole. Thus the *Puna* and *Hema* divisions of the *Ulu* line become so disproportionately longer than the *Nanaulu* straight line or its various branches. By counting upward from the present generation, having due regard to the evidence furnished by the accompanying legends as to intermarriages and other social and political relations between the chiefs of the *Nanaulu* and *Ulu* lines, it becomes an undoubted historical fact that *Maweke* and *Paumakua* were contemporaries, the former being the twenty-seventh, and the latter the twenty-sixth, generation from and inclusive of the present. If we now count from *Nanaulu* and *Ulu*, admitted by all genealogies and legends of both lines to have been brothers and sons of *Kii*, down to *Maweke* and *Paumakua*, we find only fifteen generations on the former line, and twenty-five and twenty-four respectively on the two divisions of the latter line, besides the discrepancies between the two divisions themselves, some making the *Puna* branch even longer than the *Hema* branch.

It is almost certain that a number of names on the *Ulu* line were those of chiefs in some of the southern groups, who never set foot on Hawaiian soil, but whose names and whose legends were imported by southern emigrants, and to whom dynastic ambition and national vanity afterwards assigned a *locus standi* on Hawaiian legends, and a birthplace and burialplace on the Hawaiian group. Glimpses of southern legends and genealogies in New Zealand, Tonga, Samoa, Society, and Marquesas groups confirm this proposition still more. The *Maui* legends, the *Maui* family of four brothers, and their parent *A-kalana*, *Karana*, or *Taranga*, and the grandmother *Hina-mahuia*, are found upon all those groups in slightly different versions. The legend of *Maui-kiikii* or *Maui-tiki-tiki*, the youngest of the family, being out fishing, and catching the various Hawaiian islands on his hook, attempting to drag them ashore at Hilo and join them to Hawaii, is found nearly literally the same on New Zealand. On Tonga the same legend obtained, but they ascribe the act to *Tangaloa* instead of *Maui*. Near Puuepa, district of N. Kohala, Hawaii, a stone is still shown which is said to bear the impress of Maui's fish-hook called *Manaiakalana*. Near the south end of Hawke's Bay, in the district of Heretaunga, New Zealand, Maui's fish-hook is still said to be preserved ; and at Tonga, a place called Hounga is pointed out as the spot where the hook caught in the rocks, and the hook itself was said to have still been in the possession of the *Tui-Tonga* family some thirty years before

Mariner's time and residence on that group. Maui's exploits in discovering fire are the common property, under various versions, of all the Polynesian groups. The deified ancestress and grandmother of Maui, in the New Zealand, legends called *Mahuika*, is evidently the same as his grandmother *Hina-Mahuia* on the Hawaiian *Ulu* genealogy; and the Samoan *Mafuie* betrays a confused reminiscence of the same legends. These legends were undoubtedly older than the Polynesian exodus into the Pacific. On Borneo a legend still exists that that island formerly was composed of a number of smaller islands, which by some miraculous process were joined together. It is just to conclude, therefore, that the *Maui* family and legends were not only not indigenous to Hawaiian soil or contemporary with any chiefs on the *Nanaulu* line, but it is very questionable whether their origin does not date back to the pre-Pacific period of the Polynesian race.

The next interpolation or, rather, insertion in the wrong place of the *Ulu* line, to which I will call attention, is the *Nana* family ending, or, according to the royal Hawaiian genealogy published by D. Malo, and referred to above on page 191, continued through *Heleipawa*, though several other genealogies end that family with a chief called *Kapawa*, which is no doubt the correct version. According to one genealogy there were four *Nana* preceding *Kapawa;* according to another there were three *Nana;* and according to the old genealogy above referred to, page 184, there were but two *Nana* preceding *Kapawa.* I think there is little doubt that this family and their descendant *Kapawa* were actual chiefs on the Hawaiian group. The building up and consecration of *Kukaniloko*, on the island of Oahu, that peculiarly hallowed place in all subsequent ages of Hawaiian history as the birthplace of the highest " Kapu " chiefs, is universally and continuously ascribed to Kapawa's father *Nanakaoko*. As to the time of *Kapawa*, the legend of *Paao*—a Southerner of great rank and a high-priest, whose family was established

during this *Maweke-Paumakua* period as *par excellence* the
priestly caste, and whose descendants survive to this day
—expressly confirms Kapawa's contemporaneity with this
migratory period. The legend states that when *Pili-kaiaea*
arrived from Tahiti or *Kahiki*, "the *Nana* chiefs of
Hawaii were extinct on account of the crimes of Kapawa,
the chief of Hawaii at that time :" *Ua pau na Alii Nana
o Hawaii-nei i kahewa o Kapawa, ke Alii o Hawaii ia
manawa.* What this great crime or fault may have been
is not stated. *Paao,* the high priest, who had then already
arrived and established himself, sent to *Kahiki,* that
foreign, southern land, for *Pili,* who, on his invitation and
through his instrumentality, became a king on Hawaii.
Thus *Kapawa* and *Pili* were contemporaries, and Kapawa's
grandfather, *Nana-maoa,* was contemporary with or of the
period of *Paumakua ;* and the family was probably of that
same Southern, *Ulu,* descent as *Puna* and *Paumakua,* as,
though living for some generations on the Hawaiian group
previous to *Pili,* they were never included on the original
Hawaiian *Nanaulu* line. In confirmation of this Southern
extraction of the *Kapawa* family, several legends give
strong, though inferential testimony. Thus *Hina-i-kapa-
ikua,* the wife of *Nana-maoa* and grandmother of *Kapawa,*
is also called the grandmother of *Niheu-kolohe,* who was
the recognised grandson of *Kuheailani,* the brother of *Paumakua.* Thus the same lady is called the grandmother of
Kaulu, sometimes called *Kaulu-a-Kalana,* the renowned
navigator and explorer of those days, whose astrologer and
soothsayer—*Kilo-kilo*—named *Luhau-Kapawa,* is admitted
to have been a man from *Kahiki,* and is by some said to
have introduced the "Kapu" system in the Hawaiian
group; and they are both stated to have been contemporary with *Kahiwa-kaapu,* the wife of *Hina-kai-mauli-
awa,* the grandson of *Maweke.* I feel justified, therefore,
in placing *Kapawa* within the period of Maweke's and
Paumakua's grandchildren, and as contemporary with
Pili. The *Kapawa* family, whether consisting of two or

more *Nana* previous to *Kapawa*, is evidently greatly mis-
placed on the *Ulu-Hema* genealogy, and belongs to the
latter instead of the earlier portion of the line.

Still another large excision must be made from the *Ulu*
line, as represented on the Hawaiian genealogies, previous
to the *Paumakua* period. The four first names of the
Hema division of the *Ulu* line, though referred to in song
and saga as heroes of Hawaiian birth, were really but
another importation and adaptation by that oft-mentioned
southern element of their own legends and genealogies to
their altered circumstances in the Hawaiian group.

The Hawaiian genealogies make *Puna* and *Hema* sons
of *Aikanaka* and his mythical wife *Hina-hanaiakama-*
lama, with the cognomen *Lonomoku*, and descendants on
the *Ulu* line from *Heleipawa*, or, as others say, *Kapawa*.
The longest genealogies introduce nine generations, the
shortest four, between *Puna* and *Hema* respectively and
Paumakua, whom both divisions claim as a common
ancestor for succeeding generations. The same uncer-
tainty obtains on both divisions from *Paumakua* to the
time of *Pili*, some having two, others four, and still others
five generations during that period. It is significant,
moreover, and to be observed, that no prominent name on
the *Ulu* line, previous to *Paumakua*, occurs upon the
legends connected with the *Nanaulu* line, except the
Puna family of Kauai, who claimed to be, and probably
were, of the *Ulu* descent, and with whom Maweke's grandson *Moikeha* allied himself after his return from Kahiki.
No crossings of intermarriages, no intercourse of peace or
war, are recorded as having occurred between the two
lines. They appear to have been mutually ignorant of
each other's existence; and yet the *Ulu* legends represent
the *Ulu* chiefs of this pre-*Paumakua* period as having
been born, lived, and died side by side of the *Nanaulu*
chiefs, whose bare names have been preserved through the
Maweke family, but whose legends were obliterated and
forgotten in the superior eclat and later introduction of

that southern, *Ulu*, element with its own peculiar genealogies, legends, and innovations of various kinds.

In comparing the New Zealand legends, as published by Sir George Grey, I find that the New Zealanders claim descent from the island of Sawaii in the Samoan group, which they pronounce *Hawaiki*, and that among other prominent names occurring in their ancestral tales, previous to their departure from Hawaiki, are four that appear also on the Hawaiian *Ulu* line between *Aikanaka* and *Paumakua*. In the New Zealand legends they appear as chiefs or *Ariki* of *Hawaiki*, following one another in the same succession as on the Hawaiian genealogy. Their names are—the Hawaiian pronunciation in brackets— *Hema* [Hema], *Tawhaki* [Kahai], *Wahieroa* [Wahieloa], *Raka* [Laka]. Each of these chiefs have been naturalised, so to say, and localised on the Hawaiian group by Hawaiian legends; yet as there is no reasonable probability that the New Zealanders took their departure from the Hawaiian instead of the Samoan group, and as their evidence is positive as to the residence of those chiefs on the *Hawaiki*, which they knew and from which they departed for New Zealand, I am forced to conclude that their introduction on the Hawaiian genealogies was the work of that migratory period, to which I have so often alluded, and was a local adaptation in after ages of previously existing legends, when the memory of the mothercountry had become indistinct, and when little more was known of them except the one main fact that they stood on the genealogical list of the Hawaiian chiefs of the *Ulu* line; a fact which was never allowed to be forgotten under the old system, however much local associations might be forgotten or altered.

It is hardly historically possible that there could have been two series of chiefs in the Samoan and Hawaiian groups, with identical names and in the same succession; with one transposition alone, the same identity holds good in the names of three of their wives, viz. :—

New Zealand.		Hawaiian.	
Hema, *k.*	Uru-tonga, *w.*	Hema, *k.*	Ulu-mahehoa, *w.*
Tawhaki, *k.*	Hine-piri-piri, *w.*	Kahai, *k.*	Hina-uluohia, *w.*
Wahieroa, *k.*	Kura, *w.*	Wahieloa, *k.*	Koolaukahili, *w.*
Raka, *k.*	Tongarautawhiri, *w.*	Laka, *k.*	Hikawaelena, *w.*

Thus, on the testimony of the New Zealand legends, these chiefs were not original on the North Pacific Hawaii, of which the New Zealanders knew apparently nothing, but on the South Pacific Samoan Sawaii, from which they claimed descent, from which they emigrated, and whose legends they brought with them to their new homes in *Ao-tea-roa* or New Zealand.

Thus, while the *Nanaulu* genealogy for the period between *Kii* and *Maweke* has been assailed by no doubts and by no diversity of opinion among subsequent generations of Hawaiians, the Ulu genealogy has been subject to numerous varying constructions, no two agreeing together throughout, and as a Hawaiian genealogy on Hawaiian soil is disproven in several places by its own discrepancy with the Nanaulu line, as well as by the direct testimony of the legends and genealogies of the South Pacific groups.

With these introductory remarks I will now give the Hawaiian genealogy from *Nanaulu* and *Ulu* down, as I consider it ought to be rendered, when the sources have been critically examined and properly collated; showing at the same time the collateral branches both of the *Puna* and *Hema* lines of the *Ula* division, as well as the main branches of the *Nanaulu-Maweke* division. (For Genealogical Table, see Appendix No. IX.)

Of the legends which treat of *Wakea* and his wife *Papa*, not much bearing the impress of ancient and original tradition has been preserved. What has been preserved, however, establishes the fact, as previously noticed, that *Wakea* was a chief on one of the Molucca islands (Gilolo), previous to, perhaps contemporary with, the great exodus

of the Polynesian family from the Asiatic Archipelago.
His reign seems to have been chequered by wars and reverses. Certain great changes in the social system of the
people, the strengthening of the Kapus and the introduction of new ones, are vaguely ascribed to him. His life
seems to have been troubled by rebellion at home and by
foreign pressure from without. The domestic relations
between him and his wife *Papa* appear to have been very
unfortunate, and form by far the greatest portion of the
subject-matter of the legends referring to those personages.
Wakea, however, seems not to have been without defenders
of his good name, for there were legends existing in David
Malo's time, say fifty years ago, which asserted that *Hoohokukalani*, the reputed, and on the most prevalent genealogies recognised, daughter of *Wakea* and *Papa*, was not
their child at all, but was the daughter of *Wakea's* high
priest *Komoawa* and his wife *Popokolonuha;* and I have one
genealogy which, while it recognises *Hoohokukalani* as the
daughter of *Papa* and *Wakea*, gives her *Manauluae* as
husband and *Waia* as their son. The domestic scandal of
Wakea's incest, on which later versions of the *Wakea* legends
lay so much emphasis, appears therefore not to have been
fully believed in more ancient times, and I feel justified in
considering it as an unfounded gravamen of a character
remembered only by succeeding generations for its oppres-
siveness and tyranny. I find no personal description in
the legends of *Wakea*, but *Papa* is represented as a comely
woman, " very fair and almost white." She is said to have
become crazy or distracted on account of her domestic
troubles with her husband, who publicly divorced her,
according to ancient custom, by " spitting in her face."
She is represented as having lived to a very old age, and
as having died in *Waieri*, a place in Tahiti. In after ages
she was deified under the name of *Haumea*.

Of the remaining names from *Wakea* to *Nanaulu* and
Ulu, there exist no legends of any historical value. On the
whereabouts of their residence and the exploits of their

lives, tradition is apparently silent; though some Hawaiian commentators of the ancient legends, according to D. Malo, asserted that the first six lived in *Kahiki* (Tahiti), that is in some foreign land outside of the Hawaiian group.

Of *Kii*, No. 13 on the list, and the last of the first series, nothing is known except that he was the father of the two brothers *Nanaulu* and *Ulu*, from whom the northern and southern Polynesians respectively claimed their descent, and in whose time the probable separation of the two branches took place; the *Nanaulu* branch proceeding northward and settling on the Hawaiian group with a possible sejour or rest on the Marquesas group, though nothing in the legends remain to indicate such a fact; and the *Ulu* branch remaining on the islands of the South Pacific, keeping up a not unfrequent intercourse between them, forgetting or ignoring their northern brethren for a period that may be roughly stated to have extended over ten to twelve generations.

Towards the close of this period, from *Nanaulu* to *Maweke*, as a central figure, the Hawaiian seclusion or isolation was interrupted by the arrival of sundry parties from the South, or, as the legends call it, *Kahiki*, claiming descent from *Ulu* through either the *Puna* or *Hema* division. Such were the *Puna* family established on Kauai, with whom *Maweke's* grandson *Moikeha* allied himself. Such were the *Nanamaoa* or *Nana-a-Maui* family established on Oahu, and obtaining ascendancy for some time on Hawaii. Such the *Huanuikalalailai* family, whom the *Hema* division in subsequent times claimed as the father of *Paumakua*, and probably others whose legends have perished. What particular groups of southern islands those emigrants came from no vestiges on existing legends remain to indicate. It is probable that the *Puna* family came from or through the Marquesas group. The name is familiar and common on the Marquesan genealogy in my possession about thirty-five to forty-two generations ago, and may have been the stock from which the Hawaiian *Punas* descended.

It is almost certain, taking the concurrent testimony of the legends as the arbitrium of conflicting genealogies, that several of those earlier names mentioned on the *Ulu* line, both before and after the *Puna-Hema* divisions, were contemporary. Thus the genealogies represent *Laau-alii* as the father of *Pili-kaiaea*, but the legends are unanimous that *Pili* came to Hawaii from *Kahiki* in the time of *Laaualii*, and that *Pili* succeeded *Kapawa* in the government of Hawaii. Hence *Laaualii* and *Kapawa* must have been contemporary. Thus *Hua*, or, as he is otherwise called, *Hua-a-kapuaimanaku*, who on the genealogies is placed as the grandfather of *Huanui-Kalalailai*, was in reality, according to the legends and the known contemporaneity of his associates, at least five generations later.

Discarding, therefore, the earlier portion of the *Ulu* line as of any historical value in the reconstruction of Hawaiian genealogies for the period previous to *Maweke* and *Paumakua*, the uncontested *Nanaulu* line remains for our guidance, showing a period of fifteen generations previous to *Maweke*, during which the Hawaiian group was inhabited by the Polynesian race, practising under its own line of chiefs the customs and religion which they brought with them. It is now nearly impossible to separate those customs and that religion from what subsequently obtained, after the great migratory wave of the eleventh century had passed over Polynesia and thoroughly inundated the Hawaiian group with a new order of things. Glimpses, however, of the former condition of the Hawaiian portion of the Polynesian family appear here and there in the legends immediately relating to this migratory period; and from a careful inquiry into their contents and bearing, I am led to believe that the *Kane* worship in greater simplicity, with the customs it enjoined or which grew out of it, and notices of which have been given in previous pages, was the prevalent creed of those ancient Hawaiians; that the Kapus were few and the ceremonials easy; that human sacrifices were not practised, and cannibalism unknown; and that government was more of a patriarchal than of a regal nature.

By counting upwards from the present time, the Hawaiian genealogies and legends have enabled me to establish, approximatively, the period of *Wakea* at about the middle or latter part of the second century A.D. But in examining the genealogies bearing upon the pre-Wakea period, it becomes evident that the thirty-seven generations embraced upon even the longest of them—that from *Kumuhonua*, or the first man, to *Wakea*,—is entirely inadequate to represent the continued existence of the human race during that interval, and that there must be large and important gaps in that genealogy. All the other Hawaiian genealogies, covering the pre-Wakea period, are equally if not more defective. There is evidently a large gap among the generations immediately succeeding the twelve sons of *Kinilau*. Up to that time I look upon the *Kumuhonua* genealogy as merely a reflex of the Cushite knowledge and Cushite reminiscences imparted to the Polynesians while yet sojourning in India, or during their early residence in the Asiatic Archipelago. A number of families in ancient history seem to have adopted this distant and mysterious twelve-ship as their national point of departure, and to have carried it with them wherever they spread. All previous to that was to them a common heirloom; all subsequent became national divergence, complexity, confusion, and oblivion. The manifest relation, in many places, between this genealogy (the *Kumuhonua*) and Arabian, Chaldeo-Hebraic, and other Eastern genealogies and legends, clearly proves the common origin of them all. The ten generations between the sons of *Kinilau* and the time of *Wakea* must hence cover a period of some thousands of years. They represent probably only the most prominent figures on the traditional canvass of that half-forgotten period, including the discoveries and exploits of *Hawaii-loa.* It is a period extending from their connection with, and absorption of, the Cushite element, to their expulsion from the Asiatic Archipelago by the Malays.

Having thus attempted to show who the Polynesians are, whence they came, and how connected with the old-world peoples of historic renown, I will in the next portion of this work endeavour to sketch Hawaiian history proper, from the period of *Maweke* and *Paumakua* to the times of *Kamehameha I.*—so far as such history may be gathered, from a critical research into the legends, traditions, songs, and genealogies of the Hawaiian people.

It will be observed that in this sketch of the Polynesian race I have not referred to the tribes occupying Western Polynesia, the Micronesian and Caroline groups. I am not acquainted with their languages, and very imperfectly with their traditions. That they are a branch of the same great race there can be little doubt; but they were probably of much later separation from the Asiatic Archipelago, and had been either there, or have been subsequently, subjected to intermixture with foreign elements to so great an extent as to destroy the Polynesian character of the language, and that general homogeneity of customs and traditions which is so conspicuous a link of connection between the Southern, Eastern, and Northern groups of Polynesia.

APPENDIX.

——◆——

No. I., *page 63.*

SOME writers, supporting themselves by a legend said to have come from Hawaii, that the world was produced from an egg.[1] I find a relation of that legend to the Brahminical doctrine of the World-egg. I have been unable to discover or collect such a legend on the Hawaiian group; nor do I know of any resembling it on the other island groups, unless in some distorted form it may refer to the Fiji legend which says that mankind sprang from two eggs that were hatched by the god *Ndengei.* There is a Hawaiian legend, however, which ascribes the creation of the world to *Wakea* and *Papa* in this way: "*Papa*, the wife of Wakea, begat a calabash—*ipu*—including bowl and cover. *Wakea* threw the cover upward, and it became the heaven. From the inside meat

[1] In a "Journal of a Tour around Hawaii," "by a deputation from the Mission of those islands," Boston, 1825—of which deputation Rev. Mr. Ellis, of Polynesian and Madagascar fame, was one—it is said, page 197, that in a conversation with Mr. John Young, who had resided on the islands since 1790, "Mr. Young said the natives had several traditions, one of which was, that an immense bird laid an egg on the water, which soon burst and produced the island of Hawaii, and shortly after a man and a woman, a hog and a dog, and a pair of fowls, came in a canoe from the Society Islands, landed on the eastern shores, and were the progenitors of the present inhabitants." It is much to be regretted that this tradition, of which Mr. Young gave only a meagre *resumé*, should have utterly perished from the land during the fifty years since the above "Tour around Hawaii." It certainly must have been an earlier and purer form of the subsequent tradition of Papa and her calabash.

and seeds *Wakea* made the sun, moon, stars, and sky; from the juice he made the rain, and from the bowl he made the land and the sea."

I now give the Brahminical account of creation, as gathered from an "Analysis of the Code of Menu," published in the "Asiatic Journal," November 1827. It says:—

"The universe existed only in darkness, imperceptible, undefinable, as if wholly immersed in sleep. The self-existing power, himself undiscerned, with five elements and other principles, appeared in glory, dispelling the gloom. ' He, whom the mind alone can perceive, whose essence eludes the external organs, who has no visible parts, who exists from eternity, even he, the soul of all beings, whom no being can comprehend, shone forth in person.' Having willed to produce various beings from his own divine substance, first with a thought he created the waters; 'the waters are called *nárá*, because they were the production of Nara, or the spirit of God; and since they were his first *ayana*, or place of motion, he thence is named *Náráyana*, or moving on the waters.' . . . . The Hindu legislator proceeds to tell, that the self-existing power placed a productive seed in the waters, which became 'an egg, bright as gold, blazing like the luminary with a thousand beams,' from whence he was born himself, 'the divine male, famed in all worlds under the appellation of Brahma.' "

Compare with the above the following extract from the *Manek-Maya*, the classical work on Javanese mythology before the introduction of Mohammedanism. I quote from "Oceanie," par M. de Rienzi, vol. i. p. 75.

"Avant que les cieux et la terre fussent créés, *Sang-yang-wisesa* (le Tout-Puissant) existait. Cette divinité, était placée au centre de l'univers ; elle désira intérieurement que le Régulateur suprême lui accordât un souhait. Aussitôt tous les éléments se heurterent, et il entendit, au milieu d'eux, une repetition de sons semblable au battement rapide d'une cloche. Il leva les yeux, et il vit un globe suspendu au-dessus de sa tête, il le prit et le separa en trois parties : une partie devint les cieux et la terre, une autre partie devint le soleil et la lune, et la troisième fut l'homme, ou *Manek-Maya.* La volonté de Sang-yang-wisesa ayant été accomplie, il voulut bien parler à *Manek-Maya,* et lui dit : Tu seras appleé *Sang-yang-gouron ;* je place une entiêre confiance en toi ; je te donne la terre et tout ce qui en depend, afin que tu en uses et que tu en disposes selon ton plaisir. Après ces paroles, le Tout-Puissant disparut."

The Hawaiian legend, as I have collected it, is possibly a corruption of the Javanese myth ; but whether either of them refers to Menu's account of creation for their origin, may, I think, admit of a doubt, unless the Brahminical account itself is a copy, or a compromise, of some previously existing Cushite-Dravidian cast of thought, hardened into myth or legend. The chaotic condition of the world, the *Narayana* or "moving on the waters," referred to by Menu, are certainly Cushite modes of thought, and bespeak their kindred to the Polynesian *Po,* and the Tahitian *Tino-Taata,*[1] and the Hawaiian *Lono-noho-i-ka-wai,*[2] as well as with the Egyptian *Noub* and his mysterious boat.

[1] *Vide,* p. 64.   [2] *Vide,* p. 94.

No. II., *page* 63.

Te Vanana na Tanaoa.

In the beginning, space and companions.
I te tumu ona-ona a na hoa.
Space was the high heaven.
Ona-ona oia te iku-ani,
Tanaoa filled and dwelt in the whole heavens.
Tanaoa[1] hakapi a nonoho i na ani otoa
And Mutuhei was entwined above.
A Mutuhei[2] ua hei ma una,
There was no voice, there was no sound ;
Koe na eeo, koe na tani,
No living things were moving.
Aoe e ae na mea pohoe,
There was no day, there was no light.
Koe na A, maama koe
A dark, black night.
He tano-tano ke-ke po,
O Tanaoa he ruled the night.
O Tanaoa vivini-ia o te po,
O Mutuhei was a Spirit pervading and vast.
10   *O Mutuhei uhane vae-vae a oa.*
From within Tanaoa came forth Atea.
Mei ioto Tanaoa tihe ae Atea,[3]
Life vigorous, power great.
Pohoe oko, mana nui,
O Atea he ruled the day
O Atea vivini-ia o te 'A,
And drove away Tanaoa.
A tatai pu ia Tanaoa.

---

[1] Darkness.   [2] Silence.   [3] Light, the Sun.

Between Day and Night, Atea and Tanaoa,
I vavena o te A me po, a Atea me Tanaoa
Sprang up wars, fierce and long.
Tupu ae na toua a-ha oa-oa,
Atea and Tanaoa, great wrath and contention.
Atea a Tanaoa, a-ha nui a nanaku
Tanaoa confined, Atea soared onward,
Tanaoa tamau ae, Atea hee anatu
Tanaoa dark as ever.
Tanaoa keke pe ananu
Atea very good and very active.

20   *Atea meita meitai a ta-ana-ana*
From within Atea came forth Ono.
Mei ioto o Atea taha-taha ae te Ono [1]
O Ono he ruled the sound
O Ono vivini 'ia o te tani
And broke up Mutuhei.
A ta fati-fati 'ia Mutuhei
Here a great division was made
I tenei he pahei nui haka' ia
In the company of Atanua.
I na hoa o Atanua [2]
Atanua was beautiful and good
Atanua pootu a meitai
Adorned with riches very great.
Tapi i taia tae-tae ma-iko-iko
Atanua was fair, very rich and soft.
Atanua teea, taetae nui a peehu,
Atea and Atanua embraced each other.
Atea me Atanua popoho'ia kohua
Atanua produces abundantly of living things.

30   *Atanua tupu oko i na mea pohoe*
Atea took Atanua for wife.
Atea too'ia Atanua mea vahine
Atea and Ono pass onward, pass upward.
Atea me Ono hee anatu, hee ma una
Atea the body, Ono the Spirit.
Atea tino, Uhane Ono

---

[1] Articulated sound, the voice.   [2] The Dawn.

Atea with Ono in one place.

Atea me Ono etahi ona

Atea the substance, Ono the

Atea tono, moui Ono

Atea produces the very hot fire.

Atea tupu i te ahi vea-vea

Ono is powerful and great

Ono mana oko nunui' ia

Atea is adorned with riches changeable and dazzling,

Atea tapi i te taetae take take a ponio-nio

Ono is adorned with princely wealth and power.

Ono tapi i te taetae Hakaiki me te mana

They two the same glory.

40   *Aua eua etahi koaa.*

Atea the body, Ono the Spirit.

Atea te tino, Uhane Ono

Atea the substance, Ono the

Atea te tono, o moui Ono,

And dwelt as kings in the most beautiful places

A nonoho hakaiki o na ona meitai oko

Supported on thrones, large, many-coloured, wondrous.

Hakatu mauna na paipai nui take take a-anaau

They dwelt above, they dwelt beyond.

A noho una, a nonohu atu

They ruled the space of heaven,

Mea haatoitoi te va-vae-ani

And the large entire sky,

Me na ikuani nui otoa

And all the powers thereof.

A me otoa na mana i ke ia

The first Lords dwelling on high.

Te tau Fatu o'mua nonoho tikitiki,

O wondrous thrones, good and bright

50   *E na paipai aanaau meitai ta-ana-ana*

O wondrous thrones, whereon to seat the great Lord Atea.

E na paipai aanaau mea paipai ia te Fatu-nui Atea.

O thrones placed in the middle of the upper heavens.

E na paipai hakatu i vavena o te ani una

O thrones whereon to seat the Lord of love;
E na paipai mea paipai 'ia te Fatu o te hina-nau
The great Lord Atea established in love,
Te Fatu nui Atea haatuia i te hinanau
To love the fair Atanua.
Mea hinanau 'ia te pootu Atanua,
Atanua shades the neck of Atea.
Mau kaki Atanua no Atea
A woman of great wealth is Atanua,
He vahine taetae nui Atanua
Which she brought from out of night,
Toi mai 'ia mei ioto o te po
Gathered for Atea:
Hai-hai 'ia mai no Atea
Nothing was given back to night,
60   *Aoe he mea tuu atu no te po*
Atea gave nothing back to Tanaoa,
Aoe he mea no Atea tuu atu no Tanaoa.
Who thus was chased to distant regions,
Pehea tatai 'ia vahi oa
Where the light of day was not known;
Koe e itea te ao-o-te a
No wealth, no warmth;
Taetae koe, mahanahana koe,
Confined, lying beneath the feat of Atanua,
Tamau moeana iao te tapu vae no Atanua
Very cold, dreary, dark, without companions;
Anu oko aa-naho Kevokevo koe na hoa
Nothing of all his wealth remained.
Koe to'ia taetae a na mea otoa
Cold, shivering, engulfed; behold indeed!
Anu kamaiko uuku ia aa ehoa.
O dark Tanaoa engulfed in the long nights
E keke Tanaoa uuku ia i na po a oa
Secure sits Atea on his wondrous throne,
70   *Mau Atea una to'ia paipai aanaau,*
And dwells as Chief in his domains.
Nonoho Hakaiki i to'ia pai aina

Born is his first son, his princely son.

Tupu to'ia tama mua, to'ia tama Hakaiki.

O the great Prince, O the sacred superior.

O te Hakaiki nui o te una tapu

O the princely son, first born of divine power !

O te tama Hakaiki fanau mua o te mana na etua

O the Lord of everything, here, there, and always.

O te Hakaiki o na mea otoa eia aia a e ia mai a oa

O the Lord of the heavens and the entire sky.

O te Hakaiki o te vaevaani a na ikuani otoa

O the princely son, first born of the exalted power.

O te tama Hakaiki fanau mua o te mana tiki-tiki.

O the son, equal with the father and with Ono.

O te tama tia me te motua a me Ono

Dwelling in the same place.

Etahi ona a te nonoho

Joined are they three in the same power.

80   *Poho 'ia toko tou etahi koaa.*

The Father, Ono, and the Son.

Te motua, Ono a te Tama

One tree (trunk, cause) was formed from those three.

Te tumu tahi koaa mei na toko tou

The tree producing in the heavens above

Te tumu tupu ia i te vaevaani una

All the good and wondrous families in love.

I te tau huaa meitai aanaau i te hina-nau

The tree of life, firm rooted in heaven above

Te tumu o te pohoe, mau te aka i te ani una :

The tree producing in all the heavens

Te tumu tupu i te ani otoa

The bright and sprightly sons.

I na tau tama ponionio a ta anaana

From Atea they were born as his sons.

No Atea hakatupu nui ia atou i te tama

O Atea, the exalted Lord of everything !

O Atea te Fatu tikitiki o na mea otoa

O Atea, their life, body, and spirit.

90   *O Atea to atou pohoe, tino, moui a uhane.*

The foregoing chant is extremely valuable as a relic of Polynesian folklore. It is now impossible to determine the age of its composition; but to judge from the ruggedness of its diction, it must be of very high antiquity. It is an allegory, no doubt, but the consciousness of its being an allegory had not yet faded from the mind of the composer, nor, perhaps, from the people before whom it was chanted. It points to a period of the human mind when the thoughts of sages still lingered and laboured in the border land between material facts and metaphysical abstractions; when *Tanaoa* was still half the real darkness of night, chaos, and half the deified impersonation of an evil principle, antagonistic to the powers of light; when *Atea* was still half the actual sun, springing forth from, succeeding to, and dispelling the gloom and darkness of night, and half the deified impersonation of creative power; when *Ono* was still half the mere actual sound, the busy hum of a living, active, moving world, just awakening from the torpor and silence of night, and half the deified impersonation of speech and intelligent communication, an evolution of, and a companion to, Atea; when *Atanua* was still the mere Dawn, the result of the apparent contest between Darkness and Light, "encircling the neck of the sun," as well as the goddess wife of Atea. This chant must be at least as old as the period when the Vedic poets sang the praises of Indra and the charms of Ushas. It sounds like a lost hymn of the Vedas, or, perhaps, of the pre-Vedic period. Its whole tenor, style, and imagery are thoroughly Arian. Even here the conception of a triplicate Godhead occurs: perhaps the prototype of the Chaldean Anu, Bel, Hea, as well as of the Indian Trimurti, and is but another version of the Hawaiian Kane, Ku, Lono.

No. III., *page* 63.

PROBABLY one of the grandest religious poems, once current among the Polynesians, and relating to the creation of the world, is that which Mr. Moerenheut has preserved in his " Voyage aux isles du Grand Ocean.". Though but a fragment of what was probably a series of religious poems, yet its lofty tone and archaic simplicity of expression make it extremely valuable as a testimony to the ancient belief of the Polynesians. As published by Mr. Moerenheut there are several errors of orthography which I have endeavoured to correct; but there are also some other unintelligible parts, whether owing to a bad manuscript copy or to careless printing, which I have enclosed in brackets, being unable to give an English translation of the same. Those who have an opportunity and are competent to compare Mr. Moerenheut's translation with the original and with mine, will perceive that though his is more florid and free, and mine more literal, yet the spirit of the poem is fully preserved. The poem accords so thoroughly with the Marquesan and Hawaiian poems on the same subject, that there can be no doubt of its very great antiquity, although the introduction of *Taaroa* as the Great Creator would seem to indicate a later period for its composition than that of the Hawaiian and Marquesan chants on creation and cognate subjects. I am unable, at present, to indicate the period of Polynesian life, when the attributes and powers of *Kane*, or *Tane*, or *Atea* (for they are but synonyms of the same conception) were transferred to *Taaroa* or *Tangaroa*, who, to judge from the Hawaiian and Marquesan folklore, was originally conceived of as the very opposite in attributes and functions. It is admitted even in Tahitian folklore, that at some remote period the *Tane* worship was superseded by, and subordinated to, that of *Ono* on nearly all the islands of the Society group except Huahine; and at that time probably the legend arose which made *Tane* and *Ono* to be brothers, and sons of *Taaroa.*

With these considerations, and others that have been set forth elsewhere in this work, I am satisfied that this Tahitian chant of creation is older than the period when *Taaroa* was elevated by the southern groups into the primacy of Godhead, and that its intrinsic evidence connects it with the remarkable series of ancient chants, once common to the Polynesian race as an heirloom from the past, of purer creed and loftier conceptions, and of which the Marquesans and Hawaiians have preserved such interesting relics.

For 'better reference I have interlineated the translation.

> He abides—Taaroa by name—
> *Parahi, Taaroa te ioa,*
> In the immensity of space.
> *Roto ia te aere.*
> There was no earth, there was no heaven,
> *Aita fenua, aita rai,*
> There was no sea, there was no mankind.
> *Aita tai, aita taata.*
> Taaroa calls on high;
> *T'iaoro Taaroa i nia;*
> He changed himself fully. . . .
> *Fuariro noa ihora oia (i te ohe narea ei).*
> Taaroa is the root;
> *Te tumu Taaroa ;*
> The rocks (or foundation);
> *Te papa ;*
> Taaroa is the sands;
> *Taaroa te one ;*

Taaroa stretches out the branches (is wide-spreading).
  Toro Taaroa ia naio.
Taaroa is the light;
  Taaroa tei te ao;
Taaroa is within;
  Taaroa tei roto;
Taaroa is . . .
  Taaroa (te nahora;) [1]
Taaroa is below;
  Taaroa tei raro;
Taaroa is enduring;
  Taaroa te taii;
Taaroa is wise;
  Taaroa te paari;
He created the land of Hawaii;
  Fanau fenua Hawaii;
Hawaii great and sacred,
  Hawaii nui raa,
As a crust (or shell) for Taaroa.
  Ei paa no Taaroa.
The earth is dancing (moving).
  Te ori-ori ra fenua.
O foundations, O rocks,
  E te tumu, e te papa,
O sands! here, here.
  E te one! O, o.
Brought hither, press together the earth;
  O-toina mai, pohia tei fenua;
Press, press again!
  Pohia, popohia!
They do not. . . .
  Aita ia (e farire)
Stretch out the seven heavens; let ignorance cease.
  Toro o hitu te rai; e pau maua.
Create the heavens, let darkness cease.
  Fanau ai te rai, pau mouri,

---

[1] *Nahora*, if not a misprint, probably refers to the Tahitian *Hora-hora*, "a platform, the deck of a canoe;" to the Samoan *Fola* and Hawaiian *Hola*, "to spread out, to unfold, to open."

Let anxiety cease within ; . . .
Mataroa e pau roto ; (pau ahai te pautia).
Let repose (immobility) cease ;
E pau noho ;
Let the period of messengers cease ;
E pau va arere ;
It is the time of the speaker.
E te va orero-reo.
Fill up (complete) the foundations,
E faai te tumu,
Fill up the rocks,
E faai te papa,
Fill up the sands.
E faai one.
The heavens are enclosing (surrounding),
Fa-opia rai,
And hung up are the heavens
A toto te rai
In the depths ;
Ia hohonu ;
Finished be the world of Hawaii.
E pau fenua no Hawaii.

Mr. Horatio Hale, "United States Exploration Expedition," under Commodore Wilkes, section, "Ethnography and Philology," Philadelphia, 1846, p. 125, refers to this same Tahitian chant as published by Mr Moerenhout, and sees in it another evidence of the Tahitian descent from the Samoan island of Sawaii; the more so, as in another poem, connected by Mr. Moerenhout with the former, it is said that the god *Roo* created Uporo, another island of the Samoan group. Mr. Hale is doubtless correct in tracing the Tahitians to the Samoan group, though possibly some of them came direct from the Fiji group at the time of their expulsion; but the evident relation of this Tahitian chant to those of the Marquesas group, which positively locate the "Hawaii" of which they speak far to the westward of the Fiji group, prevents me from concurring with Mr. Hale in assigning no higher or older origin to this and those chants. I regret that I have not any Samoan legends or chants comparable in date to those of the other groups. If any such exist, I shall be much deceived if they also do not refer to a Hawaii far beyond, and to the westward of their own Sawaii.

. What Mr. Hale calls "the third portion" of this chant, as arranged and published by Mr. Moerenhout, and treating of the genesis of the Tahitian gods, is evidently a separate poem, and of very much later date; in short, a local theogony, not even fully recognised on the Society group, and unknown in the neighbouring groups.

No. IV., *page 90.*

Te Tai Toko (The Deluge).

Part I.

The Lord Ocean is a going

1   *Te Fatu Moana ua hoe 'ia*

To pass over the whole dry land.

E taha ta te Moo oa

A respite is granted

He koina e vae ana

For seven days.

Na mou atea eitu

Who would have thought to bury the great earth * * *

Oai tuto e tomi 'ia te papanui Tinaku'

In a roaring flood? E.

Ma he tai-toko e hetu. *E.*

Ho, ho, in the enclosure !

Ho, ho, i te papua

Ho ! the twisted ropes !

Ho, ho, te tau hauhii

Here is confusion among

Eia e tohu 'ia i vavena

The generations (different kinds) of animals

10   *Te tai o te puaa*

O we are the kind, O we are the kind,

O maua he tai, O maua he tai

O we are reserved from the flood

O maua a ke iho e tai

Reserved on the flood,

E ke iho i tai

The flood, the roaring. E.

He tai-toko e hetu. *E.*

And it will fall over the valleys,
A e vi una i na kavai
Pass over the plains,
Taha una te tohua
It will bury the mountains,
Tomi 'ia te tau mouna
And envelop the hill-sides,
A e tupo te vau
O the flood, the roaring.   E.
O te tai-toko e hetu.   E.
Ho! in the enclosure.
20   *Ho, ho, i te papua*
Ho! the twisted ropes,
Ho, ho, te tau hauhii
For. to tie up in couples
Mea pitiki i tahuna.
The (various) kinds of animals.
Te tai o te puaa.
The white kinds,
Te tai o te mouo
The striped kinds,
Te tai o te hahei
The spotted kinds,
Te tai o te patipati
The black kinds,
Te tai o te papanu
The horned kinds,
Te tai o te kivikivi
The big lizard kinds,
Te tai o te huho-oa.
The small lizard kinds,
30   *Te tai o te huho-poto*
O the flood, the roaring.   E.
O he tai toko e hetu.   E.
High above the ocean,
Tie tie o te moana
Build a house upon it,
Haka haka he hae ma eia

A storied house, the house.
He hae papa, te hae
A house with chambers, the house.
He hae puho, te hae
A house with windows, the house.
He hae puta maama, te hae,
A very large house, the house.
He hae oa-oa, te hae
A house to keep alive
He hae mea haapohoe
The (various) kinds of animals.
Te tai o te puaa.
O the flood, the roaring.   E.
40   *O he tai toko e hetu.   E.*
Ho, ho, there in the enclosure.
Ho, ho, ina i te papua
Ho, ho, the long-twisted ropes
Ho, ho, te hauhii oa
To tie up and make fast in couples
Mea nati a haamau i tahuna
The (various) kinds of animals.
Te tai o te puaa
One man before, O Fetu-amo-amo.
He enata imua o Fetu-amo-amo.
One man behind, O Ia-fetu-tini.
He enata i mui o Ia-fetu-tini
The animals between, making great noise.
Te puaa te vavena e tani huina
O the flood, the roaring.   E.
O te tai toko c hetu.   E.
Eh; bear away (carry away); Here.
E amo E.   Eia
Carry away the animals; Here.
50   *E amo te puaa.   Eia*
Carry them away to the sea.   Here
E amo atu atou i tai.   Eia
O, the long deep wood (a name for the house or vessel).
O Kakaveie-oa.   Eia   [Here.

O the God of destruction (causing evil). Here
O te Etua o te hakanau. Eia
O Hina-touti-ani. Here
O Hina-touti-ani. Eia
O Hina-te-ao-ihi. Here
O Hina-te-ao-ihi. Eia
O Hina-te-upu-motu. Here
O Hina-te-upu-motu. Eia
O Hina-te-ao-meha. Here
O Hina-te-ao-meha. Eia
O Fetu-moana. Here.
O te Fetu-moana. Eia
O Fetu-tau-ani. Here
O te Fetu-tau-ani. Eia
O Fetu-amo-amo. Here
60 *O Fetu-amo-amo. Eia*
O Ia-fetu-tini. Here.
O Ia-fetu-tini. Eia
O the flood, the roaring. E.
O he tai toko e hetu. E.
A man before, with the offerings,
He enata i mua i te utunu
O Fetu-moana.
O te Fetu-moana
A man behind, clinging to the offerings.
He enata i mui te pikia i te utunu
O Fetu-tau-ani.
O te Fetu-tau-ani
A turtle between, making great noise
He hono te vavena-e-tani-huina
O the flood, the roaring. E.
O te tai toko e hetu E.
Cut off, cut off your ear; this is a bad house
Tipia, tipia to oe puaina, te hae pe 'ia
For to cook food for the God * * * *
70 *Mea tuna kai no te Etua ke huha ko huha*
The four-faced priests * * * *
Te tau taua mata fa ke huha ko huha

House fast asleep.   God the destroyer.
Hae momoe, Etua te hakanau
Crush, crackle, a stinking crowd.
A omi hu, tai piau
Bring together, pell-mell,
E hau 'ia kohua
All the heaven-fed animals.
Ani otoa tafau puaa
Sleeps the sacred supporter in this noise.
Moe te tapu tutui i teia mu
Noise, God, noise, with God arise !
Mu Etua mu, ma Etua va
God wills it.
Etua kaki hia.
Here is manifest the trouble (storm),
Eia ua atea te toua
A trouble that is great and manifest,
80   *He toua te mea nui i atea*
And it is roaring, and it is working,
A ua hetu e hana nei
A rain like a solid cloud.
He ua mea ata tahi
Bring together, pell-mell,
E hau ia kohua.
All the heaven-fed animals.
Ani otoa tafau puaa
Sleeps the sacred supporter.
Moe te tapu tutui
Shaken up and mixed up is the earth.
Ua upu a uu-uu te fenua
I consent and let loose
N'au e ae tuku atu
*   *   *   *   a confused noise
Te matu he mu
*   *   *   *   make a buzzing noise,
Matu a mu a mu
*   *   *   *   arise, arise
90   *Matua a va a va*
*   *   *   * I will it thus.
Matu t'au kaki tenei.

Part II.

O, the * * * new
E te kou hou
O, the mountain ridges
E te vau va-a
E, * * * *
E te mota
Some * * * men
He mou uu Enata
Are arriving here,
Tu-tu ana nei
People in the storm (war, trouble) ;
Tai i te toua
A veil on the head
He pae i te oho
A paddle in the hand
He hoe i te iima
E, arrivals, come and push back
100   *E tutu' ina amai e hoe*
The ocean to the centre.
Te moana ie vene.
E, the house, E.
E puho E.
Here I am aground.
Eia toko ae au
The Fetu-moana E.
Te Fetu-moana E.
Hearken up there
Hakaono oe una nei
The Lord-Ocean consents
Te Fatu-moana e ao-'ia
That the dry land appears.
Te fenua moo e haaitea.
The Lord-Ocean, E.
Te Fatu-moana, E.
Ah, quick the * * * new
A-ve te kou hou

The * * * new, here it is

110   *He kou hou e ia mai*

   *   *   *   *

    A te mota.

In channels receding.

    I kava miki 'ia.

The Lord-Ocean.   E.

    Te Fatu-moana.   E.

Ah! quick the * * * new

    A-ve te kou hou

 * * long, and when I * *

    Kou oa a no au e mota

I will offer seven sacred offerings

    E utunu au eitu tapu taetae

And seven sucklings that shall cry

    A eitu mamau a te ve

To the Lord-Ocean.

    No te Fatu-moana

The Lord has assented that the earth

    Te Fatu ua ao te fenua

Shall now be dry.

120   *E moo ana mai.*

E, the traveller,

    E te teetina

The traveller of Tanaoa,

    Te teetina o Tanaoa

Over the sea of Havaii,

    Una te tai o Havaii

Stretch thy bones thither,

    Te ivi a ke atu

Stretch thy bones hither,

    Te ivi a ke mai

Over the sea of Havaii,

    Una te tai o Havaii.

Tanaoa, rest on the curling wave,

    E noho Tanaoa no te hae-hae

Remain at the stern of the vessel,

    E maohe i te mui o te vaa

Strike, strike your legs, Tanaoa
E paki-pakia to vae Tanaoa
Tanaoa, I will it thus.

130　　*Tanaoa au kaki hia.*
Tanaoa, why do you return ?
Tanaoa heaha to oe hua
Returned is the North wind with the ＊　＊
A hua te tiu me te hafa
Not found is a place where to alight.
Aoe koaa e tau ae mei nei atu
Tanaoa, I will it thus.
Tanaoa au kaki hia
Alight, Tanaoa, on the sands.
E tau Tanaoa i te one-one
Call Tanaoa here　＊　＊　＊
E vevau Tanaoa nei tahu mai
Do not go away.
A umoi a hee atu
Strike, strike thy breast, Tanaoa.
E paki-pakia te vaa Tanaoa
Tanaoa, yes I will it thus.
Tanaoa ee au kaki hia
E the traveller,

140　　*E te teetina*
The traveller of Moepo,
Te teetina o Moepo
Over the sea of Havaii
Una te tai o Havaii
Thy bones stretch thither,
To ivi a ke atu
Thy bones stretch hither,
To ivi a ke mai
Over the sea of Havaii.
Una te tai o Havaii
Ah, alight, alight here.
E a a tau-tau mai.
E the Lord Ocean.　E.
E te Fatu-moana.　E.

The four bowls, and the four bowls
Te efa ipu-ipu, a te efa ipu-ipu
Are safely landed here.
Ua tau meitai nei.
Great mountain ridges, ridges of Havaii
150   *Va-va nui 'ia te va-va o Havaii*
Great mountain ridges, ridges of Matahou,
Va-va nui 'ia te va-va o Matahou.
Whereon to thread and stamp.
Mea kihahi a kahi.
Ah, here is the Moepo
A eia te Moepo
Bringing aloft what has been gathered.
E hai ina mai una kohi-kohi.

Part III.

Ask, ask, the sorcerer (the high-priest),
Ui-ui te tupua
Generations new, generations past,
Tai hou, tai hee,
Who is the flower above there ?
Oai oia te pua una nei ?
It is Atii-hau-hua.
O Atii-hau-hua.
The Tiki-vae-tahi.
Te Tiki-vae-tahi.
What is the work of that God,
160   *Heaha te hana o tena etua*
That is here revealed
Te fai mai ae
With that face that is so bright,
Me tena ao te io mai ae
And with that noise arising ?
A me tena mu ua va
E generations, E.
E, tai, E.

Generations go (spread) again,
Tai a-hee-hou
E quick over the plain,
E a-ve una te tohua
Return and stand with Tanaoa
Te hua a ua tu me Tanaoa
I shall arrive, hearken,
A tu-tu au, e ono
Hark, hark, arise, get up,
Ono, ono, tu ae va-a
Ho, Ho, arise, God wills it thus.
170   *Ho, Ho, va, Etua kaki hia.*
Ask, ask, the sorcerer,
Ui, ui te tupua
Who is the flower inland here?
Oai oia te pua iula nei?
It is Ka-ka-me-vau.
O Ka-ka-me-vau.
The God with the white teeth.
Te Etua niho teea
Hark, it is he, I arise, hearken,
Ono oia tutu au e ono
E generations, E.
E, tai, E.
Generations go again
Tai a hee hou
Quickly over the plain.
E a-ve una te tohua
Hark, hark, arise, get up,
Ono, ono, tu ae va-a
Ho, Ho, arise, God wills it thus.
180   *Ho, Ho, va Etua kaki hia.*
Ask, ask, the sorcerer,
Ui ui te tupua
Who is the flower seaward here?
Oai oia te pua tai nei?
It is the Fatu-moana,
Oia te Fatu-moana

He is going to sacrifice
Na hoe 'ia e tooo
The sorcerer here below.
Te tupua iao nei
O the black eel (water-snake)
O te puhi ke ke
The eel with ugly head.
Te puhi o oho ino.
Who is the flower tied here ?
Oai oia te pua naki nei?
It is Tu-mata-te-vai.
Oia o Tu-mata-te-vai.
Who is the flower before here ?
190 *Oai oia te pua mua nei?*
It is Au-te-una-tapu.
Oai te o Au-te-una-tapu,
Who is the flower behind here ?
Oai te pua imui nei?
It is Mau-te-anua-nua.
O Mau-te-anua-nua.
Who is the strange flower here ?
Oai te pua hiva nei ?
I am here, Tumu-tupu-fenua.
195 *O au tenei te Tumu-tupu-fenua.*

Believing that Mr. Lawson—from whose MS. collection
the foregoing chant has been copied—in his endeavour to
be literal in his translation, has sometimes become unintelligible, I have attempted a translation that would in
some measure obviate that defect, but this, like almost
all the ancient Polynesian chants, is replete with tropes
and allusions of which the original meaning is in many
instances now forgotten or only acquired with great difficulty. The words marked with asterisks in the translation
are such words as I was either unable to find in the only
Marquesan vocabulary within my reach (that by the
Abbé Mosblech. Paris 1843), or only found with a
meaning that would have made no sense of the context.

No. V., see *page* 116, n. 2.

DIEFFENBACH, in "Travels in New Zealand," p. 28, &c., describes the baptism of infants; that the priest with a green branch, dipped in a calabash of water, sprinkled the child and recited a prayer over it. The prayer differed for boys and for girls. The following are the prayers :—

For Boys.

Tohia te tama nei
Kia riri, kia nguha
Kani o tu me te nganahau
Ka riri ke tai no Tu
Ka nguha ki tai no Tu
Koropana ki tai no Tu
E pa te karanga ki tai no Tu
Me te nganahau ki tai no Tu
Taku tama nei kia tohia
Koropana ki tai no Tu
Pa mai te karanga ki tai no Tu
Ko te kawa o karaka wati
O riri ai koe, e nguha ai koe
E ngana ai koe
E toa ai koe
E kano ai koe
Ko Tu iho uhia
Ko Rongo iho uhia.

For Girls.

Tohia te tama nei
Kia riri, kia nguha te tama nei.

Kani o Tu me te nganahau
Ka riri ki tai no Tu
Ka wakataka te watu
Kania ma taratara
Te hau o Uenuku
Puha ka mama tauira o Tu
Ka mama tauira o Rongo
Ho.
Ka kai Tu
Ka kai Rongo
Ka kai te Wakariki
He haha
He hau ora
He hau rangatira
Kei runga, kei te rangi
Ka puha te rangi
E iri iria koe ki te iri iri
Hahau kai mau tangaengae ·
Haere ki te wahie mau tangaengae
Watu kakahu mou tangaengae.

I am inclined to think that Dieffenbach has not correctly
apprehended some of the words in the above prayers, or
that they have been misprinted.

No. VI., *page* 128.

The following are a number of signs and omens current among the Hawaiians in heathen times, and not yet entirely disregarded :—

Opeakua : "Hands crossed behind." If a Hawaiian was going out on business or on pleasure, and met another person with his hands crossed behind his back, it was an unlucky omen; but if it occurred twice on the same journey, it became a sign of success.

Maka-paa : "A blind person." If you met a blind person on the road, it was a bad sign. If you met two blind ones, the sign was good.

Kahea-kua-ia : "Calling after one." If, starting on a journey, you were called after or called back by somebody, it was a bad sign. Therefore, to prevent being thus troubled, the traveller always told those whom he left where he was going, his errand, &c.

Kuapuu-hohailua : "Meeting a humpback." If on your journey you met a humpbacked person, it was a bad sign. If two such were met with, the sign was good.

Hoo-kua-kii : "Arms akimbo." If you met a person with his or her arms akimbo, hands resting on the hips, it was a bad sign.

Hoihou-i-hope : "Returning." If, starting away from a place, and having actually proceeded some distance from the house, however short, you turned back after something forgotten or left, it was a bad sign.

Ku-ia o ka wawai : "Stumbling." If you stumble or stub your feet in walking, it is a bad sign.

Makole : "Sore-eyed." If you meet a person with sore or inflamed eyes, the sign is bad.

Kukue : "Lame." If you meet a lame or deformed person, it is a bad sign.

Maia : "Bananas." If you are going on business, and meet a man carrying a banana bunch, you will not prosper, and would do well to defer it; but if that cannot be done, then, to avoid the evil omen, you should either touch the bananas with your hand, or grasp them, and then proceed on your journey without looking back.

Alae : "A water-fowl." If the bird called alae was heard crying in the neighbourhood of a village, it was a sign of the death of somebody there.

Kuukuu : "Spider." If the long-legged spider drops down from above in front of you, or on your bosom, it is a good sign, foreboding either presents or strangers; if he drops on either side, or behind you, the sign brings you no good.

Hulahula o ka Maka : "Twitching of the eyes." If the eye twitches or throbs suddenly, it is the sign of the arrival of strangers, or of approaching wailing for some one that is dead.

Kani-ana o ka ula o ka pepeiaò : "Ringing sounds in the ear." If you have a ringing sound in your ears, it is a sign that you are spoken evil of by some one. If in the right ear, by a man; if in the left ear, by a woman. Sometimes it indicates approaching sickness.

Okakala or Malana o ka poo : "Shuddering, shivering of the head." If you feel a sudden shivering or itching of the scalp or skin of the head, as if a louse were crawling, it is a sign that you are spoken evil of.

Koni o na wawae : "Throbbing of the feet." If you feel a beating, creeping, throbbing sensation in the foot, it is a sign that either you will go on a sudden journey, or that strangers are arriving.

No. VII. *Vide page* 132.

THERE are numerous other customs, traits, and peculiarities observed by the Polynesians, which find remarkable analogies and coincidences among the nations to the west of them, from whom they sprang, or with whom they cohabited during unknown periods of their former national life. Each one, singly, is but a drop in the stream of evidence which tends to connect the Polynesian with the Cushite and Arian races; but, taken together, they supplement in a large measure the coincidences previously referred to, and strengthen the evidence of that connection beyond the possibility of contravention. As with my limited means of reference I am unable to say whether these coincidences ultimately refer to Arian or Cushite sources, seeing that the former borrowed so much from the latter, I merely present them *en bloc*, that men more able than myself may classify them hereafter. We find, then—

I.

The Hawaiian soothsayer or *kilo-kilo* turned always to the north when observing the heavens for signs or omens, or when regarding the flight of birds for similar purposes. The ancient Hindus turned also to the north for divining purposes, and so did the Iranians before the schism, after which they placed the devas in the north; so did the Greeks, and so did the ancient Scandinavians before their conversion to Christianity.

II.

Hogs were of the most precious offerings to Polynesian

gods, and hogs'-meat the most delicious food of the people.

While the Egyptian, the Hebrew, and the Brahmanised Hindu abominated swine, and the contact therewith, the Arian, Goth, and Scandinavian sacrificed swine as well as sheep, cattle, and horses to their gods, and the boar was a daily feast to the heroes of that northern Valhalla. The Greeks held swine in high estimation, and Homer gives to a swineherd the title " divine."

III.

The Egyptians were permitted to marry their sisters by the same father and mother, and in patriarchal times among the Hebrews a man might marry a sister, the daughter of his father only, though it was afterwards forbidden in Leviticus (chap. xviii.). According to Persian law such marriages were not permitted; but the Greeks and Romans seem to have admitted the practice in earlier times, if the proceedings of the Olympian gods are an index of primitive manners—Saturn and Rhea, Jupiter and Juno.

Among Hawaiian chiefs such marriages were not uncommon, even in earliest times, and the offspring of such unions were invested with higher rank, and called *Aliipio*, taking precedence over brothers and sisters of different unions.

IV.

In the Hawaiian, Marquesas, and Tahitian groups the first prisoner taken in war was invariably offered as a sacrifice to the particular god of the captors.

" The custom of sacrificing their first prisoner (in war) is ascribed by Procopius to the Thulitœ or Scandinavians " (" Bell. Goth." ii. 15). " The Germans made their first captive contend with a champion of their own race, and took the result as an omen of success or failure " (" Tacit. Germ." 10), *vide* Rawlinson's " Herodotus," vii., 180, n. 4.

V.

In Ceylon, and Southern India, whenever a favour is solicited, peace made, or an interview desired, presents are always sent before.[1] In Hawaii and elsewhere in Polynesia presents always accompanied the visitor, or were sent before.

VI.

In India an unhealthy country is said to "eat up the inhabitants," and a victorious or oppressive rajah is said to "eat up the country."[2] In Hawaii the expression *Ai-moku*, "eating up the land," is an epithet of chiefs.

VII.

In India the expression "to live in the shadow," *i.e.*, under the security and defence of another, is very common.[3] In Hawaiian the expression *e noho ma ka malu*, "to dwell in the shadow," *i.e.*, under the protection of such or such a chief, is frequently heard.

VIII.

In App. chap. v. book ii. of Rawlinson's edition of " Herodotus," I read that the hieroglyphic sign for a negative "is a pair of extended arms with the palms of the hands downwards, preceding the verb." Before such an action of the hands could have become a recognised hieroglyphic sign of a negative, it must have been a common and generally adopted manner of expressing a negative in actual everyday life, a gesticulation as significant and as well understood to the Egyptians, and perhaps the entire Cushite race, as a shrug of the shoulders or a shake of the head is to many nations of modern time.

[1] Oriental Illustrations, by Joseph Roberts, p. 22.   London, 1835.
[2] *Ibid.*, p. 101.   [3] *Ibid.*

I know not if such a manner of expressing a negative still obtains among the Cushite descendants in N.E. Africa, in Asia, or the Archipelago, but the self-same identical manner of inverting the hands, "palms downwards," in sign of a negative answer, prevails throughout Polynesia. Ask a person if he has such or such a thing, and, two to one, instead of saying "No," he will turn his hand or hands "palms downwards," in sign of a negative answer.

No. VIII., *page* 144.

MR. CRAWFURD, in his "Grammar and Dictionary of the Malay Language," vol. i. p. 134-35, considers that those who hold that the Polynesian "language and race are essentially the same as the Malay," are undoubtedly "under a great mistake," and advance "a gratuitous assumption." And, though he resolutely repudiates the idea that there is anything, physically or linguistically, to connect them as springing from the same race, or that the former descended from the latter—yet, in order to account for the few Malay and Javanese words which, according to him, have found entrance into the Polynesian language, he resorts to the hypothesis that at some remote period, while the Polynesians were still living in a body, before their dispersion over the East Pacific, they had been visited by a fleet of Malay rovers, who introduced to the then uncultivated Polynesians the knowledge of the taro, yam, cocoa-nut-palm, sugar-cane, and the numeral system, p. 144 *et seq.;* and he fixes upon the Tonga or Friendly Islands as the country where this encounter took place.

Mr. Crawfurd argues that, as those articles, taro, yam, &c., bear Malay names, ergo they are of Malay origin, and most probably brought by Malays to the Polynesians. Let us consider these names. Mr. Crawfurd identifies the Polynesian *taro, kalo*, arum esculentum, with the Javanese *talás*, and the Polynesian *to, ko*, sugar-cane, with the Javanese and Malay *tábu*. I would not, on slight grounds, question the conclusions arrived at by a gentleman who has done so much, and done it so worthily and well, to illumine the dark and unknown parts of the Asiatic island-world; but when Mr. Crawfurd wrote, the data bearing upon Polynesian life, language, customs, and traditions were scanty, detached, frequently one-sided, and hence not always reliable. Consequently, when Mr. Crawfurd deriving *talo* from *talás*, and *to* from *tábu*, I have no doubt that every competent Polynesian scholar of the present day, foreign or native, would dissent from such derivation as contrary to the very genius and idiom of the Polynesian. Had *talás* and *tábu* at any time been introduced as foreign words in the Polynesian language, the form the former would have assumed could not possibly have been any other than *talasa, talaha, talafa*, or even *talaka*, according to the peculiar dialect wherein adopted; and the form of the latter would have been *tapu, tafu, tahu*, or *tawu*. With one exception, I know of no single instance where a foreign word, introduced in the Polynesian, and ending with a consonant, is not invariably followed by a vowel to enable the Polynesian to pronounce it; and I know of no instance where a foreign dissyllable, ending with a vowel, has been contracted into a monosyllable in the Polynesian. The exception alluded to is in the Hawaiian dialect, where a few foreign words ending in *er* or *ar* have the *r* elided and the entire syllable sounded as *a*, as *dia* for "deer," *bea* for "bear," *wineka* for "vinegar," *leta* for "letter," and some others; though the rule is not general, for we find per contra foreign words like *hamale* for "hammer," *lepela* for "leper," and others. And so violent a contraction as *to* from *tábu* is entirely unheard of in the Polynesian. *Taro* and *tálas, to* and *tábu* may possibly be related; but if so, it is for the very opposite reason, viz., that the latter names are derived from the former, and not as Mr. Crawfurd claims it. Taro is not a staple food of the Malays or Javanese, who, when they arrived from India, brought with them their rice-eating proclivities, and spread the use of the article as well as the name, throughout the Archipelago. But taro has from time immemorial been the staple food of the Polynesians; and so with the sugar-cane. The Hawaiians ascribe the introduction of taro to their renowned ancestor *Wakea;* but, according to the most reliable and rational of their traditions, it will be seen that *Wakea* was a Gilolo chief, in times previous to the Polynesian migrations, who never put foot on any of the Pacific groups now inhabited by those who claim descent from him.

That the Polynesian *ufi, uhi,* and *u'i,* "yam," and *niu,* "cocoa-nut," are identically the same words as the Malay and Javanese *ubi, uwi,* and the Javanese *ñu,* there can be no doubt. But assuming that yams and cocoa-nuts were not indigenous on the groups of the Pacific—which, however, has yet to be proven—is it not as likely that the first Polynesian emigrants from the Archipelago (Asiatic) brought those articles with them, as that they were subsequently brought to them by Malay rovers? Besides, I am inclined to think that *kálapa* is the genuine proper Malay name for cocoa-nut, and *ñu* only adopted by them since their arrival in the Archipelago, and adopted from the previous inhabitants, the Polynesians and their congeners. Among the thirty-three names for cocoa-nut recorded in the Appendix to Mr. R. A. Wallace's "Malay Archipelago," p. 611, there are thirty-one entirely different from the Malay name, which is there given as *kálapa* or *klápa,* and twenty-three which are evidently related to the Polynesian *niu,* though more or less corrupted, of which only two, the Salibabo and Ceram (Gah), appear to have retained the Polynesian word in its purity.

In regard to the numeral system, I have shown (p. 144 *et seq.*) the sources which in all probability contributed to form the Polynesian numerals, and for which they are not beholden to either Malays or Javanese.

The notion entertained by Mr. Crawfurd, that the Tonga Islands were the cradle of the Polynesian race, from whence they spread over the Pacific Ocean, after having received the benefits of the intercourse with Malay and Javanese sea-rovers, does not at this day require consideration. I prefer to follow Mr. Horatio Hale in his excellent work on the "Ethnology and Philology of Polynesia—United States' Exploring Expedition," published 1846, wherein it is convincingly shown that the primary rendezvous of the Polynesian emigrants from the Asiatic Archipelago was at the Fiji group, and that when driven out from there they scattered east, south, and north over the Pacific Ocean. Malay and Javanese rovers may have followed them to the Fijis; but if so, there is no trace of such occurrence in the traditions, customs, or language of the Polynesians. Whatever there may be in common between the Malays and Javanese, on one hand, and the Polynesians, on the other, must be sought for in circumstances unconnected with ethnic consanguinity, and existing previous to the migrations of the latter into the Pacific.